MEASUREMENT IN EDUCATION AND PSYCHOLOGY

Measurement in Education and Psychology

Dr. PREM PRAKASH
M.A. (Psy., Eng.), M.Ed., Ph. D.

Principal
Greater Noida College of Education
Greater Noida
Distt. Gautam Buddh Nagar (U.P.)

KANISHKA PUBLISHERS, DISTRIBUTORS
NEW DELHI-110 002

KANISHKA PUBLISHERS, DISTRIBUTORS
4697/5-21A, Ansari Road, Daryaganj
New Delhi -110 002
Phones : 2327 0497, 2328 8285
Fax : 011-2328 8285
E-mail : kanishka_publishing@yahoo.co.in

Measurement in Education and Psychology
First Published-2008
Edition-2018

ISBN: 978-81-8457-092-2

PRINTED IN INDIA

Published by Madan Sachdeva for Kanishka Publishers, Distributors, 4697/5-21A, Ansari Road, Daryaganj, New Delhi-110 002, Typeset by Sunshine Graphics, Delhi, and Printed at Rajdhani Printers, Delhi.

In Loving Memory of
My Revered Mother
(The Fountain of Inspiration)

Preface

In Modern times measurement and evaluation has become the part and parcel of education and psychology. An effective teaching text book must offer comprehensive and accurate coverage.

Measurement in Education and Psychology covers the full range of important topics – from measurement, and evaluation to statistical techniques. The book aims to satisfy the student's curiosity and to provide them with an understanding of psychological testing. This book surveys the essentials techniques of item analysis, reliability, validity and statistical techniques which are required to study the problems and its psychological solution. After studying this book the students will have a grasp in the scope and content of educational and psychological measurement, a working knowledge of its vocabulary, understanding and its application. It is hoped that this book will be interesting and useful both to the students as well as teachers who plan to learn practically the art of application.

The chapters in this book are designed to stand on their own so that the teachers can deal with the topics in whatever order suits to his plan of action. This book is designed to meet the examination needs of B.A., M.A. (Education and Psychology), and B.Ed and M.Ed students studying in various universities of India. All the topics have been dealt in a very cogent and lucid manner. Wherever needed, text is supplemented by illustrations, diagrams and tables. Every effort has been made to ensure that the students may be able to grasp the basic concept of measurement efficiently and completely with the minimum efforts.

In the last, the names of a few books have been suggested for further readings. Questions (long answer, short answer and objective type) have also been provided.

This book is planned to be trustworthy, friend, philosopher and guide to all those who are interested in acquainting themselves adequately with the measurement and evaluation in the field of education and psychology. The exhaustive referential material may actualize and visualize any curious knowledge seeker to imporve and enrich his understanding in this area.

The author extends his grateful thanks to all authors and publishers whose books he had studied and quoted in preparing of this volume. Suggestions for further improvements of this book will be highly appreciated.

I shall be failing in my duty if I do not pay off debt of gratitude to Madan Sachdeva of Kanishka Publishers & Distributors who has taken keen interest in the publication of this book.

With best wishes to the readers.

Dr. Prem Prakash

Contents

1

Measurement and Evaluation

There are individual differences among individuals. It may be stated "no two individuals are alike." We are aware of this fact that the scientific study of these differences has been started. The standardized tests deal much in the field of measurement and evaluation. Mental testing has its own history in this field. It was Francis Galton who provided special statistical techniques to study and to process the data on individual differences. Cattell took an active part in the development of testing and measuring movements. He introduced the term 'mental test'. Binet and Simon designed first intelligence scale to measure the intellectual level which was revised in later years. Now-a-days measurement has become essential part of study to explain the psychological problems quantitatively. But it is also true that Psychology can never attain those functions of measurement as has been attained by the Physical Sciences.

Meaning and Definitions of Measurement

A very related term to measurement is evaluation which is used sometimes interchangeably. However, in Psychology, the both terms are used separately as both connote different meanings. Measurement means the process of assigning numerals to events or object according to some rules.

Tyler defines measurement as "assignment of numerals according to rules while evaluation refers appraisal or assessment with respect to some standard."

Thorndike and Hagan stated, "Anything that exists in some quantity is capable of being measured that measurement mean quantitative description of data as and when we assign numbers to express the quantity of an object or event or trait is called measurement."

According to Fred N. Kerlinger, "Measurement is the assignment of numerals to objects or events according to rules."

A numeral is a symbol of the form 1, 2, 3 or I, II, III. However, it has no quantitative meaning unless we give it to such a meaning. Measurement, simply uses numerals which after being assigned quantitative meaning, become numbers. *A number is a numeral that has been assigned quantitative meaning.*

The term assigned or assignment means mapping. In most Psychological and educational measurement numerals and numbers are mapped out or assigned to individuals.

A rule in the definition means a guide, a method, a command that explains what to be done, we decide rules or set of rules earlier. Effectiveness of measurement depends upon the setting of rules. Most of the human characteristics are difficult to be measured as to frame rules for them is difficult. It is also fact that we must frame rules to measure anything.

Isomorphism

It is often stated that the measurement procedure and the number system are isomorphic to reality Isomorphism refers to identity or similarity of form. It is generally stated that we measure objects but it is not so, actually we measure the properties or characteristics of the objects. However, we measure indicants of the properties of objects.

What do we Measure ?

As mentioned earlier in this chapter that we do not describe everything about an individual but description of these attributes can be made which are relevants to our concerns. We may be satisfied to describe any variable roughly and qualitatively and we may try to be more precise by describing any attribute in quantitative terms. "The more we try to make our description precise and quantitative, the more we involve measurement." Actually we measure properties or attributes of the individual. Any measurement involves three common stages:

1. To identify the properties or attributes that are to be measured.

2. Determination of set of rules through which the attribute may come to light in true sense.
3. Establishment of a set of procedures and techniques which may be quantified into quantitative statements of degree or amount.

Measurement Postulates

There are three postulates basic to measurement. A postulate is an assumption that is an essential prerequisite to carrying out some operation or line of thinking or reasoning. Although, postulates are generally assumed to be true in measurement, it is necessary to test postulates whenever possible. More than three postulates are really essential in order to make it possible to equate objects, to rank order them and to add them. The three postulates can be:

1. Either $(a = b)$ or $a \neq b$, but not both.
2. if $\{(a = b)$ and $(b = c)\}$, then $(a = c)$.
3. if $\{(a > b)$ and $(b > c)\}$ then $a > c$.

These postulates seem easy and even justifiable to make many such postulates and statements but not always, however, we cannot take it granted that the postulate is satisfied. It is remarkably difficult to find examples of simple orders among social Psychological variables, for example, *'a'* may dominate *'b'* and *'b'* may dominate *c*, but it is possible that *'a'* does not dominate *c*. If researcher is studying dominance relations, he cannot simply assume that the postulate is correct.

Measurement Scales

The scale of measurement are considered in terms of their mathematical properties. The most widely used classification of measurement scales are: *(a)* nominal scale, *(b)* ordinal scale, *(c)* interval scale, and *(d)* ratio scale.

Sources of Errors in Measurement

An investigator should be aware of the sources of errors in measurement. These sources are:

1. *Respondent:* At a time the respondent may cooperate and another time he may be reluctant to express his views.
2. *Situation:* It is also one of the factors that effect on correct measurement.

3. *Measurer:* The researcher or investigator may distort responses by rewording or reordering questions.
4. *Measuring Instrument:* One of the main sources of error i.e., unreliable and non-valid. Psychological tests as such defective instrument employed to measure any behaviour shall spoil the whole result.

Levels of Measurement

The Nominal Scale or Classificatory Scale

The measurement at it weakest level exists when numbers or other symbols are used to classify an object, person or characteristic. When numbers or other symbols are used to identify the group to which various objects belong, these numbers or symbols constitute a nominal or classificatory scale. For example, Psychiatric system of diagnostic groups constitutes a nominal scale when doctor identifies a person as 'schizophrenic', 'paranoid', or 'manic' depressive. He is using a symbol to represent the class of persons to which this person belongs, thus he is using nominal scaling. All scales have certain properties viz:

Formal Properties of Nominal Scale

In nominal scales, the only relation involved is that of equivalence. This means that the member of any one sub-class must be equivalent in the property which is being scaled. This relation is symbolized by the familiar sign (=).

The equivalence relations is reflexive, symmetrical and transitive. We may explain these terms like this.

Reflexive	:	$x = x$ for all value of x.
Symmetrical	:	If $x = y$, then $y = x$.
Transitive	:	If $x = y$ and $y = z$ then $x = z$.

The nominal scale is said to be 'unique up to one-to-one transformation. The symbol designating the various sub-class in the scale may be inter-changed if this is done consistently and completely. It is also sometimes called, "the symmetric group of transformation."

Statistics Used

The only statistics used is 'Mode', frequency. We do not measure variability. Non-parametric statistics of x^2 (chi-square) is used for hypothesis testing.

The Ordinal or Ranking Scale

It may happen that the objects in one category of a scale is not just different from the objects in other categories of that scale but they stand in some kind of relation to them. Typical relations among classes are : Higher, more preferred, more difficult, more disturbed, more mature. Such relations may be designated by the symbol (>) which in general means 'greater than '. If the relation '>' holds for all pairs of classes so that a complete ranking, ordering of classes arises, we have this level of scale of measurement. Warner and his associates describe, socio-economic status of the children/ individuals constitutes an ordinal scale.

'=' relations holds among members of the same class.

'> ' relation holds among members between any pair of classes.

Many personality inventories, tests of abilities or aptitude tests result in scores which have the strength of ranks.

Formal Properties

Axiomatically, the fundamental difference between a nominal and ordinal scale is that the ordinal scale incorporates not only the relation of equivalence '=' but also the relation 'greater than'. (>). The latter relation is 'reflexive', a symmetrical and transitive.

Irreflexive : it is not true for any x or that $x > x$.
Asymmetrical : if $x > y$, then $y \ngtr z$.
Transitive : if $x > y$ and $y > z$ then $x > z$.

The Statistics Used

The most appropriative statistics for describing the central tendency of an scores in an ordinal scale is the median. Since median is not affected by changes of any scores which are above or below, it is long as the number of scores above and below remains the same. With ordinal scaling, hypothesis can be tested by using that 'large group of non-parametric' statistical tests which are sometimes called 'order statistics' or which are sometimes called 'order statistics or ranking statistics' correlation co-efficients based on rankings (e.g., Spearman`s *rho* or the Kendall *r*) are appropriate:

The Interval Scale

When a scale has all the characteristics of an ordinal scale and when in addition to the distances between any two numbers on the scale are of known size, then measurement considerably stronger that ordinately has been achieved. In such a case measurement has been achieved in the scale of an interval scale. An interval scale is characterized by a common and constant unit of measurement which assigns a real number to all pairs of object in ordered set. In this sort of measurement, the ratio of any two intervals is independent of the unit of measurement and of the zero point. In this scale of measurement the zero point and the unit of measurement are arbitrary. For example, we measure temperature on an interval scale of two different scales i.e., centigrade and fahrenheit are commonly used. The unit of measurement and zero point in measuring, the temperature are arbitrary. However, both scales contain the same amount and the same kind of information. This is the case because they are linearly related i.e., reading on one scale can be transferred to the equivalent reading on the other by the linear transformation.

$$F = 9/5\ C + 32$$

Here freezing point (c) = o, boiling point (c) = 100.

Freezing point (F) = 32, boiling point (F) = 212.

Centigrade	0	10	30	100
Fahrenheit	32	50	86	212

It may be noted here that ratio of the differences between temperature readings on one scale equal to the ratio between the equivalent differences on the other scale, e.g.

$$\text{Centigrade: } \frac{30-10}{10-0} = \frac{20}{10} = 2$$

$$\text{Fahrenheit.: } \frac{86-50}{50-32} = \frac{36}{18} = 2$$

The ratio is the same in both cases = 2.

In an interval scale, the ratio of any two intervals is independent of the unit used and of the zero point, both of which are arbitrary. Behavioural scientists create interval scales and on infrequent occasions they get success. It is here noted that intervals can be added and subtracted, e.g.

a	*b*	*c*	*d*	*e*
1	2	3	4	5

a to *c* = 3–1 = 2.

c to *d* = 4–3 = 1.

By adding (3–1) + (4–3) = 2 + 1 = 3.

It is not quantities or amounts that are added and subtracted but it is intervals or distances.

Assumptions:

1. That the variable is being scaled is normally distributed in the individual being tested.
2. That person's answer of 'yes' on any one item is exactly equivalent to his answering affirmately on any other items. This assumption satisfies in the requirement that interval scale has a common and constant unit of measurement.

Formal Properties

Axiomatically, it can be shown that the operations and relations which give rise to the structure of an interval scale are such the difference in the scale are isomorphic to the structure of arithmetic numbers may be associated with the position of the objects on an interval scale so the operations of the arithmetic may be performed meaningfully on the differences between these numbers.

In constructing an interval scale one must not only be able to specify equivalence (nominal) greater than as (ordinal scale), but one must be able to specify the ratio of any two intervals.

Statistics Used

The interval scale is the first truly quantitative scale. All the parametric statistics are used (Central tendency, variability, '*t*' test and 'F' test etc.).

The Ratio Scale

When a scale has all the characteristics of an interval scale and in addition has a true zero point as its origin, it is called a ratio scale. In a ratio scale the ratio of any two scale points is independent of the unit of measurement.

EVALUATION

Meaning and Concept of Evaluation

Evaluation is considered both to be as the procees and products of education which is applied to know to what extent the goals of

Four Levels of Measurement

Scale	*Defining relations*	*Examples of appropriate statistics*	*Appropriate statistical test*
Nominal	1. Equivalence	Mode, Frequency, contingency coeff-icient of correlation	–
Ordinal	1. Equivalence 2. Greater than	Spearman's 'r' Median, Percentile, 'r' Kendall, 'r' Kendal W.	Non-parametric statistical tests.
Interval	1. Equivalence 2. Greater than 3. Known ratio of any two intervals.	Mean, SD, Pearson product moment correlation, Multiple product moment correlation.	Non-parametric and Parameter Statistical Tests.
Ratio	1. Equivalence 2. Greater than 3. Known ratio of any two intervals. 4. Known ratio of any two scale values.	Geometric mean coefficient of variation.	

education have been achieved. This is the only process through which a student may come to know his deficiency and weakness in the concerned subject. Similarly teacher may also evaluate him where he could not make his point clear in the class so that he may be able to remove short comings in effective teaching-learning process. It is the best way to get valuable feed back on the decision, planning and implementation of programme. Thus evaluation plays and important and significant role in programme and system.

Concept of Evaluation

The term evaluation has several meanings in education and Psychology. The evaluation is a qualitative as well as quantitative descriptions of pupil's behaviour.

Tuchman defines "evaluation is a process wherein the parts, processes or outcomes of a programme are examined to see whether they are satisfactory particularly with reference to the programme stated objectives, our own standard of excellence."

The above definition explains that evaluation involves a process of assessment of an object or event with reference to some standard.

Evaluation may be defined as a systematic process of determining the extent to which teaching learning objectives have been achieved, by the teachers and pupils.

On the analysis of this definition, it is stated that evaluation is systematic process which reveals that their is scientific-thinking in evaluation and may be assumed that teaching-learning objectives have previously been identified.

The definition also indicates that evaluation is a much comprehensive and inclusive term than measurement which is limited to quantitative descriptions of human behaviour as its results are always expressed in numbers while evaluation includes qualitative or quantitative description of pupils or both. One thing more, plus to evaluation i.e., it always has value judgements concerned to the desirability of results. It may be explained with the help of following diagram, the comprehensive nature of evaluation and the role of measurement in the evaluation process.

Evaluation = Quantitative description (measurement)
and/or
Qualitative description (non-measurement) +
Value judgement.

The significant stress in classroom evaluation is on the extent to which learning outcomes are achieved.

According to Hanna, "Evaluation is the process of gathering and interpreting evidence on changes in the behaviour of all students as they progress through school."

In Encyclopaedia of Educational Research, the evaluation has been explained as "Evaluation is a relatively new technical term introduced to designate a more comprehensive concept of measurement, that is implied in conventional tests and examinations."

This definition states that evaluation in classroom context implies in broader sense than only conventional examinations but includes, achievements, attitudes, aptitude, interest, personality traits, intelligence, and skills factors, are also taken into considerations. All the behavioural objectives (cognitive, affective, and psychomotor learning) outcomes are measured and assessed in evaluation process.

Types of Testing and Evaluation Process

One of the distinctive characteristics of the evaluation process is the use of wide variety of tests. This may be classified and described in many different ways depending on the frame of reference and purpose of evaluation in the varying contexts of use. It is the tests that are used as tools of measurements and guide us in evaluation. We may categorize on the following lines:

Maximum Performance Vs. Typical Performance

1. *Maximum Performance:* In this category, those tests are included which are used to determine a person's capacities. Procedures of this type are concerned with how well an individual performs when motivated to put forth his or her best effort. Aptitude and achievement tests are included. Aptitude tests are designed particularly to predict success in some further learning activity whereas achievement tests are designed to indicate degree of success in some post learning activity.
2. *Typical Performance:* Evaluation of typical behaviour of the persons fall in the general area of the personality evaluation. The evaluation of students' interests attitudes and various aspects of personal social adjustments are included in this category. Classification as to use in classroom.

We may classify such evaluation in the following ways:

1. *Placement evaluation:* This type of evaluation is concerned with the pupils entry based on performance.
   Placement evaluation is designed to place the right person in the right place. This type of evaluation focuses on questions such as:
   (*a*) The extent to which the learner possesses the knowledge and skills needed to begin the planned instructions.
   (*b*) The extent to which the learner already mastered the objectives of the planned instructions.
   (*c*) The what extent the learner's interest, aptitude, work habits and personality traits, indicate his success better.

The goal of placement evaluation is to determine the position in the instructional sequence and the mode of instruction that is most likely to provide optimum achievement for each learner.

2. *Formative Evaluation:* The formative assessment is concerned to identify pupils's weaknesses in attainment with a view to help him to overcome them. In other words, it may be stated that such an evaluation is used to monitor learning progress during instruction. We have the following goals:
   (*a*) To provide continuous feed back to both student and educator concerning learning successes and failures.
   (*b*) Such feedback is to provide to pupils which may enforce them for successful learning and identify the specific.
   (*c*) To identify the specific learning errors that need correction.
   (*d*) It provides feedback to the teachers to modify instructions.

Diagnostic Evaluation

This tests help us to identify the areas of learning in which learner needs a remedial teaching. This typc of evaluation is concerned with the persistent or continuous learning difficulties that are left unresolved by the standard corrective prescriptions of formative evaluation. As we know that formative evaluation provide a kind of first aid treatment for simple learning problems while diagnostic evaluations searches for the underlying causes of those problems that do not respond to first-aid treatment. Thus diagnostic evaluation is more comprehensive and detailed.

It is remarked that the main aim of diagnostic evaluation is to specify and determine the factual causes of learning problems and thus to formulate a plan of remedial action.

Summative Evaluation

This type of evaluation is designed to determine the extent to which instructional objectives have been attained and is utilized polarity to assign course grade or to certify pupils mastery of the intended learning outcomes. Thus the summative evaluation aims at certifying and grading the attainment of the learner at the end of a given course.

The teacher made achievement tests and ratings on various type of performance are generally used techniques to evaluate students at the end of the course. This type of evaluations also provide informations for judging the appropriateness of the course objectives and the effectiveness of the instructions.

Difference between Measurement and Evaluation

Measurement	*Evaluation*
1. Measurement refers to the observations that are expressed quantitatively.	1. The evaluation is expressed qualitatively.
2. Measurement answers to the question—How much ?	2. Evaluation answers—How Good?
3. Measurement is precise and objective.	3. Evaluation is subjective.
4. It assigns numerical value to quantify the data.	4. Evaluation adds value judgement to the state of quality.
5. It is concerned with the level of attainment.	5. It is concerned in improvement.

Assessment

All teaching of classroom involves evaluation. The key of evaluation is Judgement, that makes its decisions on measurement. As we have seen that measurement in evaluation put in quantitative terms. However, not all the evaluative decisions made by teachers involve measurement. There are some decisions which are based on information that is difficult to express numerically such as student preferences, information from parents, previous experiences. Modern times both evaluation and measurement experts are using the assessment to describe the process of gathering information about learner's learning. Assessment is broader than testing and measurement as it includes all kinds of ways to sample and observe students' skills, knowledge and abilities. Assessment is "any of a variety of procedure used to obtain information about student performance" (Linn and Gronlund, 2000). "Assessment may be formal (unit test) or informal (observing who emerges as a leader in a group)." The assessments usually involve testing and the reporting of scores. Test results have no meaning by themselves, we must make some kind of comparison to interpret them. There are two basic types of comparison.

Norm-referenced Tests

A test score is compared to the scores obtained by other people who have taken the some test. Every kind of a test provide the 'norms' for determining the meaning of a given individual's score. Norm is a typical level of performance for a particular group.

Norms Groups

A group whose average score serves a standard for evaluating any student's score on a test.

There are at least three types of norms groups in education (comparison groups) – The class, or school itself, the school district and national samples.

Characteristics of Norm-referenced Tests

1. Such tests cover a wide range of general objectives rather than assessing a limited number of specific objectives.
2. These tests are especially useful in measuring the overall achievement of students.
3. Non-referenced tests are also appropriate when only the top candidates are to be admitted to a programme.

Limitations

1. The results of a norm-referenced test do not tell us whether students are ready to learn more advanced material.
2. Norm-referenced tests are appropriate specifically for measuring affective and Psychomotor objectives.
3. Norm-referenced tests tend to encourage competition and comparison of scores for instance some students may compete to be the best while others realizing that being the best is impossible, may compete to be the worst.

Criterion-referenced Tests

In this type of tests, scores are compared not to those of others but to a given criterion or standard of performance. Such tests measure the mastery of very specific objectives. The result of such test should tell the teacher exactly what the students can and cannot do, at least under certain conditions.

For example, this type of test would be useful in measuring the ability to add three-digit numbers. We may design a test with 20 different problems, and the standard for mastery could be set at 17 correct out of 20 (the standard to be set is arbitrary and may be based such things as the teacher's experience). If two students receive scores of 7 and 11, it does not matter that one student did better than the other because no one reached to the standard.

Characteristics of Criterion-referenced Tests

In teaching basic skills there are many instances where comparison to a pre-set standard is more important than comparison to the performance of others.

Limitations

1. Criterion-referenced tests are not appropriate for every situation.
2. Many subjects cannot be broken down into a set of specific objectives.
3. Although standards are important in this type of testing, but they are often be arbitrary.

Deciding on the Type of Test to be Used

1. Norm-referenced tests may work when we are:
   - *(a)* Measuring general ability in certain areas such as literature, maths, and science.
   - *(b)* Assessing the range of abilities in a large group.
   - *(c)* Selecting top candidates when only a few openings are available.
2. Criterion-referenced tests—Such tests may work best when we are:
   - *(a)* Measuring mastery of basic skills.
   - *(b)* Determining if students have pre-requisites to start a new unit.
   - *(c)* Assessing affective and psychomotor objectives.
   - *(d)* Grouping students for instruction.

QUESTIONS

A. Long Answer Type Questions

1. Explain the concept of measurement. Discuss its various functions.
2. What do you understand by the levels of measurement? Discuss various levels of measurement by giving suitable examples.
3. Discuss the concept of evaluation. Why is it important?

4. 'Measurement' is meaningless without 'evaluation'. Discuss.
5. Evaluation is the most important aspect of achievements of school children. Why? Discuss various techniques of evaluation.
6. "Evaluation assists a teacher to obtain a desired goal or objectives of teaching-learning process." Discuss.
7. Differentiate between measurement and evaluation. Prove both are complementary to one and other.

B. Short Answer Type Questions

1. Define measurement and its levels.
2. Discuss concept of evaluation.
3. Functions of educational measurement.
4. Differentiate between diagnostic and prognostic evaluation.

C. Objective Answer Type Questions

1. There is a difference between measurement and evaluation. True/False
2. Evaluation is the process of gathering and interpreting the data. True/False
3. Measurement has personal errors but no constant error. True/False
4. There is no absolute zero in Psychology. True/False
5. There are three levels of measurement. True/False
6. Measurement is content centred while evaluation is objective centred. True/False
7. Evaluation is the small form of measurement. True/False
8. Measurement is the assignment of_____ to objects or events according to _________.
9. There is no________ in interval scale.
10. In measurement, when measures are expressed in equal units and are also taken from true zero. This is:
    (a) Interval scale (b) Nominal scale.
    (c) Ratio scale (d) Ordinal scale.
11. The highest level of measurement which has true zero point is known as:
    (a) Interval scale (b) Nominal scale
    (c) Ordinal scale (d) Ratio scale.
12. F = 9/5c + 32 is an example of:
    (a) Interval scale (b) Nominal scale.
    (c) Ratio scale (d) Ordinal scale.

SUGGESTED READINGS

1. Travers, R.M.W., "Educational Measurement", McMillan and Co. New York, 1955.
2. Thorndike, R.L and Hagen E., "Measurement and Evaluation in Psychology and Education", John Wiley and Sons, New York, 1955.
3. Siegal, Sidney, "Non-parametric Statistics" McGraw hill Book, Co., New York, 1956.
4. Rammers, H.H. "Educational Gage, N.L., and Rummel, J.F Measurement and Evaluation", Harper and Brothers, New York, 1943.
5. Payne, D.A and MC Marris, R.F., "Educational and Psychological Measurement" Oxford and IBH Publishing Co., New Delhi, 1972.
6. Bradfield and Mordock, "Measurement and Evaluation in Education", MacMillan, New York, 1957.

2

Item Analysis

Item Analysis, Its Procedure, and Selection

Item analysis is an integral part of any test construction. Therefore it becomes essential to have the critical knowledge of item analysis. Both reliability and validity of any tests depend on the characteristics and qualities of their test items. High reliability and validity can be built into test in advance through item analysis as the adequacy of a test. Whatever its purpose depends upon the care with which the items of the test have been chosen. Most of the psychological and educational achievement tests are made up of a large number of items. Item analysis is relevant in the construction of informal local tests too which are used in examinations prepared by the teachers to use in the classroom. Some of the general guidelines for effective item writing as well as simpler statistical techniques of item analysis can improve the quality of classroom tests.

Item analysis can be analysed qualitatively in terms of their content and form, which includes the construction of face and content validity as well as the evaluation of items for effective item writing procedures. Similarly quantitative analysis includes the measurement of item difficulty and items discrimination. It is therefore necessary to analyse each item by adopting standardized procedure in order to retain only those that suit the purpose and rationality of device being used.

According to Lamarck. "The procedure used to judge the quality of an item is called item-analysis."

Harper throws light on the importance of item analysis by describing it as the most time consuming, interesting, challenging, and rewarding part of the test analysis.

Test can be modified and improved by selecting, substituting or revising of items. It is the item analysis that makes possible to shorten a test and at the same time increase its validity and reliability.

Objectives of Item Analysis

1. The major objective of an item analysis is to obtain objective information concerning the items we collect for the test. This information is valuable as it provides the opportunity to check up on the test writer's subjective judgement in selecting the items to comprise the test.
2. The second objective of an item analysis is to select the best item to construct the final test form. The selection enables the researcher to modify the test in the direction as he desires and rejects those items which are poor and have least validity.
3. To obtain the difficulty value of each item, to classify them as difficult, moderate and easy items.
4. To obtain the discrimination power to differentiate between capable, incapable and less capable examinees in the test. At this stage items are classified on the basis of indices-positive, negative or zero discrimination.
5. To reject the items outrightly on the basis of having negative and no discrimination power.
6. To find out the powerful and poor distractors which provide the basis for the modification to be made in some of the items.
7. To provide the basis for preparing the final draft of a test.
8. Item analysis helps to fulfill the objective of the test construction which require items to be arranged in the order of difficulty.

Criterion of Item Analysis

There are two major aspects of evaluating the items which are considered to be the most important.

1. The Difficulty/level/index/value of each item.
2. Discriminatory power/value of each item.

Difficulty Level/Value/Index

This is determined by the percentage of individuals who are able to pass each item. If an item is capable to distinguish among individuals, then it should neither be so easy that all individuals can solve or answer it, nor it should be so difficult that no one may be able to answer that item. Statistically an item be passed by 50 percent of a group discriminates between more pairs of persons than does an item passed by a smaller or larger percentage. The difficulty level indicates that items to be included in the final draft that are passed by large percentages, same by small percentages with many degrees between the extremes.

According to J.P. Guilford, "The difficulty index of an item is defined as the proportion or percentage of the examinees who have answered the item correctly."

Freeman defined, "as the proportion of certain sample of subjects who actually know the answer of an item."

Analysis of these definitions indicates that difficulty index depends upon the correct answer of an item rather than answering of an item. In this regard it may be stated that definition given by freeman is the most dependable and functional because an item can even be answered correctly by guessing while examinee does not know the correct answer of an item. The difficulty of an item may be determined in different ways. H.E. Garrett mentioned it inthree ways.

(i) by the judgement of competent people who rank the items in order of their level of difficulty.
(ii) how quickly an item can to solved.
(iii) by the number of examinees in the group who get the item right.

The first two procedures are usually the first step especially when the items are for use in special aptitude test or in performance tests where qualitative distinctions and opinion serve as criteria. But the third way i.e. number right or the proportion of the group which can solve an item correctly is the 'standard' method for determining in objective type of conducting examination. This is the statistical approach as contrasted with the judgemental approach to item validity.

Discrimination Index or Validity Index

The discriminatory index of an item is determined by the extent to which the given item discriminates among individuals who differ sharply in the function measured by the test as a whole.

According to Blood and Budd, "Index of discrimination is that ability of an item on the basis of which discrimination is made between superior and inferior."

Bean defined, "the degree to which a single item separates the superior from the inferior individuals in the trait or group of traits being measured."

Marshall and Hales defined, 'The discriminatory power of an item may be defined as the extent to which success and failure on that item indicate the possession of the trait or the achievement being measured.

On the basis of the above definitions, the term discriminating of an item is used for the item reliability and validity e.g., if an item of a test is answered by all the examinees, it indicates that the item's deiscriminatory, index is zero. There is no use of its inclusion in the test, such items are outrightly be rejected. Similarly if an item is not answered correctly by all the students, i.e. neither by the superior nor by the inferior indicates that item does not discriminate between superior and inferior students. There is no use of such items to include in the test. Such items are also be rejected.

Kinds/Types of Discriminatory Power

There are two types of discriminatory powers.

1. *Item Reliability:* It is considered as the degree to which an item distinguishes between high and low groups on the basis of some test scores.
   Loevinger Terms: Item reliability as internal consistency of the test. He further States that this kind of internal consistency of the test is increased, the empirical validity of test is decreased.
2. Item Validity

Relation between difficulty index and discrimination index.

1. Both indices are complimentary to each other instead of being contradictory.
2. The aim of both indices is to choose purposeful items for the final draft of the test.
3. The items may be rejected on the basis of one index either of difficulty value or discriminatory power.
4. The items having negative discriminatory power are outrightly rejected whatever their difficulty values are.

5. The difficulty index depends on item variation and subject variation as discriminative power depends on the item variation alone, as the groups are formed on the basis of subject variation.
6. Both are considered to select item to the final draft of the test.

Process of Items Analysis

1. Item Variance and Difficulty. The proportion of passing an item is an index of an item difficulty e.g., if 95 per cent of a standard group pass an item, it is easy and if only 5 per cent among the group pass the item is considered as hard. Suppose if.

   P = The Percentage (%) of passing an item

   Q = the percentage (%) of failing an item

   Then stadard deviation (σ) of the item

   (its variability) = $\sqrt{pq}$

   Its variance = pq or σ^2

   When p = .50, q = .50

   The variance = .25

This is the maximum variance which an item can have. Therefore an item with difficulty index of .50 (p = .50) or goes above it, the variance of the item steadily decreases. This has been shown in the following Table 2.1.

Table–2.1

S. No.	*p (% of passing an item)*	*q (%) of failing an item*	*Variance of the item pq or σ^2*
1.	.50	.50	.25
2.	.60	.40	.24
3.	.70	.30	.21
4.	.80	.20	.16

Similarly if examinees in a group of 10, 5 examinees pass an item and 5 examinees fail in an item therefore p = q = .50. There are (.5 × .5 = .25) differentiation or discriminations possible at each of 5 passers is separated from each of the 5 who fail. Similarly:

P	q	Discriminations
.6	.4	.24

.7	.3	.21
.8	.2	.16

The larger the variance of the item, greater the number of separations among the individuals, the test items is able to make. Other things being equal items of moderately difficult (40%, 50%, 60% passing) are to be preferred to those items which are much easier or harder.

Items Intercorrelations and Range of Difficulty

In item difficulty we do not only consider individual item difficulty but also the intercorrelation and to compute all of the item correlations. In such circumstance the normal curve is taken, as a guide in the selection of difficulty indices (for detail see chapter normal probability curve).

Correcting Difficulty Indices for Chance Success

It is important to estimate the number of examinees who get the right answer through correct knowledge and to rule out answers which are based upon guess work. To correct chance success, it is assumed that *(a)* wrong answers are due to absence of knowledge and that *(b)* to one who does not know the right answer. Under these assumptions it is expected that some of those who really did not know the right answer but corrected it by chance. We use a formula for correcting the difficulty index of an item for chance success is:

$$P_c = \frac{R - \frac{W}{(K-1)}}{N - HR}$$

Where:

P_c = The per cent who actually know the correct answer.
R = The number who get the correct answer.
W = The number who get the wrong answer.
N = The number of examinees in the sample.
HR = The number of examinees who do not reach the item (and do not try it)
K = The number of options or choices

Illustration

Suppose that a sample of 300 examinees take a test of 10 items. Each item has 5 choices. Out of them 150 examines answered 46 items correctly 120 examines answered them incorrectly and 30 examinees do not reach the item hence do not attempt it in the time limit. Thus By substituting the value in the above formula, we get:

$$P_c = \frac{150-\frac{120}{5-1}}{300-30}$$

$P_c = .44$ or 44 per cent

This corrected value of the difficulty index is an approximation but gives more nearly true measure than does the experimentally obtained percentage.

Determination of Validity Index or Discrimination Power of an Item

A number of methods have been devised to determine the discrimination power of an item.

But biserial 'r' gives the correlation of an item with total score on the test or with scores in some independent criterion. Much preferred method of determining validity by the researchers or test maker is to set up extreme groups in computing the validity of an item.

Techniques of Dichtotomizing High and Low Groups

There are various ways to classify a sample into high (top) and low (bottom) groups. There are three main techniques which are used in classifying top and bottom groups.

(a) 25 per cent top and 25 per cent bottom dichotomy.
(b) 33 per cent top and 33 per cent bottom dichotomy.
(c) 27 per cent top and 27 per cent bottom dichotomy.
(d) The last *(c)* dichotomy was given by T.L. Kelley which is the most popular and widely used in item analysis.

The procedure. The following steps are followed in using the above mentioned techniques. Here we are giving the method of 27 per cent top and 27 per cent bottom dichotomy. However the procedure is the same for all above mentioned dichotomy except setection of its percentage of top and bottom.

Step 1. The number of examinees who answer the item correctly is selected upper and lower subgroups.

Step 2. The discriminative power of the item—its consistency with total score on the test is gauged by the biserial correlation (r_{bis}) of the item and the whole test. The biserial correlation (r_{bis}) is read from a table as shown.

Illustration

We follow the procedure in detail as below:

1. Arrangement of test papers in order of size for test scores. The test paper to be put having highest score on the top. Assuming that we have 200 examines. Now we would count 27 per cent of papers at the top and the same percentage of papers to be counted at the bottom. These 54 papers are to be put in the first pipe and another 54 in the second and the middle 92 papers are to be kept aside.
2. Now tally the number in the top group which passes each item on the test and the number in the bottom group which passes each item. The numbers are counerted into percentage.
3. The percents are to be corrected for chance success.
4. Entering table from the normalized biserial correlation (r_{bis}) as determined from proportion of correct responses in upper and lower 27 per cents of the group.
5. Average the percentage (top and bottom groups) is find the difficulty index of the item.

The following example of 5 sample items make it clear how to campute the difficulty indices and validity indices.

Table–2.2

Item No.	*% Right in the Top 27% Corrected*	*% right in the bottom 27% Corrected*	*Difficulty Index D.I.*	*Validity Index V.I.*
5	73	58	.65	.17
21	61	38	.49	.23
36	50	50	.50	.00
54	43	36	.39	.07
75	36	8	.22	.40

The Difficulty Index (D.I.): It is calculated by averaging the percents corrected in the upper and lower groups e.g., for item no 5, we have—

% right in the top 27 per cent corrected = 73

% right in the bottom 27 per cent corrected = 58

$$D.I. = \frac{73 + 58}{2} = \frac{131}{2 \times 100} = .65$$

Similarly other items may also be computed to find out its difficulty level or index.

Validity Index (V.I.): The validity index or discriminatory power of each item is read from table which is abridged from J.C. Flanagon's table of normalized biserial coefficient (r_{bis}). The r_{bis} for the split 73–58 (item No. 5 is .17 and for the split 61-38 is .23.

Acceptable Validity Index: The size of an acceptable validity index depends upon:

(*a*) Length of the test.
(*b*) The range of the difficulty indices
(*c*) The purpose for which the test is designed.

However as a general rule the items with validity indices of .20 or more are regarded as satisfactory. The items having negative validity must be discarded. If the proportion of correct responses in the lower 27 per cent exceeds that in the upper then enter the table with the lower 27 per cent at the top and put a negative signs to the coefficient.

Cross Validation: It is important that the validation of a computed test should always be computed on a new sample i.e., one different from that used in the item analysis. This process is called 'cross validation.'

Normalized biserial coefficient of correlation as determined from proportion of correct responses in upper and lower 27 per cent of the group.

Correction of Difficulties Indices for Chance Errors

Guilford Formula – Generally it happens with the students while answers the items particular in multiple choice answers, they answer correctly without knowing the answer *i.e.,* they guess the answer. In such a situation we use Guilford's correction formula to restrict them from the guessing, the formula is:

$$P_c = \left(R - \frac{W}{(K-1)}\right)\frac{1}{N}$$

P_c = Percentage of the correct answer what they really know.
R = Percentage of correct answer
W = Percentage of wrong answer.
N = No of candidates in the sample,
K = Number of choice.

Example: Suppose there are 200 students in a sample, only 140 students are able to solve item while each item has four alternatives.

Here

R = 140, W = 60

N = 200, K = 4

Substituting in the above formula, we find.

$$P_c = \left(R - \frac{W}{(K-1)}\right)\frac{1}{N} = [W = N - R]$$

$$P_c = \left(140 - \frac{60}{4-1}\right)\frac{1}{200} = (140 - 20)\frac{1}{200} = \frac{120}{200} = .75$$

Or = .75 × 100 = 75 per cent (difficulty level in per cent)

Unattempted or Unreached Items. It has been observed that students do not attempt or unable to read to some items because the shortage of time or items being difficult such items are called unattempted or unreached items.

Suppose: A student attempted 1 to 25 items in 50 items and did not attempt 26 and 27 and again solved 28 to 40 and then did not solve onward questions. In such situations.

Items no 41 to 50 will be known unattempted items no 26 and 27 shall not be known as unattempted or unreached.

In such circumstance the above menioned formula becomes:

$$P_c = \left(R - \frac{W}{K-1}\right)\frac{1}{N - NR}$$

Here NR = Number of students who could not attempt the questions.

Suppose there are 300 students in a sample and a test of 100 items has been a administered upon them. There are (five) 5 alternatives. Now further, there are 150 correct answer and 120 wrong answer and 30 unattempted.

By substituting the in the above fomula.

$$P_c = \left(150 - \frac{120}{5-1}\right)\frac{1}{300-30}$$

$$= (150 - 30)\frac{1}{270} = \frac{120 \times 1}{270} = \frac{4}{9} = .44$$

$$= .44 \times 100 = 44 \text{ per cent}$$

Kelley's Formula – When the number of students is more, we use Kelley's 27 per cent top and 27 per cent bottom formula which is gives below:

$$P_c = \frac{1}{2}\left\{\left(R_H - \frac{W_H}{K-1}\right)\frac{1}{N_L+NR_H} + \left(R_L - \frac{W_L}{K-1}\right)\frac{1}{N_L-NR_L}\right\}$$

R_H = Number of top 27 per cent examinees giving right response

W_H = Number of top 27 per cent giving wrong responses

N_H = Total Number of top 27 per cent examinees

NR_H = Number of top 27 per cent students who did not attempt that very item.

R_L = Number of bottom lower 27 per cent students giving right response.

W_L = Number of bottom or lower 27 per cent students giving wrong response.

N_L = Total number of bottom or lower 27 per cent students.

NR_L = Number of bottom or lower 27 per cent who did not attempt that very items.

Illustration

An Achievement test was administered upon a group of 300 students. The investigator was interested in calculating (D-I) Difficulty Index of item No 80 by Kelley's 27 per cent method for which the different values are as under:

$N_H = 80, R_H = 60, W_H = 10, N_{RH} = 10$

$N_L = 80, R_L = 20, W_L = 40, N_{RL} = 20$

$K = 5$

Solution. By substituting the above values in Kelley's formula given above:

$$Pc = \frac{1}{2}\left\{60 - \frac{\frac{10}{5-1}}{80-10} + 20 - \frac{\frac{40}{5-1}}{80-20}\right\} = \frac{1}{2}\left\{\frac{60-2.5}{70} + \frac{20-10}{60}\right\}$$

$$\frac{1}{2}\left(\frac{57.5}{70} + \frac{10}{60}\right) = \frac{1}{2}\left(\frac{4150}{4200}\right) = \frac{1}{2} \times .98 = .49$$

$= .49 \times 100 = 49$ per cent (difficulty index in percentage)

Calculation of discriminatory power (D.P. using chi–square Test formula.)

When there is difference in correcting difficulty indices for chance error by using above formula and becomes very difficult to study comparatively the result of the item, consequently we use chi-square test formula to calculate discriminatory power of the item. There are two forms of this formula.

1. When $R_H > R_L$
2. When $R_L > R_H$

$$D.P. = \frac{R_H - R_L - 1}{\sqrt{R_T\left(1 - \frac{R_{RT}}{N_T - N_{RT}}\right)}}$$

$$D.P. = \frac{R_H - R_L + 1}{\sqrt{R_T\left(1 - \frac{R_T}{N_T - N_{RT}}\right.}}$$

Illustration

An achievement test of artithmetic was administrated on 300 students of class VIII. The different values related to test are given below. Calculate Discriminatory power.

$N_H = 80$, $R_H = 60$, and N_{RH} 10

$N_L = 80$, $R_L = 15$, and $N_{RL} = 25$

Here, $N_T = N_H + N_L$

$R_T = R_H + R_L$

$N_{RT} = N_{RH} + N_{RL}$

By substituting given value in the above formula we find

$$D.P. = \frac{60 - 15 - 1}{\sqrt{75}\left(1 - \frac{75}{160 - 35}\right)} = \frac{60 - 16}{\sqrt{75}\left(1 - \frac{75}{125}\right)} = \frac{44}{\sqrt{75}\left(1 - \frac{3}{5}\right)}$$

$$D.P. = \frac{44}{\sqrt{75 \times \frac{2}{5}}} = \frac{44}{\sqrt{30}}$$

$$D.P. = \frac{44}{5.47} = 8.04$$

$$D.P. = 8.04$$

Horst's formula correction for guessing Horst stressed on the importance of powerful distractor and evolved the following formula-correction for guessing

$S = R - D_P$

S = Actual correct responses on the item

R = Right responses on the item

DP = Powerful distractor in the item.

Illustration

The following item is administered on a group of 50 students of psychology. The responses are obtained on different alternatives of the item indicated against:

Item – individuals differ from one another in

1.	Kind	7
2.	Quality	8
3.	Personality	15
4.	Degree	20

The correct alternative is (4). The powerful distracter is (3) which is answered by 15 subjects.

Here we would like to apply both *(i)* Guilford's formula-correction for guessing and *(ii)* Horsts formula-correction for guessing to compare the utility in their application.

First Guilford's formula-correction for guessing:

Where R = 20, W = 30, n = 4

$$S = R - \frac{W}{n - 1} = 20 - \frac{30}{3} = 20 - 10 = 10$$

$$S = 20 - 10 = 10$$

S = 10 indicates that 10 subjects of the group actually know the answer of the item and 10 subject guessed the right response Guilford's formula-correction or guessing is based upon the following assumptions:

(i) All the distractors of an item are qually attractive. Therefore the average of wrong responses is to be subtracted from the right responses.

(ii) All the subjects try to attempt answer correctly by guessing. They apply guessing for the item for which they do not know the actual answer.

This formula seems appropriate but imposes the high penalty to the subjects who have small number of right responses and less penalty to those who have large number of right responses. There is no uniformity in the penalty.

Horst's formula-correction for guessing as per example given above.

S = R – Dp
S = 20 – 15 = 5

It indicates that 5 subjects out of 50 actually know the correct answer of the item and 15 subjects used guessing for the right responses.

The Horst's formula correction for guessing is based upon the following two assumptions:

1. All the distractors of an item are not equally attractive for the subjects. There is an order of attraction of alternatives.
2. The correct alternative may attract the subjects equally as the power distractor.

If we compare the utility and application of both guessing formulae we reach to this conclusion that Guilford's formula-correction for guessing is more appropriate and imposes less penalty on the subjects as campared to Horst's formula-correction for guessing.

Item Analysis by Point Biserial Correlation Technique

When items are scored as 1 if right and 0 if wrong and the assumption of normality in the distribution of right or wrong responses in unwarranted. In such cases point biserial *r* is appropriate. The point biserial *r* assumes that the variable which has been classified into two categories can be thought of as concentrated at two distinct points along a continuum. The formula for the point biserial *r* is:

$$r_{\text{pbis}} = \frac{\text{Mp} - \text{Mq}}{\sigma}\sqrt{\text{pq}}$$

Mp and Mq are the means of the two categories.

P = is the proportion of first sample in the first group.
q = proportion in the second group.
σ = SD of entire sample.

The point biserial *r* is especially useful in the analysis of the items of a test i.e., in item test correlations. The example makes it clear the kind of data used in item analysis.

Example – calculation of point biserial *r* (1 = item passed, 0 = item failed:

Table–2.3
Item Analysis with the Help of Point Biserial Correlation

Subject	*Test Score*	*Item Score*	x^2	y^2	xy
1.	25	1	625	1	25
2.	23	1	529	1	23
3.	18	0	324	0	0
4.	24	0	576	0	0
5.	23	1	529	1	23
6.	20	0	400	0	0
7.	19	0	361	0	0
8.	22	1	484	1	22
9.	21	1	441	1	21
10.	23	1	509	1	23
11.	21	0	441	0	0
12.	20	0	400	0	0
13.	21	1	441	1	21
14.	21	1	441	1	21
15.	20	1	484	1	20
16.	323	9	7005	9	201

Number of passing item = 9

$$M_p = \frac{201}{9} = 22.33$$

Number of failing item = q = 15 – 9 = 6

$$M_p = \frac{323 - 201}{6} = \frac{122}{6} = 20.33$$

$$\sigma = \sqrt{\frac{N\sum x^2 - x(\sum x)^2}{N}} = \sqrt{\frac{15 \times 7005 - (323)^2}{15}}$$

$$= \sqrt{\frac{105075 - 104329}{15}} = \sqrt{\frac{746}{15}} = \frac{27.31}{15} 1.82$$

$$P = \frac{9}{15} = .60 \qquad q = \frac{6}{15} = .40$$

Substituting the values in the formula of point bisenal *r*

$$r_{pbis} = \frac{Mp - Mq}{\sigma}\sqrt{pq} = \frac{22.33 - 20.33}{1.82}\sqrt{.60 \times .40}$$

$$\frac{2}{1.82}\sqrt{.24}$$

$$= 1.09 \times .48 = .52$$

D.P. = .52 is substantially correlated with *catenating list* score—passed by high scores more often than by low scores. The $r_{pbis} = 0.52$ is the discriminative index of the item.

The difficulty index is the (P = 0.60), it indicates that 60 per cent examinees have answered the item correctly.

The items D.V. is .60 and D.P. = 0.52. It seems to be good item and it should be selected for the final draft.

B. 50 per cent top and 50 per cent below—Right Response Method Description of the Procedure

Illustration—A Teacher desires to prepare an objective test having 10 items. He preliminary prepared 16 items and administered upon 10 students. He is to find out the difficulty level and power of discrimination of each item.

Table-2.4
Item Analysis

Sl.No. Items	*1*	*2*	*3*	*4*	*5*	*6*	*7*	*8*	*9*	*10*	*11*	*12*	*13*	*14*	*15*	*16*	*Score obtained*
A	✓	✓	✓	✓	×	✓	✓	×	✓	✓	×	✓	✓	✓	✓	✓	13
B	✓	✓	✓	✓	✓	✓	✓	✓	✓	✓	✓	✓	✓	✓	✓	✓	14
C	✓	✓	✓	✓	✓	✓	✓	✓	✓	✓	✓	✓	✓	✓	✓	✓	12
D	✓	✓	×	✓	✓	✓	×	×	✓	✓	✓	×	×	✓	✓	✓	13
E	✓	✓	✓	×	×	✓	×	×	✓	✓	×	×	✓	×	×	×	7
F	✓	×	×	×	✓	×	×	×	✓	×	×	×	×	×	×	×	4
G	✓	✓	✓	✓	×	✓	×	✓	✓	✓	×	×	✓	×	✓	×	10
H	✓	✓	✓	×	×	×	×	×	✓	×	×	×	✓	×	×	×	5
I	×	×	✓	✓	✓	×	×	×	×	✓	✓	✓	✓	✓	×	×	8
J	×	✓	✓	✓	×	×	✓	✓	✓	×	×	✓	✓	×	×	✓	9

Since total No. of Student 10. Therefore 5 students shall be counted as upper group and 5 students shall be lower group according to their score obained. *When we put up scores in descending order.*

Table–2.5

Student	*Scores*	*Obtained*
B	14	50%
A	13	Upper or
D	13	superior group
C	12	
G	11	
J	9	50%
I	8	Inferior or
E	6	lower group
H	5	
E	4	

Table–2.6
Difficulty Index and Validity Index

Higher Group or Upper Group			*Lower of Infenor Group*		*Difficulty Level Index and Discrimination Power*			
Sl. No.	*No. of Right Answers* R_H	R_H *Pro Diffculty Level*	*No. of Right Answers*	R_L *Pro Diffculty Level*	*D.V.* $\frac{R_H + R_L}{2}$	*V.I. or D.V.* $R_H - R_L$,	$R_H - R_L$ *Proportion*	
1.	5	5/5 1.00	3	3/5 .60	.80	+2	.40	AV.
2.	5	5/5 1.00	3	3/5 .60	.80	+2	.40	AV.
3.	5	5/5 1.00	3	3/5 .60	.80	+2	.40	AV.
4.	3	3/5 .06	2	3/5 .40	.50	+1	.20	Poor
5.	5	5/5 1.00	1	1/5 .20	.60	+4	.40	AV.
6.	5	5/5 1.00	0	0/5 .00	.50	+5	.50	Sup.
7.	2	2/5 .40	1	1/5 .20	.30	+1	.20	Poor
8.	3	3/5 .60	1	1/5 .20	.40	+2	.40	AV.
9.	4	4/5 .80	1	1/5 .20	.50	+3	.60	Good
10.	4	4/5 .80	1	1/5 .20	.50	+3	.60	Good
11.	4	4/5 .80	1	1/5 .20	.50	+3	.60	Good
12.	5	5/5 1.00	3	3/5 .60	.80	+2	.40	AV.
13.	5	5/5 1.00	3	3/5 .60	.80	+2	.40	AV.
14.	3	3/5 .60	3	3/5 .60	.60	0	.00	AV.
15.	1	1/5 .20	3	3/5 .60	.40	– 2	.40	Neg.
16.	4	4/5 .80	3	3/5 .60	.70	+1	.20	Poor

Difficulty Index D.I. = $\frac{R_H + R_L}{2}$

In the above table the items that have index level more than .70 are easy items while index level less than .35 are considered difficult items.

Discriminating Power/Value/or Validity Index

The difference between the right responses in higher or upper group and right responses in lower a bottom group is know as the validity index. We can calculate the Validity Index V.I. with the following formula:

V.I. = $R_H - R_L$ (When N being the same for both groups)

Table–2.7
Validity Index

Item No.	*Right responses in higher group*	*Right responses is lower group*	R_H–R_L	*Degree*
1	5	3	+2	Average
2	5	3	+2	Average
3	5	3	+2	Average
4	3	2	+1	Poor
5	5	1	+4	Above average
6	5	0	+5	Superior
7	2	1	+1	Poor
8	3	1	+2	Average
9	4	1	+3	Good
10	4	1	+3	Good
11	4	1	+3	Good
12	5	3	+2	Average
13	5	3	+2	Average
14	3	3	0	V. Poor
15	1	3	–2	Negative
16	4	3	+1	Poor

Negative Validity Index

It indicates that the right responses of the lower group are more than the right responses of the higher group. Therefore such items should never be included or selected in the final form of the test. See the Validity Index table 2.7, the item No. 15 has the negative value, this item should immediately be rejected.

Similarly Item No. 14th has the validity index 'O' this shows that this item does not discriminate between superior and inferior students such an item should also not get any place in the final form of the test. Similarly item No. 4th, 7th and 16th have not validity index satisfactory therefore these items should also be discarded from the final form of the test. Remaining items, are selected on the basis of their 'difficulty level' and discriminating power value.

Table–2.8

Selection of Items for Final form of the Test

Item No.	*Difficulty Level Value*	*Discriminating*	*Result*
1	.80	+2	Selected
2	.80	+2	Selected
3	.80	+2	Selected
4	.50	+1	Rejected
5	.60	+4	Selected
6	.50	+5	Selected
7	.30	+1	Rejected
8	.40	+2	May be or may not selected
9	.50	+3	Selected
10	.50	+3	Selected
11	.50	+3	Selected
12	.80	+2	Selected
13	.80	+2	Selected
14	.60	0	Rejected
15	.40	–2	Rejected
16	.70	+1	Rejected

Using Formula

(Difficulty Index) We can use the following formula to calculate difficulty level of the items.

$$D.I. \frac{N_R}{N_T} \times 100$$

Where, D.I. = Difficulty Index

N_R = No. of students having right responses

N_T = Total No. of students

Example—Suppose in any test, 120 students solved an item correctly out of 150 students and 30 students solved that item wrongly then the difficulty index of that item will be

$$D.I. = \frac{120}{150} \times 100 = 80$$

Using formula (Discriminating Power or Validity Index)

We use the following formula to find out the discriminating power or validity index of the item.

$$D.P. = \frac{P_1 - P_2}{\frac{P_1 - Q_1}{N} + \frac{P_2 - Q_2}{N}}$$

Where, D.P. = Discriminating power on value

P_1 = % of Right responses in higher group

Q_1 = % of wrong responses in higher group

P_2 = % of right responses in lower group

Q_2 = % of wrong responses in lower group

If the value of D.P. is 1.96 or more than item is capable to discriminate good and poor students. In this way we can calculate discriminating power of each item and select accordingly.

We can also use the following formula to calculate discriminating power of the item.

D.P. = PQ.

D.P. = Discriminating power of the item

P = % of the students solved correctly the item

Q = % of the students solved wrongly the item

Example—In a test an item has been solved correctly by the 45 students out of 75 students. What will be the D.P. of the item.

$$D.P. = PQ = P = \frac{R}{N} \times 100$$

$$= \frac{45}{75} \times 100$$

$$Q = 100 - 60 = 40 \text{ or } \frac{30}{75} \times 100 = 40$$

$$D.P. = 60 \times 40 = 2400 \text{ App.}$$

D.P. equal to 2500 approximate are considered suitable according to the formula:

Item Analysis of Diagnostic Test Items

We use Davis method of item analysis for Diagnostic test items. Stanley developed a method for diagnostic test item analysis. The main purpose of diagnostic test is to identify the weaknesses of the students in their study subjects. Stanley considered the wrong responses of the items in procedure of item analysis.

Procedure

Step I: The try out group is divided into high and low groups

Step II: The 27 top and 27 per cent bottom dichotomy of Kelley is used for this purpose.

Step III: The items proportions of wrong responses are calculated separately for high and low groups.

Step IV: The percentage of wrong responses on items are calculated for high and low groups of examinees.

These proportions/percentages are used for calculating difficulty values and discriminative powers. The following table 2.8 illustrates this method.

There is a significant difference in the interpretation of difficulty values (DVs) of the items between Davis and Stanley method. In Stanley method the high index of difficulty value of an item indicates that the item is difficult while the low values indicate that the item is easy. In the following Table 2.9 the item No. 4 is the most difficult as D.V. is .90 because 90 per cent of students did not response correctly and item No. 5 is the easiest as its D.V. is .15 which indicates only 15 per cent students did not answer correctly. In Davis method interpretation of D.V. is the reverse to the value of difficulty of an item.

Final Form of the Test

After preliminary and original correction and evaluation of the test, tester/researcher prepares, the test in its formal form. Those items are selected in the final forms of the test whose difficulty level and discrimiantory power is upto the mark keeping in view their both values.

Table–2.8
Stanley Method of Item Analysis

(N = 10) in each group

Item No.	*High Group Wrong Response*	*Low Group Wrong Responses*	P_H	P_L	*D.V.* $\frac{P_H + P_L}{2}$	*D.P.* $P_H - P_L$
1	1	5	.10	.50	.30	.40
2	2	7	.20	.70	.45	.50
3	4	8	.40	.80	.60	.40
4	8	10	.80	1.00	.90	.20
5	1	2	.10	.20	.15	.10 (×)
6	2	8	.20	.80	.50	.60
7	7	3	.70	.30	.50	.40 (×)
8	3	5	.30	.50	.40	.20
9	8	8	.80	.80	.80	.60 (×)
10	2	9	.20	.90	.55	.70

Factors Influencing the Item Indices of Test

There are factors which affect on the difficulty value and discriminate power of an item. Some of the following factors have been enumerated.

1. Form of an item: If the formation of an item is complex and ambiguous, the item automatically will become difficult. Item has two parts (a) the stem (b) the solution or alternative.

Secondly if the distractors are poweful, the item difficulty would be high and D.V. index would be low.

2. Awareness of the students about the structure of the items.

Non awareness of forms of the items and its way of answering the items students would not be able to answer correctly although they know it and that item would become difficult and index would be low.

Technique of Dichotomizing into High and Low Groups

There are several techniques of dichotomizing into high and low groups. The most extreme case of high and low groups would yield high discriminating power, therefore 27 per cent top and bottom dichotomy of Kelley is considered most appropriate technique.

Formulae-Correction for Guessing

There are various formulae-correction for guessing which are based upon their own assumptions, characteristics and limitation. Some of the formulae have high penalty on students who scored low and low penalty on those students who scored high. It may be observed from Horst and Guilfored formula correction for guessing.

Homogeneity and Heterogeneity of the Students

It influences great on item analysis. If the sample of examinees is homogeneous the discriminating power of the item would be low and if the sample of students is heterogeneous, the discriminating power would be high.

Speed of the Test

The item analysis is usually conducted on of the power test rather than speed test but in each power test time limit is allotted for the test. This time duration of the test is decided by the test designers empirically that most efficient and intelligent examinees should reach to the last item whether it may be prognostic or diagnostic test. The difficulty value and discriminating power would be changed as both are related to time limit of the test.

Some Problems

There are some problems and difficulties in selecting the process of item analysis such as:

1. Selection of the technique
2. Using of formula-correction for guessing.
3. Speededness of the test.
4. Correlation between item and total scores yields D.P.

The difficulty and discriminative indices are calculated on the basis of P_H and P_L value of an item. The scores of an item are correlated with total test scores. It is the internal consistency or reliability of the item.

The total test scores depend on the item and other items which may be rejected because they are not good item. Therefore total test scores is used as criterion which is not justifiable in the procedure of item analysis.

Merits of Item Analysis

There are some main characteristic in the process of item analysis.

1. During first tryout of the test, we become aware of the main difficulties, suitability of the items and ambiguity of the instruction of the test which can be removed after that.
2. We come to know earlier the efficiency of examinees.
3. We can understand the appropriateness of each item for the test and select items accordingly.
4. Item analysis helps to convert long form test into brief form.
5. Item analysis is helpful in the selection of proper and effective methodology of teaching.

QUESTIONS

A. Long Answer Type Questions

1. Explain the term 'Item Analysis'. Describe its functions and objectives in test construction.
2. Describe the relationship between difficulty and discriminative indices of items of a test. How do these indices contribute to the test of validity?
3. Describe the importance of guessing factor in objective type test. Compare Guilford and Horst formula correction for guessing. Explain its utility in item analysis.
4. Describe any method of item analysis for calculating the indices of difficulty and discriminative power.

B. Short Answer Type Questions

1. Describe the basis of item selection.
2. Enumerate main useful method of item analysis.
3. Explain technique of dichotomising high and low groups.
4. Need of 'Item Analysis' in the construction of a test.
5. Problems of a researcher face while analysing items.
6. Explain the term 'difficulty value' of an item.
7. Explain the term 'discriminating power' of an item.
8. Enumerate factors affecting item analysis.

C. Objective Type Questions

1. An item analysis considers both item difficulty values and discriminating power. True/False
2. In item analysis Kelley's dichotomy is used. True/False
3. Guessing formula is not used in item analysis. True/False
4. Item analysis is used for selecting and .... items.
5. Item analysis technique is used for .... type test items.

6. Item analysis is done to calculate.
   (a) Difficulty value *(b)* Discriminating power
   (c) Item validity *(d)* All the above.
7. Kelley's dichotomy employed as:
   (a) 33% top and 33% bottom.
   (b) 27% top and 27% bottom.
   (c) 25% top and 25% bottom.
   (d) 50% top and 50% bottom.
8. The purpose of item analysis technique is to modify items. True/False
9. An item has two characteristics item validity and .... value.
10. Guilfords formula-correction for Guessing is:
   (a) $S = R - \frac{W}{n-1}$ *(b)* $S = R - DP$
   (c) $S = \frac{\frac{R-W}{N-1}}{R+W}$ *(d)* $S = R - \frac{\frac{W}{n-1}}{J-NR}$

3

Test and Reliability

There are differences in abilities, aptitudes, and interests etc. among individuals. Each individual behaves differently in the different situations. In other words we can say that individuals differ in their cognitive, affective and psycho motor abilities as well as in physical traits. They are invariably different. It was Sir Francis Galton who for the first time in 1806 conducted studies on the extent of genetic inheritance in human beings. He had desived sensory motor tests is examine differences among individuals. Another outstanding contributor to the developent of psychological testing was the American Psychologist James Mckeen Cattell who prepared a dissertation on individual difference in 'reaction time'. In 1905, the Binet in collaboration with Simon prepared the first intelligence scale designed to yield a global index of intellectual level. Psychological tests have had very extensive use in educational classificaton, selection and planning from the first grade (and some times earlier too) through the University.

Meaning and Definition of Psychological Test

Psychological tests and testing play a significant role in a variety of situations and affect significantly on the lives of many persons. It may be stated that a test is a series of items or other means of measuring the skill, efficiency, proficiency, knowledge, intelligence, attitude and aptitude of an individual or group of individuals.

Definitions

According to Frank S. Freeman, "A Psychological test is a standardized instrument designed to measure objectively one or more aspects of a total personality by means of samples of verbal or nonverbal responses or by means of other behaviour."

Fredrick G. Brown defines, "A test is a systematic procedure for measuring a sample of behaviour."

Anastasi defined, "A psychological test is essentially an objective and standardized measure of sample of behaviour."

L.J. Cronbach defined, "A test is a systematic procedure for comparing the behaviour of two or more persons."

If we analyse above definitions we find that the test covers the behaviour under consideration depends on the number and nature of items in the sample and the diagnostic or predictive value of a psychological test depends on the degree to which it serves as an indicator of a relatively broad and significant area of behaviour. However the main objective of standardizing a test is to give it objectivity i.e., to provide freedom from personal judgements as much as possible. Every test is designed for use on a specified population and that must be standardized on a group which contains the representative sample of the total population for which a test is intended to construct.

Characteristics of a Good Psychological Test

Followings are the main characteristics of a psychological test.

1. Standardization
2. Reliability
3. Validity
4. Norms.

Standardization

It implies the uniformity of procedure or set of procedure. Test constructor provides detailed directions for administering each newly developed test.

Process of Standardization

In the process of standardization a test, it is administered to a large representative sample of persons for whom the test is designed. The following centre part are to be explained in the manual in detail by the constructor of the test.

(i) Oral instructions to subjects
(ii) Time limit
(iii) A key to score the responses

(iv) Exact material
(v) Preliminary demonstration
(vi) Establishment of rapport.
(vii) Good surroundings
(viii) Established norms for in interpretation of the result.

Other three characteristics of a psychological test shall be discussed in detail.

Reliability

Of all achievements by psychologists in making tests useful, the most important and essential characteristics of a good measuring instrument are their reliability and validity. The reliability has synonyms such as dependability, trustworthiness, consistency stability and accuracy. We can explain the concept of reliability in three ways. First, if we measure the same set of objects again and again with the same or comparable measuring instrument, we will get the same or similar results. This explanation of reliability implies the terms stability, dependability and predictability. Secondly the scores or measures obtained from a measuring instruments are the 'true' indicator of measures of the property measured. This is an explanation of 'accuracy'. Thirdly the reliability may be termed as the relative absence of errors of measurement in a measuring intrument.

The first explanation is generally given in the general discuss as and the second is more fundamental while third helps us to define and solve both theoretical and practical problems as well as implies other approaches and definitions. Thus we can state that reliability is the accuracy or precision of a measuring instrument.

Definitions of Reliability

The followings are the some important definitions of reliability.

According to Anastasi, "Reliability refers to the consistency of scores obtained by the same persons when they are reexamined with the same test on different occasions or with different set of equivalent items, or made other variable examining conditions."

Here the concept of reliability has been used to cover several aspects of score consistency.

Frank S. Freeman defined, 'The reliability of a test is its ability to yield consistent results from one set of measures to another. It is the extent to which the obtained test scores are free from internal defects.

The term reliability has two closely related but somewhat different connotations in psychological testing. First, it refers to the extent to which a test is internally consistent i.e., consistency of results obtained throughout the test when administered once. Secondly reliability refers to the extent to which a measuring device yields consistent results upon testing and retesting.

These two aspects of reliability are intimately related.

H.E. Garrett defines, "The reliability of a test or any measuring instrument depends upon the consistency with which it gauges the ability to whom it is applied."

Ghiselle defined, "Reliability of measurement is defined as the extent of unsystematic variation in scores on individual on same trait when the trait is measured number of times.

Reliability is also defined through error i.e., the more errors the greater the unreliability, the less errors, the greater the reliability. It means that if we can estimate the error variance of a measure we can also estimate the measure' of reliability. Fred Kerlinger defined reliability in the following two, ways.

1. Reliability is the proportion of the true variance to the total obtained variance of the data yielded by a measuring instrument.
2. Reliability is the proportion of error variance to the total obtained variance yielded by a measuring instrument subtracted from 1.00. The index 1.00 indicating perfect reliability.

This can be explained with the help of the following equations.

$$r_{tt} = \frac{V_{\infty}}{V_t} \qquad (1)$$

where V_{∞} = true variance component
r_{tt} = reliability coefficient
V_t = total obtained variance

Now it may be stated –

$$r_{tt} = 1 - \frac{V_e}{V_t} \qquad (2)$$

where V_e = error variance component.

Equation (1) is theoretical and can not be used for calculation.

Equation (2) is theoretical and practical.

Second equation can be used to conceptualize the idea of reliability and to estimate the reliability of an instrument. An alternate equation to (ii) is

$$r_{tt} = \frac{V_t - V_e}{V_t} \quad (3)$$

This alternative definition is useful in understanding the concept of reliability statistically.

If we analyse the above definitions of reliability we find the following characteristics:

1. It is a consistency of scores.
2. It is the measure of variable error or chance error or measurement error.
3. It is the measurement of unsystematic variation in scores.
4. The smaller the variability (S.D./σ), higher the reliability and larger the variability, lower the reliability.
5. It is coefficient of consistency.
6. It is the accuracy or precision of measuring instrument.
7. Coefficient of correlation of test administer at two occasion indicates its reliability coefficient.
8. There are various conditions/factors that may affect reliability such as differences in general ability and specific ability as being measured by the test.
9. Reliability does not ensure the validity of the test.
10. The reliability is the characteristics of the test scores not the property of the test itself.

Statistical Definition of Reliability

The measurement involves some kinds of errors such as personal, constant, variable and interpretive errors. If the measurement is perfectly accurate, it indicates that there is no error and the reliability will be perfectly +1.00. This is an ideal situation which is never achieved at least in social and behavioural sciences. The Guilford defined the reliability logically.

"Reliability is the proportion of the true variance in obtained test scores."

This means Reliability = True variance/Total variance

According to Guilford, the socre of each individual consists of two components – 1. true score, 2. error score i.e.

Total score (X) = True score (T) + Error score (E)

Components of Test Scores

Subject	*X*	*T*	*E*
1	60	45	15
2	75	55	20
3	50	60	-10

True score of the score of an individual which is free from errors of all kinds. Total score may vary from trial to trial because error score influences the total score in each trial. Here

X = The actual obtained or Test score

T = True score

E = Error score (may be plus or minus)

The logical reliability as stated by Guilford may be explained as under:

$$\text{Reliability} = \frac{\text{Variance of Total Scores}}{\text{Variance of Obtained scores or test scores}}$$

$$r_{tt} = \frac{\sigma_t^2}{\sigma_x^2} = 1- \frac{\sigma_t^2}{\sigma_x^2} \quad (1)$$

where r_{tt} = Reliability coefficient

σ_t^2 = Variance of True scores

σ_x^2 = Variance of Total scores or Obtained scores.

As indicated above X = T + E, i.e. Total scores = True scores + Error scores (±)

$$\sigma_t^2 = \sigma_t^2 + \sigma_e^2$$

If we divide all by σ_x^2 then

$$\frac{\sigma_x^2}{\sigma_x^2} = \frac{\sigma_t^2}{\sigma_x^2} + \frac{\sigma_e^2}{\sigma_x^2}$$

$$\text{we get } 1 = r_{tt} + \frac{\sigma_e^2}{\sigma_x^2} \quad (2)$$

Since equation $r_{tt} = \frac{\sigma_t^2}{\sigma_x^2}$ (From equation No. 1)

$$\text{Then } r_{tt} = \frac{\text{True Variance}}{\text{Total Variance}} = \text{Reliability}$$

Now from equations No. (2) we get

$$\frac{\sigma_e^2}{\sigma_x^2} = 1 - r_{tt}$$

$$\sigma_e^2 = \sigma_x^2 = (1 - r_{tt}) \quad \text{OR}$$

$$\sigma_e = \sigma_x \sqrt{1 - r_{tt}} \quad \text{Here } SE_M = \sigma x \sqrt{1 - r_{tt}}$$

SE_M = Standard error of measurement.

Where σ_e = Standard deviation of error scores.

σ_x = standard deviation of total scores.

It is evident from the above describe formula that variable error or error of measurement influences the reliability of a test. There are two types of errors which have been identified:

1. Chance errors or random errors or error of measurement.
2. Systematic errors or biased errors.

(1) Errors of Measurement or chance errors: Such errors sometimes decrease the score. In other words it may be stated that it works randomly in both directions i.e., positive and negative. The reasons of such errors may be followings:

(i) Non-inclusion of large number of items in the test.

(ii) Failure to administer the test at a large number of times and to maintain the same conditions.

(iii) Not to utilize the sufficient number of examiners when scoring the students responses.

(iv) It has already been stated that if we use the large sample, the positive and negative errors would tend to cancel each other. Thus the sum of obtained or total score would be equal to sum of true scores. In this way chance error may be reduced.

(v) It is not possible to administer the test on the population, therefore chance errors creep into it.

(vi) X = T + E

Where X = Total variance, T = True variance/
E = error variance

$\sigma_x^2 = \sigma_t^2 + \sigma_e^2$ i.e., Total variance = True variance + error variance

According to Guilford

$$r_{tt} = \frac{\sigma_t^2}{\sigma_x^2}$$

Table-3.1
Error of Measurement

Subjects	*T*	*T-M*	*T²*	*E*	*E-M*	*E²*	*X*	*X-M*	*X²*
1.	5	–20	400	–2	± 2	4	3	22	484
2.	15	–10	100	+2	+2	4	17	–8	64
3.	20	–5	25	–4	+4	16	16	–9	81
4.	25	0	0	–2	+2	4	23	–2	4
5.	25	0	0	+2	2	4	27	2	4
6.	25	0	0	0	0	0	25	0	0
7.	25	0	0	+10	10	100	35	10	100
8.	30	5	25	–4	4	16	26	1	1
9.	35	10	100	–2	2	4	33	8	64
10.	45	20	400	0	0	0	45	20	400
Σ	250		1050	0		152	250		1202
M	25			0		15.2	25		120.2

$\sigma_t^2 = 105.0$ $\sigma_e^2 = 15.2$

X = T + E Where
X = Total variance
T = True variance
E = Error variance

$\Sigma T = 250$
$\Sigma E = 0$
$\Sigma X = 250$
$\sigma_x^2 = \sigma_t^2 + \sigma_e^2$
$\sigma_t^2 = 105.00$
$\sigma_e^2 = 15.20$
$\sigma_x^2 = 120.2$
$\sigma_x^2 = 105.00 + 15.2$
$\sigma^2 = 120.2$

Total variance = True variance + Error Variance

According to Guilford

$$r_{tt} = \frac{\sigma_t^2}{\sigma_x^2} \quad \text{where } r_{tt} = \text{reliability}$$

$$r_{tt} = \frac{105.00}{120.2} \quad 0.88$$

The assumption of this formula is that all the terms are of the same difficulty.

2. Systematic Errors or Biased Errors

This type of errors works constantly in one direction. This indicates that they would either tend to increase or decrease the score. This type of errors may be due to the following reasons:

1. Failure to breakdown the factor attributed to be measured the point of its homogeneous properly.
2. To select the terms that measure the attribute is in question.
3. Poor selection of test items.
4. Poor weightage to the test items.
5. Defective scoring of the responses.

As we know that any obtained score is dividied into the true score and the error score—X = T + E. Similarly the total variance of the test is also divided into components–true variance and the error variance i.e. $\sigma_x^2 = \sigma_t^2 + \sigma_e^2$.

Variance is defined as standard deviation square σ^2 (SD^2) which is also the index of variability.

The reliability of a test score is logically is the proportion of true variance. The correlation between true scores (x_t) and error scores (x_e) is assurned to be zero.

$$\sigma_x^2 = \sigma_t^2 + \sigma_e^2$$

Now the reliability coefficient (r_{tt}) logically can be shown.

$$r_{tt} = \frac{\sigma_t^2}{\sigma_x^2} = \frac{\text{True Varivance of the Score}}{\text{Total Variance of the Score}}$$

The reliability coefficient can also be computed in a substitute way where coefficient becomes equal to one minus that part of the total variance which is error variance. The substitute formula becomes.

$$r_{tt} = 1 - \frac{\sigma_t^2}{\sigma_x^2}$$

3. Sampling Error—We use different sampling techniques to estimate the true mean of population. The size of sample is the important components for minimizing this type of error.

Here

$M_x = M_t + M_e$ $\quad\quad$ M_x = Sample mean

M_t = True mean

M_e = Error mean.

It is true that by increasing the size of sample chance error is reduced. Both these errors (sample and chance error) are related to each other.

Components of Test Scores:

Total score = ΣX = True Score T (ΣT) Error score E i.e. $\pm$ value of E is + or – $\Sigma E = 0$

Hence $\Sigma X = \Sigma T : EE = 0$

Sample mean $= \frac{\Sigma X}{N} = \frac{\Sigma T}{N}$

$M_x = M_E$, obtained score = True Mean.

The sample error is estimated by employing the following formula:

$$SE_M = \frac{\sigma}{\sqrt{N}} = \frac{\text{S.D. of the population}}{\sqrt{\text{Size of the sample}}}$$

If we increase the sample size upto infinity (∞). The sample error will be zero.

$$SE_M = \frac{\sigma}{\sqrt{\infty}} = 0; N = \infty \text{ (infinity)}$$

This indicates that the obtained mean of sample is equal to the population mean.

Psychological tests can roughly be divided into two classes.

1. *Homogeneous:* It indicates internally consistent all parts of the list and measure the same thing i.e., speed test. Such tests are functionally uniform and measure of one factor, one ability or one trait.
2. *Heterogenous:* This means that different parts of test measure different traits, the inter consistency index is low.

Types of Test

1. *Power Test:* A pure power test is one in which unlimited time is allowed and every one is able to try all items and the score will depend entirely upon the number of items the examinee was able to answer correctly. But practically, almost all test have a time limit. The time limit is given in such a way that between 75 to 90 per cent

of the subjects are able to complete the test. Item variation is there.

2. *Speed Test:* A pure speed test if it is such that every one who reaches an item gets it correct. None may be able to reach the last item. With a time limit, every item reached, is usually answered correctly, and thus the score will depend almost entirely upon how many items are attempted. No errors are made on the items variation.
3. *Speeded Test*: There is no pure power test in which unlimited time is provided as for the practical reasons. A power test has great item variation and there is also time limit (75% to 90%). Therefore all the power test are speeded test.

Methods or Types or Kinds of Reliability

Methods or types or kinds of reliability are based on the estimating or computing reliability coefficient of a test scores. There is no one best method of estimating reliability. The method's preference depends upon its purpose, meaning and use, researchers wishes to attach to reliability. However while estimating and computing reliability, researcher must keep the following two factors into considerations.

According to Freeman the methods of estimating reliability fall into two general classifications:

(i) relative reliability, and
(ii) absolute reliability.

The first of these is generally stated in terms of a coefficient of correlations, known as the reliability coefficient. It is also reported at times, though infrequently, in terms of analysis of variance.

The second i.e., absolute reliability is stated in terms of the standard error of measurement, which is an estimate of the deviation of a set of obtained scores from the 'true scores'.

According to Lee J. Cronbach. These are four methods of computing reliability of a test scores.

1. Coefficient of stability
2. Coefficient of equivalence
3. Coefficient of stability and equivalence
4. Coefficient of internal consistency.

J.P. Guilford suggested three methods of computing reliability of test score.

1. Internal consistency or simple internal consistency.
2. Alternative forms or parallel forms reliability.
3. Retest or test – retest reliability.

The following methods which are used for estimating reliability of a test scores depends on two considerations

(i) Type of test – Speeded or speed tests.
(ii) Purpose – Heterogeneous or homogeneous tests.

Kinds of Relaibility

1. Test-Retest Reliability coefficient of stability.
2. Alternative or parallel forms – Coefficient of equivalence reliability.
3. Split half method – Coefficient of stability and equivalence.
4. Rationale equivalence reliability – Coefficient of internal consistency.
5. Hoyt's analysis variance method reliability.

Assumptions

The first three methods of reliability have the same assumption.

I. All items of a test have the same difficulty value but the difficulty of an item depends on the knowing aspect of an individual. This means if the student knows the item it is considered an easy item for him, if he does not know the item, it is difficult item for him.

II. The last two methods of estimating reliability assume the item difficulty or item variation and at no subject variation. The items of a test have the variation with regard to its difficulty values.

Test-Retest Reliability or Coefficient of Stability

Retest method is a repetition of a test to determine agreement between two sets of scores the tests given and repeated with in a reasonable gap on the same group and the correlation computed between the first and second set of scores. It is the simplest form of estimating reliability index of a test scores. Thus the correlation coefficient calculated between the two sets of scores is the reliability index. It is known as coefficient of stability which shows to what extent the subjects retain their relative position as measured in terms of the test score over a gap of time interval. The error variance contributes inversely to the coefficient of reliability or stability.

Assumption of the Method

1. Number of items in the test are large therefore, meaning, practice and learning will not effect the retest scores.
2. Innate ability of the subject remains constant so the growth will not effect the retest scores.
3. Time gap of retest should not be more than six months.

Limitations

1. This method of estimating the reliability is less accurate therefore it is less useful than the other method.
2. Changes in the score multidimensional are no actually error, and to this extent reliability is under estimated.

   The method has several deficiences if not properly used—1. Memory, 2. Practice, 3. Fatigue will certainly effect if the test is repeated immediately and if the interval is rather long more than six months.

   In general growth increases initial score by various amounts and tends to lower the reliability coefficient.

   (1) Growth factor (2) Maturity and (3) Experience may affect the retest score and tend to lower down the index of reliability.
3. It is time consuming method of estimating reliability.
4. The subjects physical and mental health, emotional, motivational conditions and mental set do not remain the same in both the occasions of administration of test.

Characteristics of Coefficient Stability

Following are the advantages of this method.

1. It is simplest and easy method.
2. It is the most appropriate method of estimating reliability of speed test, it is also used adequately for speeded test.
3. Simple Pearson's method of correlation is used for computing.
4. It is an economical too.
5. It requires a fortnight as a time gap for retesting to obtain an accurate index of reliability.

Alternate Form Reliability or Coefficient of Equivalence

According to Thorndibe alternate forms or equivalent forms—by which he means tests having identical true variance and no overlap of error variances. Gultiksen speaks of parallel test which he defines statistically have equal means, equal variances and equal inter correlation with one other.

There is a way of avoiding difficulties faced in test-retest reliability is through the use of alternate forms of the test. In this form of test, the same person is tested with one form on the first occasion and with another equivalent parallel or alternate form is used on the second. The correlation between the scores obtained on the two forms shows its reliability coefficient. It is important to understand here that such a reliability coefficient is a measure of both temporal stability and consistency of response to different item samples (test forms).

This coefficient of correlation combines two types of reliability as both are significant for most testing purposes as this equivalent form reliability gives us a useful measure for evaluating many tests. This coefficient of correlation is termed as the coefficient of correlation of equivalence. The major problem is to develop the two parallel forms of the test. So in its development care should be taken to ensure that they are truly parallel. The test should have *(i)* the same number of items, *(ii)* items should be expressed in the same form, and *(iii)* items and cover the same type of content, *(iv)*. The range and level of difficulty of the item should be equal such as instruction, time length, illustrative examples and all other factors of the tests. While applying this method of estimating reliability researcher kept in mind that:

1. Practice, memorization, carry over factors can be controlled.
2. To construct parallel forms of test of item is a difficult task. More care and hardwork require.
3. Time interval for administration should not be more than two weeks.
4. Error variance is contributed by the change due to some unavoidable factors as it is not possible to provide like situation to measure the true score.

Freeman enumerated that both forms should meet all of the test's specifications as follows:

1. The number of items in both forms should be equal or same.
2. There should be uniformity in respect of content, operations or traits involved, levels and range of difficulty and adequacy of sampling in kinds of items.
3. The items should be similarly distributed as to difficulty.

4. Both test form should have the same degree of item homogeneity in the operations or traits being measured.
5. The means and standard deviation of both forms should be or nearly to be equal.
6. Methods of administration and scoring should be the same.

Merits

This method has the following advantages as compared to test-retest method of estimating reliability.

1. This method is an improvement over the test-retest method of estimating reliability.
2. The practice, memory and maturity effects are mostly or genuinely controlled.
3. It is economical and speedy method for computing coefficient of reliability.
4. The simple descriptive statistical method used for calculating the coefficient of equivalent.
5. It is useful in obtaining reliability of achievements test.

Split Half Reliability

This technique is used to find internal consistency—the items of a whole test are divided into two halves which should be equivalent or very nearly so. It provides a measure of consistency as indicated above with regard to content sampling. Temporal stability of the scores does not creep into such reliability as only one test session is involved. There are a few problems to find out split reliability such as.

1. How to split the test in order to obtain the most nearly equivalent halves as test can be divided into two halves in different ways.
2. There may be cumulative effects of practice, fatigue, boredom and any other factors varying from the beginning to the last items of test.

A very important factor should be kept is mind while using this technique i.e. items should have been arranged in their order of increasing difficulty. In using this method common practice is to make the division by taking the odd numbered items as one part and the even numbered as the other. The score is found for each individual for each half and two set are paired and then correlation once the two half scores have been obtained for each person. These scores are derived correlation actually gives the reliability of only a half test.

For example if the entire test consists of 50 items, the correlation is computed between two sets of scores each of which is based on only 25 items. Since the correlation coefficient for the two sets of scores is based upon sub-divisions of the full test. A statistical formula (Speanian-Brown) is used to correct for the reduced lengths of the subdivisions from which the correlated scores have been determined. The generalized formula which operates is :

$$r_n = \frac{nr}{1 + (n-1)\,r}$$

where r = the coefficient of reliability obtained between the parts of the divided test.

r_n = the reliability of the test n times as long as half the original test

Suppose, $r = .70$

by substituting the values in the formula

$$r_n = \frac{2 \times .70}{1 + (2-1)\ .70} = \frac{1.40}{1.70} = .82$$

The reliability of the whole test = .82

The reliability coefficient of the whole test may also bc estimated from the following formula:

$$r_{11} = \frac{2\,r_{\frac{1}{2}\frac{1}{11}}}{1+_{\frac{r1}{2}\frac{1}{11}}}$$

where r_{11} = reliability coefficient of the whole test.

$r_{\frac{1}{2}\frac{1}{11}}$ = reliability coefficient of the half test.

By substituting the above mentioned values in the formula i.e.,

$r_{\frac{1}{2}\frac{1}{11}} = .70$

$$r_{11} = \frac{2\,r_{\frac{1}{2}\frac{1}{11}}}{1+_{\frac{r1}{2}\frac{1}{11}}} = \frac{2 \times .70}{1 + .70} = \frac{1.40}{1.70} = .82$$

Another formula that yields nearly the same results as the Spearman-Brown for estimating reliability by the split half method is:

$$r_{tt} = 2\ (1- \frac{\sigma_a^2 + \sigma_b^2}{\sigma_t^2})$$

σ_a and σ_b = standard deviation of the scores of the half test.
σ_t = S.D. of the scores of the whold test.

The advantage of this formula is that it is not necessary to correlate the half-tests them solves.

The Rulon Formula

We can calculate reliability coefficient of correlation based upon the definition of reliability with the help of formula given by Rulon (1939) which is as follows. The basic definition of reliability that it is the proportion of true variance in a test.

$$r_{11} = 1- \frac{\sigma_d^2}{\sigma_t^2}$$

d = difference between two half score for an examinee
σ_d = standard deviation of those differences
σ_t = SD of total scores

This gives the reliability for the total score not for the half scores and therefore S-B formula would not be applied. Suppose

$\sigma_d^2 = 1.05$ and $\sigma_t^2 = 7.5$

therefore $r_{11} = 1 - \frac{\sigma_d^2}{\sigma_t^2} = 1-(\frac{1.05}{7.5}) = 1-.14$

$r_{11} = 1-.14 = .86$

The Flanagan Formula—Flanagan gives a formula parallel to Rulon's. It estimates the error variance as the sum of the variances of the two halves. This can be observed in the following forms where the sum $\sigma_t^2 + \sigma_t^2$ is used is place of Rulon's σ_d^2.

$$r_{tt} = 2\ (1- \frac{\sigma_1^2 + \sigma_2^2}{\sigma_t^2})$$

where σ_1 and σ_2 are SD's of two halves.

As in the case of the Rulon formula this provides an estimate of total score reliability suppose—$\sigma_1^2 = 2.25$ $\sigma_2^2 = 3.00$, $\sigma_t^2 = 9.45$

$$r_{tt} = 2\ (1- \frac{2.25 + 3}{9.45}) = .89 \qquad r_{tt} = .890$$

Merits

1. This method is employed when it is not possible to construct parallel forms of the test.
2. When it is not advisable to repeat the test itself such as performance tests as well as questionnaires inventories dealing with personality variables, attitudes and interest.
3. This method is regarded as the best of the methods for measuring reliability.
4. One of the main advantages is that all data for computing reliability are obtained upon one occasion so that variation brought about by differences between the two testing situations are eliminated.

Limitations

1. With the fact that chance errors may affect scores on the two halves of the test, in the same way, therefore it tends to make the reliability coefficient too high.
2. A test can be divided into two parts in a number of ways, so that reliability coefficient of correlation however this is true only when items are all of equal difficulty.
3. This method can not be used in estimating reliability of a pure speed test.
4. 'Rational Equivalent' Method of Reliability or Kuder-Richardson Reliability and coefficient Alpha.

This method represents an attmept to get an estimate of the reliability of a test. This method is free from the objections raised against the above described methods. Two forms of a test are defined as equivalent. When corresponding items, x, X, y, Y, z, Z are inter changeable and when the inter-item correlations are the same for both forms. This method stresses the inter correlations of the items in the test and the correlation of the items with the test as a whole. There are four formula to determine test relibility, out of them, following is the most useful.

$$r_{11} = \frac{n}{n-1} \times \frac{\sigma_t^2 - \Sigma pq}{\sigma_t^2}$$

where r_{11} = reliability coefficient of the whole test

n = number of items in the test

σ_t^2 = S.D. of the test scores

p = the proportions of the group answering a test item correctly q = (1 – p) = the proportion of the group answering the test item incorrectly.

To apply this formula, following calculations are necessary.

1. Computation of the S.D. of the test scores for the whole group i.e. σ_t.
2. To find out proportions passing each item (p) and its proportion failing each item (q).
3. Multiplicaton of p & q for each item and their sum for all item i.e. Σpq.
4. Substitiution of the Values in the above formula

Illustration

A test containing 50 items has been administered to a group of 80 subjects $\sigma_t = 7.50$ and $\Sigma pq = 10.25$. Applying these values.

$$r_{11} = \frac{50}{49} \times \frac{56.25 - 10.25}{56.25} = .83$$

There is another formula which may be used by the teachers who want to calculate quickly the reliability of short objective classroom examinations. It is the approximation to above formula.

$$r_{11} = \frac{n\,\sigma_t^2 - M\,(n - M)}{\sigma_t^2\,(n - 1)}$$

r_{11} = reliability of the whole test
n = number of the items in the test
(σ_t) = SD of the test scores
M = Mean of the test scores.

Illustration – An objective test of 50 multiple-choice items has been administered to a small class of students. The mean test score is 35 and $\sigma = 8.00$. What is the reliability coefficient of the test.

By substituting this values in the above formula.

$$r_{11} = \frac{50 \times 8 \times 8 - 35\,(50 - 35)}{8 \times 8\,(50 - 1)}$$

$$= \frac{3200 - 525}{64 \times 49} = \frac{2675}{3136} = .85$$

The assumption is made in the above formula that all test items have the same difficulty i.e., that the same proportions of the subjects, but not necessarily the same person, solve each item correctly.

Factors Influencing Reliability of a Test

1. *Range of Ages*: If a reliability cofficient of correlation is found with homogenous group that has a small variation of the trait or ability being measured, the coefficient will be low if the group is heterogenes the coefficient will be higher. It is necessary to know the range of ages upon which the test was standardized while interpreting a reliability coefficient.
2. *Range of Scores*: If a reliability coefficient is found when the range of scores is narrow, the correlation between two sets of scores may also be lowered by chance and minor factors but if the range of scores is higher, the correlation between two sets of scores may also be higher. The following illustration will make the point clear.

Table–3.2

Rank of Subjects on Two forms of the Test i.e. x and y

Subjects	*Rank is x*	*Rank is y*	*D*	D^2
*1.	1	2	1	1
2.	2	1	1	1
3.	3	5	2	4
*4.	4	4	0	0
5.	5	3	2	4
6.	6	7	1	1
7.	7	8	1	1
8.	8	6	2	4
9.	9	10	1	1
*10.	10	9	1	1
11.	11	11	0	0
12.	12	14	2	4
13.	13	12	1	1
14.	14	13	1	1
*15.	15	15	0	0
16.	16	16	0	0

(Contd.)

Subjects	*Rank is x*	*Rank is y*	*D*	D^2	
17.	17	17	0	0	
18.	18	20	2	4	
19.	19	18	1	1	
20.	20	19	1	1	$\Sigma D^2 = 30$

$$p(rho) = 1 - \frac{\sigma\Sigma + \sigma^2}{N(N^2 - 1)} \quad 1 - \frac{6 \times 30}{20 \times 399}$$

$$\Sigma D^2 = 10 \quad 1 - \frac{6 \times 10}{5 \times 24} = .50$$ (When the range of the score is narrow)

Ranking at Random—1, 5, 10, 15, 20

$$(rhop,) = 1 - \frac{6\Sigma D^2}{N(N^2 - 1)}$$

$$= 1 - \frac{6 \times 7}{5 \times 24}$$

$$= 1 - .35 = .65$$

$$p(rho) = 1 - \frac{6\Sigma + D^2}{N(N^2 - 1)}$$ (When the number of subject is 20)

$$p(rho) = 1 - \frac{6\Sigma D^2}{N(N^2 - 1)} = 1 - \frac{6 \times 30}{20 \times 399}$$

$$p(rho) = 1 - .22 = .78$$
$$1 - .22 = .78$$

If we take narrow range i.e., top ranking for 5 subjects we find (rho/ P = .5) If we take 5 subjects ranking at randon i.e. 1, 5, 10, 15, and 20 P (rho) = .65.

Table indicates the rho of narrow

Top 5 subjects = .50
5 subjects at random = .65
wide range i.e., from 1 to 20 = .78

It is concluded that Range of scores affect upon the reliability, coefficient.

3. The Time Interval Between Testing. The time interval between and retesting testing affect on reliability coefficient as it normally expected fluctuation in individual performances and by changes in

environmental conditions. The reliability coefficients obtained at a single sitting or in a single day are most likely to estimate best the consistency of the test.

4. The effect of Practice and Learning. This effect depends upon the content of the test the length of the interval and upon the subject's experience during the interval.

5. Method of Estimating Reliability. Reliability coefficient depends upon the method of estimating reliability as each method has its merits and limitations. Investigator is to select best method to compute in reliability coefficient depending upon the construction the test in hand.

(i) Lengthening or Repeating a Test

If the size of test is increased by adding the same difficulty value and same content the reliability index will increase on the other hand if the size of test is reduced the reliability index would decrease. Increasing the length of a test or averaging the scores obtained from several applications of the test or form parallel forms will also increase reliability. A good estimate of the effect of lengthening or repeating a test can be obtained by using to Spearman-Brown prophecy formula.

$$r_{nn} = \frac{n\, r_{it}}{1 + (n-1)\, r_{1t}}$$

where r_{nn} = the correlation between n forms of a test and n alternate forms.

and r_{it} = the reliability coefficienct of test 1

Illustration—Suppose that in a group of 50 college students the reliability coefficient of an achievement tests is .60. What will be the effect upon the test reliability of tripling the length of the test. Substituting these values is above formula, we find.

Here n = 3

$$r_{nn} = \frac{3 \times .60}{1 + (3-1)\,.60} = \frac{1.8}{1 + 1.2} = \frac{1.80}{2.20} = .81$$

(ii) Lengthening the Test to a Desired Degree of Reliability

The Spearman-Brown prophecy formula may also be used to find how many times a test should be lengthened or repeated in order to reach a given standard of reliability.

Suppose that an arithmetic achievement test has a reliability coefficient of .60. How much should it be lenghtened in order to get a reliability coefficient of .85. By substituting the values in the formula $r_{nn} = .85$

$$r_{nn} = \frac{nr_{it}}{1 + (n-1)\, r_{it}} = .85 = \frac{.60\, n}{1 +.\, 60n - .60}$$

$n = 3.75 = 4$

The test may be lenghtened 4 times its present length.

Percentage to be observed while using Spearman-Brown prophecy formula—

Predictions of increased reliability by this formula are valid when the questions added to the test cover the same ground i.e. *(i)* are of equal range of difficulty *(ii)* are comparable in other respect is to the items is the original test. If it is so this prophecy formula must be taken as approximative rather than at face value.

7. Guessing by Examiners. This is an important source of getting reliability coefficient in reality. As guessing has two important effects on total scores. It raises the reliability index high but it contributes to the error of measurement. The formula of guessing correction should be used.

8. Administration of the Test. Although each test is standardized test but even then it has some problems which may affect on reliability coefficient such as *(i)* lack of familiarity with the type of items, *(ii)* general attitude of the subject *(iii)* examinees physical well being *(iv)* examinees mental conditions *(v)* administering condition of the environment. These condition certainly will lower down the reliability index.

Some Other Factors Related to Reliability

1. Satisfactory level of reliability coefficient.

The satisfactory level of reliability coefficient required, depends upon the *(i)* nature of the test *(ii)* the size and variability of the group *(iii)* the puspose which the test is constructed. The following minimum reliabilities are required for different purposes.

1. The means of two school grades of reliability narrow range, the reliability. Coefficient should be between .50 to .60.
2. The test means to make individual diagnosis its reliability coefficient should be more than .90.

3. To evaluate differences in level of group performance, the reliability coefficient should be .90.

Table–3.3

Range of Reliabilties for Different Type of Tests as Reported

Kinds of test	*Low*	*Average*	*High*
1. Attitude scales	.45	.75	.95
2. Achievement test	.60	.90	.98
3. Aptitude test	.25	.85	.92
4. Objective personality	.42	.80	.90
5. Interest inventing	.46	.82	.92
6. Scholaslic ability	.55	.92	.96

The Index of Reliability

The coefficient of correlation of individual's true scores and obtained scores is known index of reliability. It is computed from the following formula.

$r_{1\infty} = \sqrt{r_{it}}$

is which $r_{1\infty}$ = the correlation of obtained and true scores

r_{it} = the reliability coefficient of the Test 1.

The symbol ∞ (infinity) indicates true scores.

The coefficient $r_{1\pm}$ is called the index of reliability.

This measures the dependability of test scores by showing to what extent obtained scores agree with their true scores. This index of reliability gives maximum correlation which the given test is capable to yield into its present form.

If we square both sides of equation (above formula) we get = $r_{1\infty}^2$ = r_{1t}

This reliability coefficient shows the proportion of the variance of the obtained scores which is determined by the variance of the true score.

Illustration—Suppose that the reliability coefficient of certain test is .72. Then 72 per cent of the variance of obtained scores is attributable to the variance of the true scores.

Since $r_{1\infty} \sqrt{.72}$ = .84. This .84 is the highest correlation when the test is capable of yielding in its present form. If the reliability coefficient of a test is as low as .25 so that $r_{1\infty} = \sqrt{.25} = .50$. It would be wastage of time to use it without lengthening or improving it.

The index of reliability is useful mainly as a means of showing how r_{it} is a measure is a measure of the variance.

Estimating true scores by way of Regression equations and the reliability coefficient.

We know that reliability coefficient is an index of the degree which obtained score variance is a measue of true score variance and is free of error variance. It is to be kept in mind that true scores can not be found experimentally but only we can estimatic true score by way of regression equiation if we know the reliability coefficient. It can be seen mathematically that

$$x_{\infty} = r_{it} X_t + (1 - r_{it}) M_1$$

This is a regression equation which estimates true score of the individual in which X_{∞} = estimated true score on a test.

x_1 = obtained score on Test I
M_1 = mean of Test I
r_{it} = reliability coefficient of Test 1
The standard error of an estimated true score is:
$SE_{\infty 1} = \sigma_1 \sqrt{r_{it} - r^2_{it}}$
Here $SE_{\infty 1}$ = standard error of an estimated true score in Test 1
r_{1t} = the reliability coefficient of Test 1.

Illustration—The reliability coefficient of a test is .65, the M is 50 and S.D. (σ) 8. If Ramesh has a score of 40 on the test what will be his estimated true score and its error of estimate? Compute the .95 confidence interval for Ramesh's true score

Here $r_{it} = .65, X_1 = 40$

$\sigma = 8, M = 50$

By substituting this value in the following equation as we find.

$$x_{\infty} = r_{it} x_1 + (1 - r_{it}) M_1$$
$$= .65 \times 40 + (1 - .65)\, 50$$
$$= 26.00 + (.35 \times 50)$$
$$= 26.0 + (17.50 = 43.5 = 44$$

From the following equation

$$SE_{\infty 1} = \sigma_1 \sqrt{r_{it} - r_{it}^2} = 8\sqrt{.65 - .42} = 8 \times .48$$

$= 8 \times .48 = 3.84 = 4$ (to the nearest whole number).

The .95 confidence interval for Ramesh's true score is $44 + 1.96 \times 4$ or 44 ± 7.84 the interval 36 to 52 contains Ramesh true score.

The Analysis of Variance Approach to Reliability or Hoyt's Reliability

It is well known fact that the estimation of reliability can be computed by conventional analysis of variance approach, like K-R approach. This approach also starts from the item level. The data in the following table are set up for application of Hoyt's method of estimating reliability. He regards the matrix of item scores as a two-way factorial design for analysis-of-variance without replication.

Table-3.4

Item Scores and Total Scores of 10 Examinees in a 12 Items Test with Data Needed for Estimating Reliability by Several Approaches

	Items													
STUDENTS	1	2	3	4	5	6	7	8	9	10	11	12	X_i	X^2_i
1	1	0	1	0	0	0	0	0	0	0	0	0	2	4
2	1	1	1	0	0	1	0	0	0	0	0	0	4	16
3	1	1	1	1	0	0	0	0	0	0	0	0	4	16
4	1	1	0	1	1	0	0	1	0	0	0	0	5	25
5	1	1	1	1	1	0	0	0	0	0	0	0	5	25
6	1	1	1	0	1	1	1	0	0	0	0	0	6	36
7	1	1	1	1	1	1	1	0	0	0	0	0	7	49
8	1	1	1	1	0	1	1	1	1	0	1	0	9	81
9	1	1	1	1	1	1	1	1	1	1	1	0	11	121
10	1	1	1	1	1	1	1	1	1	1	1	1	12	144
Ri	10	9	9	7	6	6	5	4	3	3	2	1	ΣRi	$\Sigma xi^2 = 517$
Wi	0	1	1	3	4	4	5	6	7	7	8	9		$\Sigma wi = 55$
P_i	1.0	.90	.90	.70	.60	.60	.50	.40	.20	.30	.20	.10		$\Sigma pi = 6.5$
P^2_d	1	.81	.81	.49	.36	.36	.25	.16	.09	.09	.04	.01		$\Sigma p^2 = 4.47$
R^2_i	100	81	81	49	36	36	25	16	9	9	4	1		$\Sigma Ri^2 = 447$
p_iq_i	0	.9	.09	21	.24	.24	.25	.24	.21	.21	.16	.09		$\Sigma Piq_i = 2.03$

$$\sigma_i^2 = \frac{\Sigma x_i^2}{N} \ (\frac{\Sigma x_i^2}{N})$$

Hoyt's Basic Formula for reliability is:

$$r_{tt} = 1 - \frac{V_r}{V_e} = \frac{V_e - V_r}{V_e} \quad (1)$$

Here V_r = Variance of remainder sum of squares

V_e = Variance of examinees

The variance sum of squares are calculated by the formula:

$$\Sigma d_e^2 = \frac{\Sigma x_t^2}{n} - (\frac{\Sigma x}{nN})^2 \quad (2)$$

Here Σd^2_e = sum of squares for examinees

x_t = total score for each examinee

n = number of items

$$\Sigma d_i^2 = \frac{\Sigma R_i^2}{N} - (\frac{\Sigma xt}{nN}) \quad (3)$$

Σd^2_i = sum of squares for items

R_i = number of correct responses for item 12 and other symbols are the same as earlier

$$\Sigma x^2_t = \frac{(\Sigma R_i)(\Sigma W_i)}{\Sigma R_i + \Sigma W_i} \quad (4)$$

where Σd^2_t = total sum of squares

W_i = number of wrong responses to item 12

The sum of square for remainder is given

$$\Sigma x^2_r = \Sigma x^2_t - \Sigma d^2_e - \Sigma d^2_t \quad (5)$$

Computation of examinees sum of squares by applying formula (2)

$$\Sigma d^2_e = \frac{\Sigma x_t^2}{n} - (\frac{\Sigma x_i^2}{n\,N}) = \Sigma x_i^2 = 517,\ \Sigma x_1 = 65$$

n = 12, N = 10

$$\Sigma d^2_e = \frac{517}{12} - \frac{65 \times 65}{10 \times 12} = 43.08 - 35.20 = 7.88$$

Computation of sum of squares of items – Application of formula (3)

$$\Sigma d^2_i \ \frac{\Sigma R_i^2}{N} - (\frac{\Sigma x_i^2}{n\,N}) = \Sigma R_i^2 = 447 = \Sigma x_i = 65, N = 10$$

$$\frac{447}{10} \quad \frac{65 \times 65}{10 \times 12} = 44.70 - 35.20 = 9.50$$

$$\Sigma d_i^2 = 9.50$$

Degree of freedom of item n – 1 i.e., 12 – 1 = 11

Total sum of squares =

$$\Sigma x^2_i = \frac{(\Sigma R_i)(\Sigma W_i)}{\Sigma R_i + \Sigma W_i} = \frac{65 \times 55}{65 \times 55}$$

$$\frac{3575}{120} = 29.79$$

Sum of squares for remainder

$$\Sigma x^2_r = \Sigma x^2_t - \Sigma d^2_i - \Sigma d^2_e$$
$$= 29.79 - 9.50 - 7.88$$
$$= 29.79 - 17.38 = 12.41$$
$$\Sigma x^2_r = 12.41$$

The various sums of squares computed for the illustration data given in the first column of values in the following table

Table–3.5

Solution for the Variances in a Short Test Preparation to Estimate Reliability

Sources of Variance	*Sum of Squares*	*Degree of freedom*	*Variance*
Examinees	7.88	9	.875
Items	9.50	11	.863
Remainder	12.41	99	.125
Total	29.79	119	

$$r_{tt} = \frac{Ve - Vr}{Ve} = \frac{.875 - .125}{Ve} = .857 \text{ or } .86$$

If we compute the reliability coefficient with that from K – R formula the result would be identical. It is true that Hoyt method like K– R formula gives biased result i.e., (under estimation in a short test but it is considerd safe as reliability of this test is probably not lower than .86. By K.R. formula we get

$$r_{tt} = \left(\frac{n}{n-1}\right) \frac{\sigma_1^2 - \Sigma pq}{\sigma_i^2} = \frac{12}{11} \left(\frac{9.45 - 2.03}{9.45}\right)$$

$$= \frac{12}{11} \times \frac{7.42}{9.45} = \frac{89.04}{103.95} = .857 \text{ or } .86$$

Merits of this Approach

1. It is a modified method of reliability and overcomes the limitations of the earlier methods of estimating reliability coefficient.
2. It computes accurate index of reliability as compared to other methods.
3. It is a sufficient value for estimating reliability index of speeded and power test.

Limitations

1. It employes analysis variance technique therefore its assumptions are to be strictly observed alongwith other assumptions.
2. The Method of calculating analysis variance is essential for its using to estimate reliability coefficient.
3. Two dimensional matrix table is difficult to prepare.
4. It is very time consuming method of reliability.

QUESTIONS

A. Long Answer Type Questions

1. Explain the concept of reliability. Discuss its relationship with error of measurement.
2. Discuss various types of estimating reliability coefficient. Indicate the method of computing the reliability index.
3. Enumerate the factors influencing the reliability of a test. Can we improve the reliability of test? If yes. How?
4. Define reliability of a test. Discuss advantages and disadvantages of various methods of estimating reliability of a test.
5. The reliability of a test refers to the consistency of scores." Anastasi. Discuss. What are the factors that may affect reliability of a test.

B. Short Answer Type Questions

1. Discuss coefficient of reliability.

2. Utility of Psychological tests.
3. Characteristics of a pshychological test.
4. What is a test.
5. Discuss test-retest method of reliability.
6. Discuss effect of lengthening a test on reliability.
7. Discuss factors influencing reliability of a test.
8. Rational equivalence method of estimating reliability.

C. Objective Type of Questions

1. Reliability refers to the consistency of scores. True/False
2. A test is a systematic procedure for comparing the behaviour of two or more persons. True/False
3. Consistency, stability and trustworthiness of scores are the characteristics of
   (*a*) Reliability (*b*) Validity
   (*c*) Objectivity (*d*) All the above.
4. Validity refers to the consistency of the scores. True/False
5. Standardization is ....procedure.
6. Match List I with List II

List I	*List II*
A. Coefficient of equivalence method.	1. Rational equivalence
B. Coefficient of reliability	2. Split-half method
C. Spearmans' Brown prophecy	3. Test-Retest method
D. Coefficient of internal consistency	4. Parallel form.

7. Match List I with List II

A. Consistency of the scores	1. Rational equivalence
B. Uniformity in procedure	2. *a*, A, *b*, B, *c*, C
C. Parallel form	3. Standardization
D. Kuder Richardson method	4. Reliability

8. Most accurate method of estimative reliability is.
   (*a*) Kuder-R method (*b*) Split-half method
   (*c*) Hyots method (*d*) Test-retest method
9. Reliability is the measure of
   (*a*) Personal error (*b*) Constant error
   (*c*) Variable error (*d*) Interpretive error
10. Reliability is proportion of ....
11. Reliability is also known as self correlation. True/False
12. Reliability indicates the extent of .... error.

13. Reliability is affected by:
    (*a*) Number of test items (*b*) Method of reliability
    (*c*) Speededness of a test (*d*) All the above.

14. Reliability index indicates the extent of constant error.
    True/False

15. Reliability index indicate the extent of
    (*a*) Constant error (*b*) Variable error
    (*c*) Personal error (*d*) All the above.

4

Validity

Validity is one of the most important characteristics of a standardized test. It indicates the purpose of the measuring instrument, it is considered as the ability of a test to measure only what is supposed to measure. A researcher who designed a test to measure mechanical aptitude must measure that not musical aptitude or personality characteristics. Similarly an intelligence test should measure intelligence, not musical training or socio-economic status. The term validity refers to the degree to which test scores or other measures predict some practical criterion measures. In broad sense, validity is considered to do with the question of what test scores measure and what they would predict. A score is considered valid for predicting anything with which it correlates. It is very important to select validation criteria and demonstration of satisfactory degree of validity are fundamental in psychological and educational testing. The most and essential quality of a valid test is it be highly reliable, if it is zero in any test, it would not be correlated with any other thing.

Definitions of Validity

Cronbach L.J. defines, "Validity is the extent to which a test measures what it pursports to measure."

Garret H.E. is of the view, "The validity of a test or any measuring instrument depends upon the fidelity with which it measures what it purports to measure."

Thorndike R.L. and Hagen E.P. defined, "A measurement procedure is valid in so far as it correlates with some measurement of success in the job for which it is being used as a predictor."

In the words of Brown F.G., "Validity is defined as the proportion of true variance that is relevant to the purposes of the testing."

According to Gullikson H., "It is the correlation of test with some criterion."

Freeman, Frank S. stated, "An index of validity shows the degree to which a test measures what it purports to measure, when compared with accepted criteria."

Anastasi, A. and Urtrima, S. are of the view, "The validity of a test concerns what the test measures and how will it does so. It tells us what can be inferred from test scores."

Lindquist, E.F. defined, "Validity is the accuracy with which it measures that is intended to measure or as the degree to which it approaches infallibility in measuring what it purports to measure."

Ghiselli, E.E. defined, "Validity refers to the extent to which a test of a set of operation measures what is supposed to measure."

If we analyse the above mentioned definitions and views, it can be concluded that validity of any test is concerns what it measures or what it purports to measure. There are accepted criteria to campare the same. It is observed fundamentally that all methods to determine test validity are concerned with the reliationships between performance on the test and other independent factors about the behavioural characteristics under the consideration. Carrell stated that validity is relative term. A test is valid for a particular purpose or in a particular situation, it is not generally valid.

Features of Validity

1. Validity measures 'constant error', while reliability measures 'variable error'.
2. It is an index of external correlation.
3. The criteria are 'set of operation' or success in the job or as a predictor for future cause of performance.
4. It is an indicator of psychological construct of a variable which indirectly measures with the help of behaviours.
5. No test is perfectly valid in behavioural sciences as measurement is indirect.
6. **Validity ensures the reliability of a test. If test is valid, it must be reliable.**
7. It indicates purposiveness of the test scores.

Characteristics of Validity

D.A. Payne and Morris distinguished following three kinds of validity which indicates the degree to which the test is capable of achieving certain objectives.

1. The test user wishes to determine how an individual performs at present in a universe of situations that the test situation claims to represent.
   Example: Most achievement tests measure the performance on a sample of questions which are certain educational objective or educational achievement. It is known as the content or objective validity.
2. The test user wishes to forecast an individual's future performance or standing or to estimate an individual's present standing or some variables for particular significance that is different from the test. It is empirical validity for example—academic aptitude or teaching aptitude may forecast the future academic teaching performance. It is predictive validity.
   An adjustment inventory may estimate the outcomes would be of careful psychological examination. It is concurrent or criterian related validity.
3. The test user issues to infer the degree to which the individual possesses some hypothetical traits or ability or quality (construct) presumed to be reflected in the test performance.
   For example: Abstract traits such as intelligence or creativity that can not be directly observed. It is psychological validity, factorial validity or construct validity.

Statistical Definition of Validity

Statistical definition of validity is based on a variance which has its relation with reliability. We know from the previous chapter that reliability was defined as:

$$r_{tt} = \frac{V\infty}{V_t} \qquad (1)$$

The proportion of 'true' variance to total variance. Similarly validity to defined.

$$val = \frac{V_{co}}{V_t} \qquad (2)$$

Where, val = validity

V_{co} = common factor variance

V_t = total variance of a measure

Now validity is defined as the proportion of the total variance of a measure that is common factor variance.

Common Factor Variance

It is the variance of a measure that is shared with other measures. In other words, it may be stated that common factor variance is the variance that two or more tests have in common.

In contrast to the common factor variance of a measure is its specific variance (V_{sp}), the systematic variance of a measure that is not shared by any other measure. For example, if a test measures verbal ability that other tests measure we have common factor variance, it also measure a verbal ability no other test does, it is special variance.

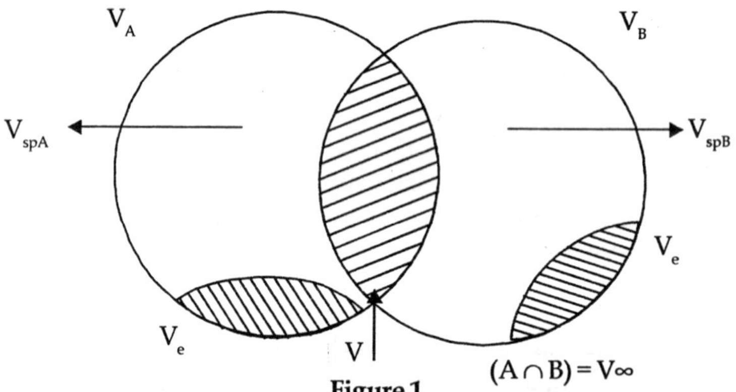

Figure 1

Above figure (1) indicates these ideas and also adds in motion of error variances. The A and B circles shows the variance of Test A and Test B. The interaction of A and B, (A ∩ B) is the common factor variances. The specific variances and the error variances of both, tests are also indicated. Any measure of total variance has several components i.e. common factor variance, specific variance and error variance. This may be expressed by the equation.

$$V_t = V_{co} + V_{sp} + V_e \quad (3)$$

If we divide the variance by of above equation by V_t

$$\frac{V_t}{V_t} = \frac{V_{co}}{V_t} + \frac{V_{sp}}{V_t} + \frac{V_e}{V_t} \quad (4)$$

The validity can be viewed as that part of the total variance of a measure that is not specific variances and not error variances. This may be algebraically written like:

$$\frac{V_{co}}{V_t} = \frac{V_t}{V_t} - \frac{V_{sp}}{V_t} - \frac{V_e}{V_t} \quad (5)$$

and we know by a definition of reliability which is

$$r_{tt} = 1 - \frac{V_e}{V_t} \quad (6)$$

This can be written

$$r_{tt} = \frac{V_t}{V_t} - \frac{V_e}{V_t} \quad (7)$$

Equation (5) may also be rewritten

$$\frac{V_{co}}{V_t} = \frac{V_t}{V_t} - \frac{V_e}{V_t} - \frac{V_{sp}}{V_t} \quad (8)$$

This shows that validity and reliability have close variance relation.

Reliability is equal to the first two right hand member of equation (8) bringing in equation (1)

$$r_{tt} = \frac{V_t}{V_t} - \frac{V_e}{V_t} = \frac{V_{\infty}}{V_t} \quad (9)$$

If we substitute (8) we get

$$\frac{V_{co}}{V_t} = \frac{V_{\infty}}{V_t} - \frac{V_{sp}}{V_t} \quad (10)$$

Now we can define validity statistically that the validity of a measure is that portion of the total variance of the measure that shares variance with other measures. Theoretically it may be stated that valid variance include no variance due to error, nor does it include variance that is specific to this measure only.

Let us assume that we have a method of determining the common factor variance or (variances) of a test. Suppose there are two sources of common factor variance is a test and no others. We may call factors A & B might be verbal (A) and arithmatic (B) ability.

If we add the variances of A and variance of B, we obtain the common factor variance of the test, which may be expressed by the equation

$$V_{co} = V_A + V_B \tag{11}$$

$$\frac{V_{co}}{V_t} = \frac{V_A}{V_t} + \frac{V_B}{V_t} \tag{12}$$

Using equation (2) and substituting in equation (12), we find

$$\text{val} = \frac{V_A}{V_t} + \frac{V_B}{V_t} \tag{13}$$

The total variances of a test includes the common factor variance, the variance specific to the test and no other test and error variances. Equations (3) and (4) express it and now substituting in (4) the equality of equation (12) we obtain

$$\frac{V_t}{V_t} = \frac{V_A}{V_t} + \frac{V_B}{V_t} + \frac{V_{sp}}{V_t} + \frac{V_e}{V_t} \tag{14}$$

The first two terms and the right hand side of equation are associated with the validity of the measure and the three terms on the right are associated with reliability of the measure. These relation have been indicated, common factor variance or the validity component of the measure is labelled (h^2) commonality a symbol used to indicate the common factor variance of a test. r_{tt} is reliability as expressed usually. The following figure diagrammatically express equation (14).

$V_{\infty} = 80\%$

$h^2 = V_{co}$ 55%		25%	Ve = 20 %
V_A	V_B	V_{sp}	V_e
30%	25%	25%	20%

Figure 2

The figure shows the contribution of the different variances to the total variance (out of four variances three are systematic variance and one is error variance comprise the total variances theoretically. The contribution of each one indicated is the figure 2.

Types of Validity

There are several ways of classifications of validity but their interpretion and explanation are the same. According to Lee J. cronbach *(a)* content validity, *(b)* concurrent validity, *(c)* predictive validity, (4) construct validity.

According to Freeman

1. Operational validity—It includes *(a)* Practical, *(b)* content and *(c)* construct validity.
2. Predictive validity, *(a)* Theoretical validity, *(b)* Empirical Validity, and *(c)* Concurrent
3. According to G.C. Helmadler (i) Test—Taking behaviour—Main type are *(a)* content, *(b)* operational, and *(c)* intrinsic validity, and (4) face validity.

2. Mental Traits. It includes (1) construct validity, (2) Factorial validity, and (3) Theoretical validity.

3. Criterion Behaviour *(a)* Empirical validity, *(b)* predictive, and *(c)* Concurrent.

Types of Validity

Operational and Predictive Validity

'Operational validity' means that the task required by the test are upto the mark to measure and evaluatic certain defined psychological traits or activities.

Predictive validity measures to the extent that they are efficient in predicting subsequent development of various degree of skill and competence in the several aspects of the activity. Such tests indicate to the extent it is efficient is forecasting and differentiating behaviour or performance in a specified field under original working and living conditions.

Predictive validity is dependent though in part upon the operational validity of the test. Most achievement tests are used to determine an individual, is level and quality of achievement in a subject of study at a specified time but also helps to plan his subsequent education.

Face Validity

This term is used to charaterize test materials that appear to measure what the tests author desires to measure. In other words, the test contains items that seems to be related to the variable being measured. Face validity was most often used with tests of educational achievement and of personality but to a lesser extent with tests aptitude and intelligence. Tests are validated at face value when there is an urgent need. Face validity is not sufficient to warrant the use of a test.

Content Validity

D.A. Payne and Morris define content validty, "The test user wishes to determine how an individual performs at present in an universe of situations that the test situation is claimed to measure is known 'content validity."

G.C. Helmadter defined, "Test scores can be interpreted in terms of school ability or the performance of today is well defined type of situation or subject matter that it is called content validity."

According to Anastasi, "Content validity involves essentially the systematic examination of the test content to determine whether it covers a representative sample of the behaviour domain to be measured."

R. Ebel defined, "Content validity is the representativeness or sampling adequacy of the content—the substance, the matter, the topic of a measuring instrument."

F.J. Freeman, explained. This type of validity is estimated by evaluating the relevance of the test items individually as well as a whole. Each items should be included to have a sampling of the knowledge or performance which test purports to measure. If taken collectively the items should constitute a representing sample of the variable to be tested.

Features of Content Validity

1. This type of validity should only be applied to tests of proficiency and of educational achievement, it should be supplemented by several types of statistical analysis.
2. It should not depend upon the subjective judgement of only one specialist.
3. It should be based upon careful analysis of several specialists.
4. The statistical analysis should be based on
   (a) determining which items discriminating best between individual at the upper and lower level of performance.

(*b*) determining the percent that answer each item correctly.
(*c*) determining significance of increases in average scores from our school grade to the next.
(*d*) determining for each item or for each subject its correlation with educational progress.

6. Content validation is basically judgemental.
7. Each item of a test must be studied and weighed for its presumed representativeness of the universe.
8. Competent judges should judge the content of the items.
9. The universe of content must clearly be defined i.e. judges must be furnished with specific directions for making judgements.

Factorial Validity

According to factorial analysists a test is said to have high factorial validity if it is a measure of one functional unity (for example, arithmetic ability to the exclusion of other elements) as far as possible. The factorial process aims to identify a list of functional unities (also called primary mental abilities) with in a test and the weight contributed by each of these to total performance on the test.

Functional unities are identified by analysing the inter correlations among a number of separate relatively restricted measures.

Factorial validity is determined by the weights called loadings contributed to the total test scores by each of the derived factors. The merit of this type of validity depends upon the appropriateness of the statistical procedure and upon the tester's initial psychological insights in selecting items and also in the interpretation of his findings. Factorial analysis assists in identifying the more restricted and immediatly relevant aspects of ability required in a given activity.

Construct Validity

The English dictionary of psychology states that a construct is a concept formally proposed with definition and limits explicitly related to empirical data.' If this criteria of validity is applied in the development of a test, this definition shows that the instrument's validity is to be judged by the extent to which it measures or assesses the psychological processes or the personality traits as defined and analyzed by the author of the test. Construct validity depends upon the degree to which the test items individual and collectively sample the range or class of activities or traits as defined by the mental process or the personality trait being measured.

Construct validity means that the test scores are examined in terms of a construct. Anastasi defined it as "the extent to which the test may be said to measure a theoretical construct or trait a psychological variable."

This Construct also means the idea that developed in one's mind to define, identify or explain objects phenomena.

According to Nunnaly, construct indicates a hypothesis which tells us that 'a variety of behaviours will correlation with one another in studies of individual differences and/or will similarly be affected by experimental treatments.

The measurement experts actually inquire into the construct validity of a test generally want to know what psychological or other property or properties can explain the variance of the test. For example, if the test is an intelligence test, they really want to know what factors lie behind test performance. They may specifically ask. Does this test measure verbal ability and abstract reasoning ability? In other words we may state that their interest are usually more in the property being measured than in the test itself.

There is difference between construct and content validity as in former each trait to be measured must be analysed and made explicit, and each item of the test must belong to the trait in question. In developing any type of inventory to assess the trait (dimensions), the investigator must define the syndromes of the concept to be tested. Investigator is to interpret the result obtained primarily in terms of the mental processes as defined and sampled with reference to the population sample upon whom the instrument has been standardized.

Convergence and Discrimination

Convergence and discriminability both are required importantly in construct validation.

Convergence means that evidence from different sources gathered in different ways. All indicate the same or similar meaning of the content. Different methods of measurement should converge on the construct.

Discriminability means that one can empirically differentiate the construct from other constructs that may be similar and that one can point out what is correlated to the construct.

In the analysis of construct validation, D.T. Campbell pointed out that construct validity must show not only that a test correlates highly with other variables with which it should theoretically correlates but also that it does not correlate significantly with variables from which it should differ. Campbell and Fiske described the former process as convergent validation and the latter as discriminant validities.

Factor analysis also developed as a means of identifying psychological traits relevant to construct validation procedure. It is a refined statistical technique for analysing the inter relationship of behaviour data. In the process of factor analysis, the number of variables in terms of which each individuals performance can be described, is reduced from the number of original tests to a relatively small number of factors or comon traits. After the factors have been identified they can be utilized in describing the factorial composition of a test such a correlation is reported as the factorial validity of the test.

Concurrent Validity

The term 'concurrent validity' indicates the process of validating the new tests by correlating it, or otherwise comparing it for agreement, with some present source of information. For example, in standardizing a new test of intelligence may be correlated with a sound standardized achievement test.

Empirical Validity

When the test user desires to predict or forecast an individual's future performance or to estimate an individual present standing on some variable of particular significance that is different from the test. It is called an empirical or predicting validity. This is also known as the 'criterion related validity'. The criterion is defined as an external and independent measure of measures essentially the same variable that the test claims to measure.

Cureton defined, "The empirical validity is an estimate of the correlation coefficient between the test scores and the true criterion scores."

Methods of Calculating Validity

Following statistical methods are used and to predict or to estimate the validity of any test.

1. Simple correlation.
2. Biserial correlation
3. Tetrachoric correlation

Factors Influencing Validity of Test

1. Length of the test
2. Dependence of validity
3. Method of estimating validity index on reliability.
4. Crterion of validation
5. Speededness of the test
6. Homogenecity of the sample

Length of the Test

Lengthening a test not only increases reliability but also increases validity of the test. The effect upon the validity coefficient of increasing a test's length may be measured by the following formula.

$$r_{cnx1} = \frac{n_{rcx1}}{\sqrt{n + n\,(n-1)\,r_{11}}}$$

Where

r_{cnx1} = the correlation between the criterion (c) and n forms of Test X or Text X_1 lengthened n times

r_{cx1} = the correlation between criterion (c) and the given test X_1.

r_{11} = reliability coefficient of Test X_1

n = number of times it is lengthened.

Illustration—Example—Test A has a 'reliability coefficient of .60 and a correlation of .30 with the criterion (c) what would be the correlation of Test A with the same criterion (its validity coefficient) if the test were trippled in length.

Here $r_{11} = .60$ $r_{cx1} = .30$

n = 3 and by substituting these values we have

$$r_{xx1} = \frac{3 \times .30}{\sqrt{3 + 3 \times 2 \times .60}} = \frac{.90}{\sqrt{6.6}} = \frac{.90}{2.57}$$

$= .36$

This tripling the length of the test or averaging 3 administrations of the same test should increase the validity coefficient from .30 to .36. In order to reach a given level of validity. How much the test would have to be lenghtened. We can rearrange the above formula.

$$n = \frac{r^2_{cxx1}\ (1-r_{it})}{r^2_{cx} - r^2_{cnx1}\ Xr_{it}}$$

Suppose a test has a reliability coefficient of .40 in a narrow range and a criterion correlation of .30. How much lengthening is necessary in order that this test will yield a validity coefficient of .40.

By substituting

$r_{cnx.t} = .40$, $r_{it} = .40$, $r_{c \times 1} = .30$

$$n = \frac{.16 \times .60}{.09 - .16 \times .40} = \frac{.096}{.09 - 0.64}$$

$$= \frac{.096}{.03} = 3$$

Test must be 3 times its present length in order for the validity coefficient to go from .30 to .40.

Dependence of Validity on Reliability

The correlation between a test and its criteria is reduced or attenuated if either the test or criterion or both are unreliable such a correction is given by the formula.

$$r_{\infty 1 \infty 2} = \frac{r_{12}}{\sqrt{r_{11} \times r_{211}}}$$

This formula gives correlation between test 1 and 2 corrected for attenuation.

In which:

$r_{\infty 1 \infty 2}$ = correlation between true measures in 1 and 2
r_{12} = correlation between obtained score in 1 and 2
r_{11} = reliability coefficient of Test 1
r_{211} = reliability coefficient of Test 2

Illustration—Suppose the correlation between criterion (c) and Test A is .50 the reliability coefficient of (c) is .70 and reliability coefficient of Test A is .80. What is corrected correlation between C and A. Substituting these values in the above equation.

$$r_{\infty 1 \infty 2} = \frac{.50}{\sqrt{.70 \times .80}} = \frac{.50}{\sqrt{.56}} = \frac{.50}{.75} = .66$$

corrected correlation is .66.

Correcting from chance errors will always raise the correlation between two tests—unless the reliability coefficient are both 1.00 chance errors therefore always lower or attenuate an obtained correlation coefficient.

3. *Methods of estimating validity index.* Cross validaton is the most popular methods of estimating validity although there are several methods of estimating validity. There are different statistical methods of estimating validity of the test through coefficient. Each method of correlation yields difficult index of validity. It is upto the researcher who is to decide which method of correlation is to be applied for estimating validity index as it depends on the test to be constructed.

Speededness of a Test

The speededness undoubtedly is very nearly related with the validity of test. If the duration of a test is increased so that most of the examinees may solve the last item of the test. Consequently the validity index will be increased as the speededness has been decreased. In other words it may be stated that the validity index is inversely proportional to speededness of the test.

5. Type of sample. If the sample of examinees is homogeneous in ability, the validity of the test scores is likely to be lowered while if the sample of the examinee is heterogeneous the validity of the test is likely to be high.

Relation of Validity and Reliability

The practical validity of a test is directly proportional to its reliability, the more reliable a test, the more it is valid. As earlier stated statistically that the greater the error variance in a test, there will be less common factor variance in a test is the source of validity.

When reliability and validity are independent. There are important exceptions too. If a test is administered at a heterogenous group there will be a low interconsistency or reliability and yet a high practical validity and if a test administered on a homogeneous group, it would be possible that its reliability may increase without affecting its validity.

Reliability and validity are incompatible in many ways such as:

1. Maximal reliability requires high-inter correlations among items while maximal validity requires low inter-correlations.
2. Maximal reliability requires items of equal difficulty maximal validity requires items differing in difficulty.
3. Reliability is attributed by true variance of the test scores while validity is attributed by common factor variance.
4. These two concepts reliability and validity refer to different aspects but measures the same thing i.e., test efficiency.
5. A reliable test may be theoretically valid but may be practically invalid as judged by its correlations with various independent criteria.
6. A highly valid test cannot be unreliable as its correlations with a criteria is limited by its own index of reliability.

QUESTIONS

A. Long Answer Type Questions?

1. What is validity? Explain various methods of estimating validity of a test.
2. Define the content validity. Indicate its use in the test.
3. Explain 'Empirical validity.' Differentiate between concurrent and predictive validity of a test.
4. Describe the advantage and use of the validity of a test and enumerate the factors affecting validity.
5. Explain statistical definition of validity. Discuss operational and predictive validity.

B. Short Answer Type Questions

1. Define the term validity.
2. Explain the factors affecting validity of a test.
3. What is the need of validity of a test.
4. Discuss relationship between reliability and validity.
5. Enumerate the methods of estimating validity.

C. Objective Type Questions

1. Validity has no relationship with constant error. True/False
2. A valid test can not be reliable. True/False
3. An achievement test requires content validity. True/False
4. An achievement test has the .... validity.
5. Validity of a test means—
   (*a*) Purposiveness (*b*) Consistency
   (*c*) Stability (*d*) All of the above.

6. An intelligence test should have
   (*a*) Construct validity (*b*) Factorial validity
   (*c*) Psychological validity (*d*) All the above.
7. An attitude scale should have
   (*a*) Content validity (*b*) Operational validity
   (*c*) Face validity (*d*) Concurrent validity
8. An aptitude test should have
   (*a*) Face validity (*b*) Logical validity
   (*c*) Predictive validity (*d*) All the above.
9. Validity index is the proportion of
   (*a*) True variance (*b*) Error variance
   (*c*) Common factor variance (*d*) Specific variance.
10. A reliable test is also valid. True/False
11. Essay type tests are valid. True/False
12. Match list I with list II

List I	*List II*
(*a*) The extent to which a test reflects a sample of actual behaviour to be measured	1. Predictive validity
(*b*) The extent to which a test looks appropriate from a reading of the items.	2. Content validity
(*c*) The extent to which a test can tell a person's behaviour in same other settings.	3. Face validity
(*d*) The extent to which a test actually measures a particular traits.	4. Construct validity

13. Validity index shows the degree to which a test measures what its purports to measure. It has been defined by.
    (*a*) F.S. Freeman (*b*) Chaplin
    (*c*) Anastasi (*d*) Lee J. Chronbach
14. Validity is the extent to which a test measures what it purports to measure. It has been defined by
    (*a*) F.S. Freeman (*b*) Chaplin
    (*c*) Anastasi (*d*) Lee J. Chronbach
15. Validity and reliability are the same. True/False

5

Norms

Norms

The raw score obtained by any individual on any test has no significance in itself. Researcher has to establish the average score for the constructed test which may be compared with the score obtained by another individual. In other words if scores obtained on each test are to be compared, the indices must be used which may express the relative significance of any given score. Meaningful index must be established to facilitate interpretation. Any standardized and sound psychological or achievement test would provide tables of age norms, or grade norms or percentage ranks or decile ranks or standard scores. It all depends on the purpose of the test. There may be other kinds of norms which are suitable to the test.

In order to find out more exactly the individual's exact position with reference to the standardization sample, the raw scores are transformed into some relative measure. These derived scores serve two purposes.

1. These derived scores indicate the individual's relative standing in the normative sample and in this way it permits an evaluation for individual's performance in reference to other individuals.
2. These derived scores provide us comparable measures that permits directly comparison of the individual's performance on different tests.

Suppose a student has a raw score of 50 on a numerical ability test and a raw score of 20 on an vocabulary test – These raw scores indicate nothing about his relative performance on the two tests. We can not say, whether he is better in numerical ability as compared to vocabulary or vice-versa or equally good in both. As the raw scores on different tests are usually expressed in different units as such a direct comparison of such scores is not possible.

Definitions of Norms

Freeman, Frank S., "A norm is the average or typical score (mean or median) on a particular tests made by a specified population."

Garrett Henry E. defines, "Norms are measures of achievement which represent the typical performance of some designated group or groups."

According to Thorndike and Hagen, "Norms are defined as the average performance an a particular test made by standardized sample."

If we analyse the definition and the concept of the norm we can enumerate the following characteristics.

1. A norm is considered as the average performance of a group.
2. A norm indicates its transformation from the raw scores into standard scores.
3. A norm is a base for interpretation of raw scores obtained by an individual in a test.
4. Without norms a test has no usability.
5. Objectivity in interpretation of the obtained score requires standardized norms of the test.
6. Norm indicates the criterion level of a test.
7. It is a process which is also known as norm referencing test.
8. Norms are the indicators of standardized score obtained from the sample of the population.
9. A norms minimizes interpretive errors of a measuring instrument.
10. Norm is a significant and important characteristics of a test.
11. Norms are quantitative criterion for different levels.
12. Norms are averages determined under prevailing conditions.
13. Test norms represent the test's standardization.
14. Norms are the actual achievement of students at standardized levels.

Norm-Referencing Test

All types of raw scores are meaningless. There are two reference points that are applied in interpreting the test scores.

(i) Norm-referencing *(ii)* criterion-referencing

Norm-referencing

It is the first way of interpreting the examinee's test score with standard score of a specific group of examinees on the test. This process is known as the norms-referencing. This type of norm is the average performance on a particular test made by standardization of sample.

To interpret the raw scores with the performance of the standardization sample and the obtained raw score is converted into the derived scores or standard scores. There are two ways and purposes for converting of scores.

1. The derived scores provide the basis for direct comparison of the examinees own performance on different tests.
2. The derived scores indicate the relative position in the standardization sample and therefore his or her performance may be evaluated accordingly.

Creterion Referencing

It is a way of interpreting a test scores it is to evolve an external criterion or standard and compare the test scores of the examinees with it. This process is known as criterion-referencing. Glaser defined, "The criterion-referenced test may be defined as one in which the test performance is linked or related to some behaviour measures or referents."

Cox and Vargos defined, "A major criterion for referencing a test is the training which results in an increase in the skill or proficiency."

The definitions indicate that the tests are usually based upon a set of behaviour referent which intends to measure and the performance on a test can be explained in terms of predetermined cut-off scores whereas a norm referenced test is always based upon the performance of a group of standardized sample.

Fundamentally derived scores are expressed in one of two major ways.

1. Developmental level attained or norms.
2. Relative position within a specified group.

Developmental Norms

(i) Mental Age

The 'mental age' norms have widely been popularized through the Binet-Siman scale although they used the term, 'mental level'. In such age norms or age levels, items were grouped into year levels. For example, the items which were passed by the majority of 9 years olds in the standardisation sample were placed in the 9 years level and those who passed majority of 10 years olds were assigned to the 10 years level and so on so forth. Mental age norms have also been used with tests that are not divided into year levels. In such a case raw score of the individual is first determined. The mean raw scores obtained by the individuals in each year or group within the standardization sample constitute the all norms for such a test. It is essential here to be noted that the mental age unit does not remain constant with age but tends to shrink with advancing years.

Definition of Age Norms or Mental Age

The age norm is defind as the average performance of a representative sample of certain age level on the measure of intelligence or a certain activity.

Mental age norms are suitable for those traits or abilities which increase systematically with chronological age.

Advantage of Age Norms

1. It has the great applicability in intelligence test and achievement test.
2. It is most appropriate for its abilities which increase systematically with chronological age.
3. It is easy to interpret score.

Limitations

1. It has only been used in intelligence and achievement tests.
2. Age norms lack a standard and uniform unit throughout the period of growth of physical and psychological traits.
3. It is difficult and time consuming task to develop the age norms and mental age norms.

(ii) ***Grade Norms or Grade Equivalents*** The scores on educational achievement test are often interpretated in terms of grade equivalents. Grade norms are found by computing the mean raw scores obtained by the students in each grade. Thus if

the average number of problems solved correctly on an arithmetic test by the fifth-graders in the standardization sample is 25, then a raw score of 25 corresponds to a grade equivalent of 5. Grade norms are popular in school settings. Grade norms have several shortcomings, such as

(i) The content of instruction varies some what grade to grade, therefore grade norms are appropriate only for common subjects taught throughout the grade levels covered by the list.

(ii) Grade norms are generally applicable at the high school level. However, the emphasis placed on different subjects may vary from grade to grade and therefore progress may be more rapid in one subject than in another during particular grade.

(iii) Grade norms are subject to misinterpretation unless the test user keeps of firmly and carefully in mind the manner in which they were derived.

Characteristics of Grade Norms

1. It is widely used in educational institutions to design the grades to the students.
2. It is easy to interpret and understand.
3. It is suitable for the measurement of educational abilities.
4. The grade norms facilitate the open education system.

Within Group Norms

All the standardized tests now provide some form of within-group norms. Within group scores have a uniform and clearly defined quantitative meaning and can approximately be employed in most type of statistical analysis.

Percentile

Percentile scores are expressed in terms of the percentage of persons in the standardization sample who fall below a given raw score. A percentile indicates the individual's relative position in the standardization sample. For example if 30 per cent of the persons obtain fewer than 20 per cent problems correct on a vocabulary test then a raw score of 20 corresponds to the 30th percentile (P_{30}).

The 50th percentile (P_{50}) corresponds to the median.

J.P. Guilford defined the term percentile, "A score or percentile is a value on the scoring scale below which are any percentage of the cases."

Percentile norms provide for interpreting the score of an individual in terms of his/her standing in some particular group.

Percentile Rank (PR) of an individual on his position on a scale of 100 to which the subject's score entitles him or her.

The distinction between percentile and percentile rank, in calculating percentile one starts with a certain per cent of N, e.g., 15 or 60 per cent one then counts into the distribution the given per cent and the point reached is the required percentile e.g. P_{15} or P_{60}.

The procedure followed in computing percentile ranks is the reverse of this process.

E.F. Lindquist the percentile rank of a given point on score scale is the percentage of measures in the whole distribution which are below this given point.

Freeman defines Percentile Rank. "An individual's percentile rank on a test designates the percentage of cases or scores lying below it."

A person having a percentile rank of 30 is situated above 30 percent of the group of which he is a member or thirty percent of the group fall below this person's rank.

It is to be noted here and it should not be confused with the familiar percentage scores expressed is terms of percentage of persons. The percentiles do not imply a zero raw score and perfect raw score. Percentile scores have the following advantages:

1. They are easy to compute and can be readily understand even by technically untrained persons.
2. Percentile are universally applicable.
3. They can be used equally well with adults and children.
4. They are suitable for any type of test whether it measures aptitude or personality variables.

Drawbacks

The chief drawback of percentile scores arise from the marked inequality of their units, especially at the extremes of the distribution. If the distribution of raw scores approximates the normal curve then raw score differences near the median or center of distribution are exaggerated in the percentile conversion, whereas raw scores differences near the ends of the distribution are greatly shrunk.

The percentile show each individual's relative position in the normative sample but not the amount of difference between scores.

Decile Rank

The decile rank is the same in principle as the percentile but instead of designating the one-hundreth part of a distribution, it designates the one-tenth part of the group (N/10) in which any tested person is placed by his score.

The term decile is used to mean a dividing point 'Decile rank' signifies a range of scores between two dividing points. If a testee has a decile rank of 10 (D_{10}) shows that he is located in highest 10 percent of the group, one whose decile rank is 9 (D_9) is in the second highest 10 per cent.

When the number of scores in a distribution is small, percentiles are not used because there is little or no significance in making fine distinction in rank. The decile ranking method may be used.

The Standard Score and Variants

Standard Score

Standard scores are the most satisfactory type of derived score. They express the individual's distance from the mean in terms of the standard deviation of the distribution. Standard scores may be obtained either linear or nonlinear transformation of the original raw scores.

If the distribution of scores of two or more tests are approximately normal standard scores derived from one distribution may be compared with those derived from the others. The formula is:

$$z = \frac{X - M}{\sigma\,(S.D.)}$$

Here z = standard score, X = An individual score

M = Mean of the distribution
(σ) S.D. = Standard deviation

Linearly derived standard scores are often designated simply as 'standard score' or 'z score'.

Comparison and computation of standard scores.

We know $z = \frac{X - M}{(S.D.)}$ Where M = 60, S.D. = 5

Sheila's score is

$X_1 = 65$

$$z = \frac{65 - 60}{5}$$

$z = +1.00$

Veena's score

$X_2 = 55$

$$z = \frac{55 - 60}{5} = -1.00$$

$z = -1.00$

In a normal curve. Sheila falls 1 SD above the group mean while the other Veena falls – 1 SD below the group mean.

Any raw score that is exactly equal to the mean is equivalent to a z score of zero.

One of the reasons for converting raw scores into any derived score is to render scores on different test. Comparable as indicated above linearly standard scores are comparable only when they are found from distributions that have approximately the same form.

To achieve comparability of scores from dissimilarly shaped distribution nonlinear transformations may be employed to fit the scores to any specified type of distributed curve.

Normalized standard scores are standard scores expressed in terms of a distribution that has been transformed to fit a normal curve. Such scores can be computed by reference to tables giving the percentage of cases falling at different SD distances from the mean of a normal curve.

Deviation I.Q.

The standard score principle has been utilized in deriving what is known as deviation intelligence quotient. Among the first test to express scores in terms of deviation IQs was the Wechsler Intelligence scale. In these tests, the mean is 100 and the SD 15. Deviation IQs are also used in a number of current group tests of intelligence and in the third (1960) revision of the Stanford Binet itself. It is to be noted importantly that deviation IQs from different tests are comparable only when they employ the same or closely similar values for the S.D.

The standardized sample mean is 100 I.Q. and SD (s) usually 16. The raw scores are converted into Deviation IQ with the help of the following formula.

$$F = \frac{DIQ - 100}{16} = \frac{X - M}{\sigma}$$

or DIQ = 16 z + 100

DIQ = Deviation I.Q.

X = Raw score of an individual

M = Mean of raw scores of the sample

(σ) = standard deviation

Suppose the mean of the distribution is 55 and (SD) σ = 15 and an examinee obtained 25 raw scores. Calculate DI.Q. of the examinee.

By substituting these values in the above formula.

$$DIQ = 16\left(\frac{X - M}{\sigma}\right) + 100$$

$$= 16\left(\frac{25 - 55}{15}\right) + 100$$

$$= 16\left(\frac{30}{15}\right) + 100$$

$$= 16 \times (-2 + 100 = -32 + 100)$$

DIQ = 68.

T = Score : A variant of the standard score, known as a T-score. It was suggested by McCall using the T-score method, the mean is set at 50 whereas in terms of standard score the value of the mean is zero. To obtain a T-score, the standard score is multiplied by 10 and then added to or subtracted from the mean T-score of 50. For example, a standard score of +1.00 becomes a T-score of 60 while –1.00 becomes 40. The justified assumption of this method is that nearly all scores will be within a range of five standard deviations from the mean. Since each SD is divided into ten units, the T-score is based upon a scale of 100 units.

The formula of T-score is as follows:

$$\frac{T - 50}{10} = \frac{X - M}{\sigma}$$

$$T - 50 = 10\left(\frac{X - M}{\sigma}\right)$$

$$T = 10z + 50$$

$$z = \left(\frac{X - M}{\sigma}\right)$$

T = T-scores or standard score

X = Raw scores of an examinee

M = Mean of the raw scores

σ = standard deviation

Illustration—The mean of a test is 54.00 and examinee gets raw score only 10 and standard deviation = 15

By substituting these values in the above formula

$$T = 10\left(\frac{X - M}{\sigma}\right) + 50$$

$$10\left(\frac{10 - 54}{15}\right) + 50, = 10\left(\frac{-44}{15}\right) + 50$$

$$= 10\,(-2.93) + 50$$

$$= -29.30 + 50 = 20.7 \qquad \text{T-score} = 20.7$$

Stanine

Another variant of the standard score technique is known the stanine. This term was coined by psychologists in the Army Air Force during World War II. According to this techniques, the standard population is divided into nine groups, thus it is called standard nine contracted to 'Stanine'. Except the ranks of stanine 1 (lowest) and 9 (highest) each unit is euqal to one half of a standard deviation. A score of 5 represents the median group defined as those whose scores are within $\pm.25$ SD of the mean i.e., a range of a half sigma at the centre of distribution. A rank of stanine 6 represents the group whose scores fall between + 0.25 σ and + 0.75 σ.

This scale provides a single-digit system of scores with a mean of 5 and an SD of approximately 2.

Raw scores can readily be converted to stanine by arranging the original scores in order of size and then assigning stanines in accordance with the normal curve percentage as f reproduced in the following table.

Table-5.1

Normal Curve Percentages for Use in Stanine Conversion

Percentage	4	7	12	17	20	17	12	7	4
Stanine	1	2	3	4	5	6	7	8	9

Relativity of Norms

Test scores can not be properly interpreted in the abstract, they must be referred to particular tests.

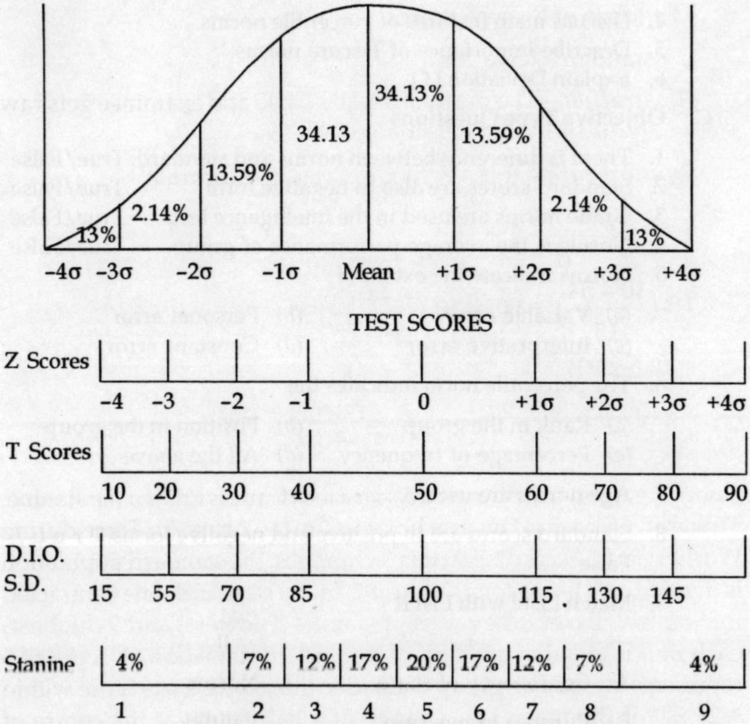

Figure: Relationship Among Different Types of Test Scores in a Normal Distribution

---

QUESTIONS

A. Long Answer Type Questions

1. Define the term 'Norms'. Enumerate the significance of Norms.
2. Differentiate between non-referencing and criterion referencing test. Describe the need and importance for using a test.
3. Explain the term 'stanine'. Establish the relationship with standard score and T-score norms.
4. Distinguish between age norms and grade norms. Illustrate your answer with suitable examples.

B. Short Answer Type Questions

1. Define the term 'Norms'.
2. Explain different types of norms.
3. What is stanine 'norms'.

4. Discuss main features of percentile norms.
5. Describe importance of T-score norms.
6. Explain Deviation I.Q.

C. **Objective Type Questions**

1. There is difference between norms and standard. True/False
2. Standard scores are also in negative form. True/False
3. Grade norms are used in the intelligence test. True/False
4. Norms is the average performance of group. True/False
5. Norms indicate the extent of

   (*a*) Variable error (*b*) Personal error
   (*c*) Interpretive error (*d*) Constant error

6. The percentile norm indicates the

   (*a*) Rank in the group (*b*) Position in the group
   (*c*) Percentage of frequency (*d*) All the above

7. Age norms are used .... test.
8. Standard scores are in positive and negative forms. True / False
9. Match List I with List II

	I		II
A	Consistency of score	1.	Norms
B	Purpose to measure	2.	Validity
C	Raw scores	3.	Standardization
D	Uniformity in procedure	4.	Reliability

10. Match List I with List II

	I		II
A	Quantitative	1.	Reliability
B	Qualitative	2.	Measurement
C	Consistency and stability	3.	Meaningless
D	Raw scores	4.	Evaluation

6

Statistics, Frequency Distribution and Graphic Representation

Statistics

Statistics summarizes data in meaningful way so that a researcher can be able to draw inferences about a large population from a small sample of subjects.

Statistics is used not only to describe the resutls but also to make references. One of the principal uses of statistics is to summarize and understand data.

Definition and Importance of Statistics

A major objective of statistics is to organize and summarise quantitative data in order to facilitate their understanding. In the behavioural sciences we conduct research in order to determine the acceptability of hypothesis which we derive from our theories of behaviour. Statistics helps to arrive at scientific conclusions which is one of the requirements of scientific method based on the objectivity.

Measurement of a group of individuals or objects almost always produces a variety of collection of numbers, which must be ordered and summarised in order to be intelligible. Statistics is an indispensible tool to solve this purpose.

Statistics is also indispensible when we try to infer the characteristics of an entire population from samples of that population. As it is so impractical and expensive and probably impossible to test entire population. We obtained the data or required information from a representative sample of the population. But it is to be kept in mind that sample can be assumed to mirror the population. Here we use statistical techniques to make our inferences reasonable about the population's characteristics from a sample's data.

Definitions of Statistics

Different statisticians have defined statistics differently.

W.G. Sutcliffer, "statistics comprises the collection, tabulation, presentation and analysis of an aggregate of facts, collected in a methodical manner, without bias and related to a predetermined purpose."

Ferguson defined, "Statistics deals with the collection, classification, description and interpretation of data obtained by conduct of survey and experiments."

A.L. Bowley defined, "Statistics may be called the science of counting."

According to Lovitt, "Statistics is the science which deals with the collection, classification and tabulation of numerical facts as the basis for explanation, description and comparison of phenomena."

Boddington defined, "Statistics to the science of estimates and probabilities."

If we analyse the above definitions of statistics we find the following characteristics/functions of the statistics:

1. *Collection*—The foremost function of statistics is to collect the facts (data) regarding the phenomena or problem under consideration.
2. *Classification*—This means to classify the collected data in a desirable manner so that it may come to us in a condensed form.
3. *Tabulation*—The classified data in order to give it in such a shape that we can easily comprehend.
4. *Analysis*—The tabulated data is analysed by using various technique of statistics.
5. *Interpretation and Description*—After analysis the results of the calculated data are described and presented in simple manner so that one can easily comprehend and conclude effectively.

According to Fred N. Kerlinger, "Statistics is the theory and method of analyzing quantitative data obtained from samples of observations in order to study and compare sources of variance of phenomena, to help make decisions to accept or reject hypothesized relation between the phenomenon, and to aid in making reliable inferences from empirical observations."

The above definition indicates four purposes of statistics

1. It helps to reduce large quantities of data to manageable and understandable form. A statistic is a measure calculated from a sample in contrast with a parameter which is a population value. In other words it may be stated that statistics are epitomes or summaries of the samples and often presumably, of the populations from which they are calculated.
2. It helps in the study of populations and samples. Here inferential statistics are calculated with the help of sample statistics.
3. It helps in decision making i.e., in accepting and rejecting hypothesis framed to study the problem.
4. It aids in making reliable inferences from the observational data.

Continuous and Discrete Series

A continuous series is one which is capable of any degree of subdivision though in practice we accept divisions to some convenient unit. In psychology and education I.Q.'s are usually thought by increment of one unit along an ability continuum which runs from idiots to genius.

Physical scores as well as mental test scores fall into this category.

Discrete series—Series which exhibit real gaps are called discrete.

The meaning of test Scores in a continuous series.

Scores in continuous series are considered of as distance along a continuum rather than discrete point. A score in a mental test is a unit distance between two limits. A score of 100 upon an intelligence test represents the interval 99.5 upto 100.5 and the exact midpoint of this score interval is 100 as indicated below:

score 100

100

99.5 100.5

The usual mathematical meaning of a score is an interval which extends along some dimension from. 5 unit below to .5 unit above the face value of the score.

There is a second view which has different meaning of a test score. According to a score of 100 means that a person has done atleast 100 items correctly but not 101. Therefore a score of 100 reperesents any value between 100 to 101 i.e., any fractional value greater than 100 but less than 101 is scored simply as 100. The middle of the score is 100.5

score 100

100.5

100 101

Both ways of defining a score are valid and useful for the calculations. The point to remember is that results obtained from treating scores under a second definition will always be .5 unit higher than result obtained when scores are taken under the first or mathematical definition.

Preparing of Frequency Distribution

The following original scores collected from intelligence test have little meaning to the researcher until he arranged or classified them in some systematic way:

100	52	98	72	99	67
95	62	96	55	97	65
45	65	88	47	56	64
60	49	87	48	57	95
90	46	70	55	47	96
85	61	75	79	57	85
87	46	79	82	57	49
92	47	80	84	92	55
45	56	72	65	82	92
95	86	75	69	57	48

We follow the following steps to classify scores into a frequency distribution steps.

1. We first determine the range or the gap between the highest and the lowest scores.

Range = Highest score-lowest score.

In the above scores highest score is 100 and lowest score is 45

Therefore Range = 100 – 45 = 55

Step 2. Now decide on the size and number of classes for dividing the data. We generally use grouping intervals are 3, 5, 10 units in length being easier to work with in later calculations. However the number of classes depends on the number of data points and the range of the data collected. As a rule statisticians rarely use fewer than 6 or more than 15 classes. The range in the above data is 55, divided by 5 give 11 class interval which is in our purview of smooth calculation and is chosen as best ruled data as in the following table.

$$\text{Number of class interval} = \frac{\text{Range}}{\text{Size of class interval}}$$

Here Range = 55 and we want 5 as the numbers of class interval

$$\frac{55}{5} = 11$$

Step 3. Tally the scores in their proper interval as shown in the table. In the first column of the table, the class intervals are listed serially from the smallest scores at the bottom of the column to the largest scores at the top.

The above scores grouped into frequency distribution

Table–6.1

Class intervals	*Mid point*	*Tallies*	*f (frequency)*
1	2	3	4
105-109	107	0	0
100-104	102	|	1
95-99	97	~~||||~~ |||	8
90-94	92	||||	4
85-89	87	~~||||~~ |	6
80-84	82	||||	4
75-79	77	||||	4
70-74	72	|||	3
65-69	67	~~||||~~	5

(Contd.)

Class intervals	*Mid point*	*Tallies*	*(frequency)*
60-64	62	||||	4
55-59	57	~~||||~~ ||||	9
50-54	52	|	1
45-49	47	~~||||~~ ~~||||~~ |	11
40-44	42		0
			N = 60

Methods of Describing the Limits of Class Intervals in a Frequency Distribution

The following table illustrates three ways of expressing the limits of the class interval in a frequency distribution.

Table–6.2
Methods of Grouping Scores into a Frequency Distribution

(Exclusive Series) A		*(Exact Series)* B		*(Inclusive Series)* C	
C.L.	*f*	C.L.	*f*	C.L.	*f*
100-105	1	99.5-104.5	1	100-104	1
95-100	8	94.5-99.5	8	95.99	8
90-95	4	89.5-94.5	4	90-94	4
85-90	6	84.5-89.5	6	85-89	6
80-85	4	79.5-84.5	4	80-84	4
75-80	4	74.5-79.5	4	75-79	4
70-75	3	69.5-74.5	3	70-74	3
65-70	5	64.5-69.5	5	65-69	5
60-65	4	59.5-64.5	4	60-64	4
55-60	9	54.5-59.5	9	55-59	9
50-55	1	49.5-54.5	1	50-54	1
45-50	11	44.5-49.5	11	45-49	11
	N = 60		N = 60		N = 60

In A—The interval 45-50 shows that all scores from 45 upto but not including 50 fall within this grouping. This is known as the exclusive series of class intervals.

In B—The intervals in B covers the same distances as in A but the upper and lower limits of each interval are defined more exactly.

As explained earlier that a score of 100 in a continuous series ordinarily means the interval 99.5 upto 100.5. This is knownas exact series of class intervals.

In C—The class intervals in (C) express the same facts more clearly than in (A) and less exactly than in (B). Thus '45-49' indicates that this interval begins with score 45 and ends with score 49.

The method (C) is as accurate as (B) or (A) but (C) is generally more used.

The Midpoint of an Interval in a Frequency Distribution

A simple rule to find out the mid point of an interval is:

$$\text{Mid point} = l + \frac{UL - LL}{2}$$

In our illustration In a Class interval of 45 – 49

$$\text{Mindpoint} = 44.5 + \frac{49.5 - 44.5}{2} = 44.5 + 2.5 = 47$$

It is known fact that interval is 5 units therefore midpoint must be 2.5 units from the lower limit of the class i.e., 44.5 + 2.5 = 47 or from the upper limit of class i.e., 49.5 – 2.5 = 47.

Graphic Frequency Distribution

Analysis of the data may often be obtained from a graphic or pictorial treatment of the frequency distribution. Graphs give data in a two dimensional picture on the horizontal axis, we can show the values of the variable (the characteristics we are measuring i.e., class intervals) on the vertical axis we mark the frequencies of the class interval shown on the horizontal axis. The graphs of frequency distribution are useful because they stress and clarify patterns that are not so readily discernible tables. They attract a reader's attention to patterns in the data. Graphs also enable us to estimate some values at a glance and provide us with a pictorial check on the accuracy of our solutions.

There are four methods of representing a frequency distribution graphically which are generally used.

1. The histogram
2. The frequency polygon.
3. The cumulative frequency graph.
4. The cumulative percentage curve or ogive.

The Histogram or column diagram. A histrogram or column diagram is a series of rectangles, each proportional in width to the range of values within a class interval and proportional in heighest to the number of scores (frequencies) following in that class interval. This type of graph is illustrated in the following figure.

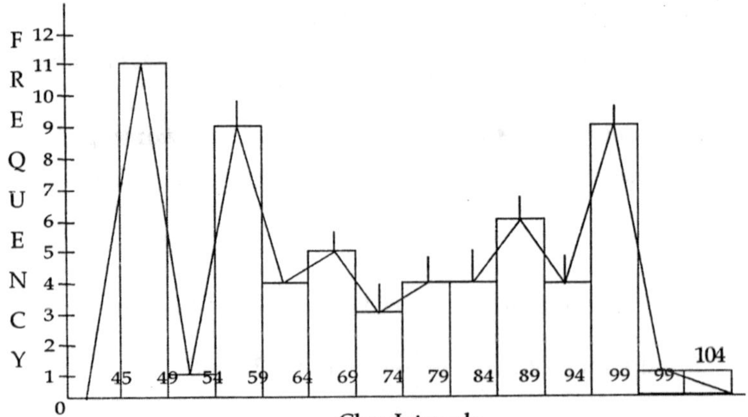

Figure 6.1 : Histogram of 60 Students from an Intelligence Test Depicted in Table 6.1

Within each interval of a histogram frequency is shown by a rectangle, the base of which is the length and the height of which is the number of scores within the interval. In the above figure 6.1.

The base line is labelled with the score intervals rather than with the exact limits. Thus the first interval in the histogram actually begins at 44.5, the exact lower limit of the interval and ends at 49.5 the exact upper limit of the interval. The one score on interval 45–49 is represented by a rectangle the base of which is the length of the interval and the height of which is eleven unit up on the y axis.

The Frequency Polygon

Construction of the Frequency Polygon

The polygon means 'many angled figure'

The procedure in plotting is as follows:

(a) *Labeling the points on the base line:* We have several ways of labeling the intervals along the baseline or *x* axis of the frequency polygon. Exact score limits are some times used. The distribution in table 6.1 begins at 45 and ends with

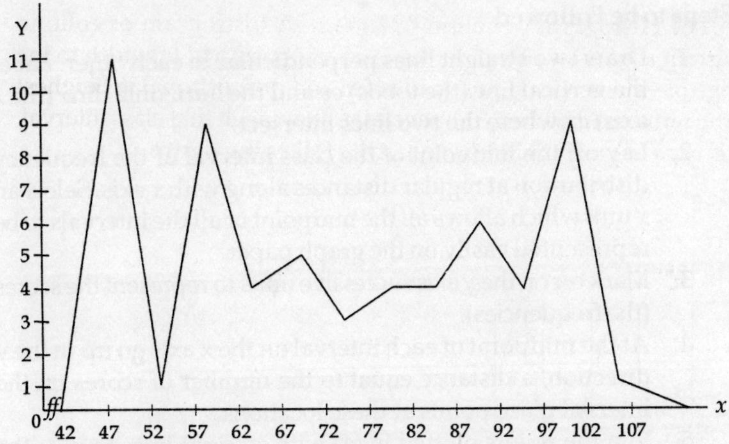

Figure 6.2

score 104. Two additional points one just below 45 (at 40) and one just above 104 (at 109) have been added.

The break in x axis (*ff*) indicates that the vertical axis has been moved in for convenience.

(b) *Plotting midpoint:* We plot frequencies on each interval above the midpoints of the interval on the x axis. There are 11 scores on the first interval 45 to 49. To represent this frequency, go out to 47; midpoint of the interval and we put a dot a distance of 11 unit up on the y axis above this midpoint. In this way we proceed till all the midpoint of class interval are exhausted.

(c) *Drawing in the frequency polygon:* When all the points are located in the diagram they are found by a series of short lines to form the frequency polygon, shown in (figure 6.2). In order to complete the figure (i.e., to bring it down to the baseline) one additional interval (40 to 44) at low end and one additional interval (105 to 109) of the distribution are included on the x scale.

This is done only to draw a diagram of polygon (as defined earlier).

(d) *Dimensions of the frequency polygon:* In order to give symmetry and balance to the polygon, for this purpose as a general we select x and y units which will make the height of the figure approximately 75 per cent of its width. This ratio may vary from 60-80 per cent.

Steps to be Followed

1. Draw two straight lines perpendicular to each other. Label the vertical line (the y axis) oy and the horizontal line (the x axis) ox where the two lines intersect.
2. Lay off the midpoint of the class interval of the frequency distribution at regular distances along with x axis. Select an x unit which allows all the midpoint of all the intervals to be represented easily on the graph paper.
3. Mark off on the y axis successive units to represent the scores (the frequencies).
4. At the midpoint of each interval on the x axis go up in the y direction, a distance equal to the number of scores on the interval place points at these locations.
5. Join the points plotted in (4) with straight lines to give the frequency surface.

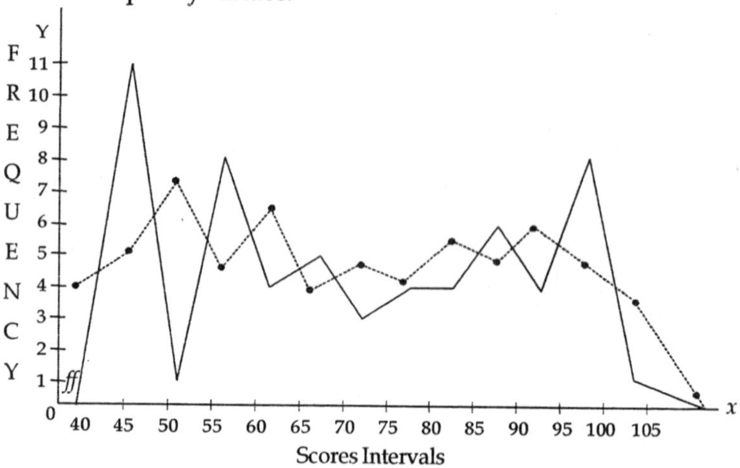

Figure 6.3 Original and Smoothed Frequency Polygons
The Original and Smoothed f's are given in Table No. 6.3.

Smoothing the Frequency Polygon

To find an adjusted or 'smoothed' frequency, we add the frequency on the given interval and the frequencies on the two adjacent intervals (the interval just below and the interval just above) and the sum is divided by 3. For example the smoothed f for interval 45-49 is:

$$\frac{1+11+0}{3} = 4 \text{ for interval 50-54 it would be: } \frac{9+1+11}{3} = \frac{21}{3} = 7$$

The smoothed *f*'s is for other intervals are found out in the table below :

Table-6.3

C.L.	*f*	*Smoothed Frequency*
105-109	0	.33
100-104	1	3.00
95-99	8	4.33
90-94	4	6.00
85-89	6	4.67
80-84	4	4.67
75-79	4	3.67
70-74	3	4.00
65-69	5	4.00
60-64	4	6.00
55-59	9	4.67
50-54	1	7.00
45-49	11	4.00
40-44	0	3.67
	N = 60	N = 60

Advantages of Histrograms

Histograms and frequency polygons are similar but the advantages of histograms are:

1. The rectangle clearly shows each separate class in the distribution.
2. The area of each rectangle, relative to all the other rectangles, shows the proportion of the total number of observations that occur in that class.

Advantages of Polygons

Frequency polygons however have certain advantages, too:

1. The frequency polygon is simpler than its histogram counterpart.
2. It sketches an outline of the data pattern more clearly.
3. The polygon becomes increasingly smooth and curvelike as we increase the number of classes and the number of observations.

A polygon smoothed by added classes and data points is called frequency curve.

The Cumulative Frequency Graph

The cumulative frequency graph is also another way of presenting a frequency distribution by means of a diagram.

Table–6.4
Cumulative Frequencies for the Distribution

C.I.	*f*	*Cum. f.*
100-104	1	60
95-99	8	59
90-94	4	51
85-89	6	47
80-84	4	41
75-79	4	37
70-74	3	33
65-69	5	30
60-64	4	25
55-59	9	21
50-54	1	12
45-49	11	11
		N = 60

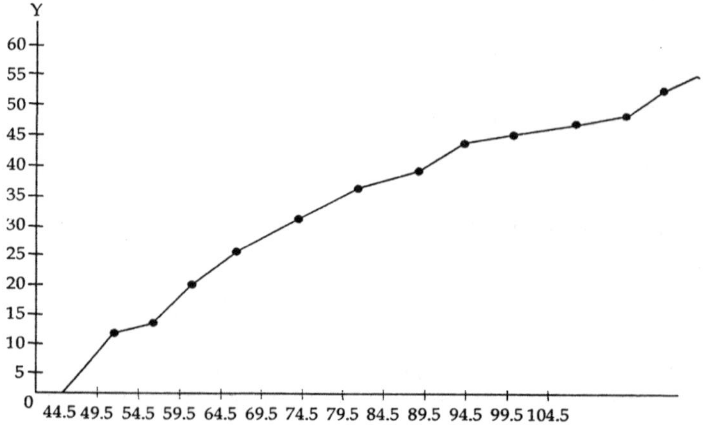

Figure 6.5. Cumulative Frequency Graph

In the above Table 6.4, the first cumulative frequency is 11 (11 + 1 = 12) from the low and of the distribution and gives 12 as the next entry and then 11 + 1 + 9 = 21, 11 + 1 + 9 + 4 = 25 etc. The last cumulative *f* is equal to 60 or N, the total frequency.

In constructing a cumulative frequency curve each cumulative frequency is plotted at the exact upper limit of the interval upon which it falls. This is because in adding progressively from the bottom up each cumulatie frequency carries through to the exact upper limit of the interval.

Construction of the Ogive

The frequencies in the cumulative percentage curve or ogive are expressed as cumulative percents of N on the *y* axis instead of as cumulative frequencies Table 5 shows how cumulative frequencies turned into percentage of N.

Table–6.5
The Cumulative Percentage Curve or Ogive

C.I.	*f*	*Cumulative f*	*Cumulative per cent f*
99.5-104.5	1	60	100.00
94.5-99.5	8	59	98.33
89.5-94.5	4	51	85.00
84.5-89.5	6	47	78.33
79.5-84.5	4	41	68.33
74.5-49-5	4	37	61.67
69.5-74.5	3	33	55.00
64.5-69.5	5	30	50.00
59.5-64.5	4	25	41.67
54.5-59.5	9	21	35.00
49.5-54.5	1	12	20.16
44.5-49.5	11	11	18.33
	N = 60		

We can calcula'e cumulative per cent *f* with the help of cumulative frequency of the exact class interval divided by N(60) and multiplied by 100 e.g.

$$\frac{11 \times 100}{60} = 18.33$$

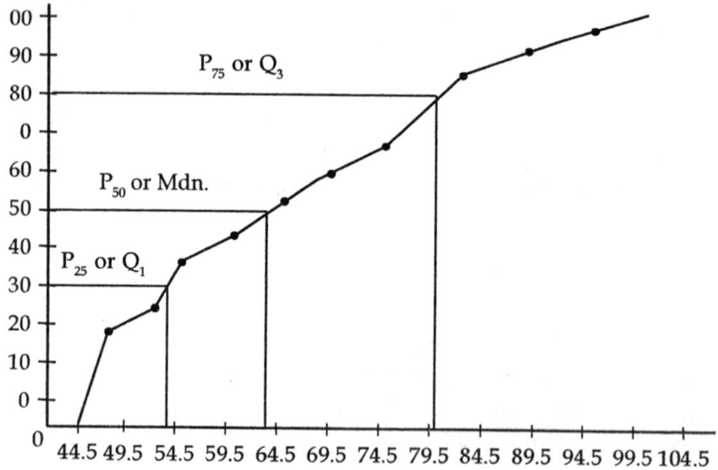

Figure 6.5. Cumulative Percentage Curve or Ogive

Problems

1. Tabulate the following scores into two frequency distribution using (1) an interval of five and (2) an interval of seven units.

72	78	100	95	98	60	52	80
79	68	98	69	88	68	95	84
82	55	58	73	92	58	92	87
65	62	92	59	90	65	85	91
89	75	87	68	70	62	87	96
79	72	77	79	75	61	65	55
88	82						

2. Prepare a histogram frequency, polygon, and smoothed frequency polygon of the data given in question 1.
3. Explain Advantages of histograms, frequency polygon and the cumulative frequency graph.
4. Define statistics. Disucss its utility in education and psychology.
5. Explain continuous and discrete series.

7

Measures of Central Tendency

In the previous chapter, we constructed tables and graphs from raw data. The resulting 'pictures' of frequency distribution illustrated trends and patterns in the data. In most cases, however, we need more exact measures. In such cases we can use single numbers called summary statistics to describe characteristics of a data set. Two of these characteristics are particularly important to the investigators (1) central tendency and (2) dispersion. In this chapter we will learn the concept of central tendency and their calculations. And in the next chapter we will learn the concept of dispersion and their calculations.

Central Tendency

Central tendency is the middle point of a distribution. Measures of central tendency are also called measures of location or central position. The value of a measure of central tendency is two fold:

1. It is an average which represents all of the scores made by the group.
2. It enables us to compare two or more groups in relation to their performance According to Ross, "It is the tendency of the scores to bunch or concentrate somewhere near the centre .... It is that value which typifies or best represents the whole distribution."

Measures of Central Tendency

There are three mesures of central tendency *(i)* The Mean *(ii)* The Median *(iii)* The Mode.

The average is the popular term for the arithmetic mean. However in statistical work we use average for any measure of central tendency.

Calculation of Measures of Central Tendency

The Arithmetic Mean (M)

The mean may be defined as the sum of a set of data divided by the number of subjects in the set. In other words we can say that mean is the sum of the separate scores or data divided by their number.

1. Calculation of the Mean when data are ungrouped.

The mean of a distribution of scores is the value on the scores scale corresponding to the sum of scores divided by their numbers or size of sample.

$$\text{Mean} = \frac{\Sigma X}{N}$$

where Σ = sum of

$X = X_1 + X_2 + X_3 .... Xn$

N = Total number of scores.

Example: Calculate mean of the scores of obtained by the five individual as given below: 10, 12, 15, 18, 20

$$M = \frac{\Sigma X}{N} = \frac{10 + 12 + 15 + 18 + 20}{5} = \frac{75}{5}$$

$$M = \frac{75}{5} = 15$$

Scores deviation (d) from the mean = $(X_1 - M)\ (X_2 - M)$ ...

i.e. $(10 - 15), + (12 - 15), + (15 - 15) + (18 - 15) + (20 + 5)$

$= (-5) + (-3) + 0 + (3) + (5)$

$\Sigma d = -8 + 8 = 0$

Note: The sum of deviations from the mean of data is always zero.

It may be stated that the mean is the value of a score which has equal deviatioins of its both sides as illustrated in the above example.

where $\Sigma d = \Sigma(X_1 - M) + \Sigma(X_2 - M)$ ...

d = deviation (X – M) or (score – mean)

X = score obtained by an individual

M = Mean

Σ = sum of

This method explained above is used for small sample (N < 30)

Example. The score of 10 students in English test are as follows:

15, 17, 19, 21, 23, 25, 27, 29, 30, 32, 34, 38

$$\text{Mean} = \frac{\Sigma X}{N}$$

$$= \frac{15 + 17 + 19 + 21 + 23 + 25 + 27 + 29 + 30 + 32 + 34 + 38}{5}$$

ΣX = Sum of scores = 240

N = Number of subjects = 10

$$\text{Mean } \frac{240}{10} = 24$$

Sometimes ungrouped data are also organized in a frequency distribution which does not involve class interval. We use the following method to compute mean.

Table–7.1
A Frequency Distribution

x	*f*	*fx*
22	1	22
18	2	36
15	3	45
12	5	60
10	4	40
9	3	27
8	1	8
7	1	7
Total	N = 20	Σfx = 245

$$M = \frac{\Sigma f x}{N} = \frac{245}{20} = 12.25$$

(b) Computation of Mean form Grouped Data or Frequency Distribution Table.

This method is generally used for large sample when the data organised in frequency distribution table. There are two methods to calculate mean from frequency distribution table (1) Long method (2) Short method.

Table–7.2
Calculation of Mean from Frequency Distribution Using Long Method

Class Interval	*Midpoint* X	*Midpoint* *f*	*fX*
95-99	97	1	97
90-94	92	2	184
85-89	87	4	348
80-84	82	6	492
75-79	77	6	462
70-74	72	11	792
65-69	67	6	402
60-64	62	4	248
55-59	57	5	285
50-54	52	3	156
45-49	47	1	47
40-44	42	1	42
		N = 50	$\Sigma fX = 3555$

The *fX* column is found by multiplying the midpoint (here X) of each interval by the number of scores (f) on it. The mean is simply the sum of the ΣfX viz (3555) divided by N (50)

One thing here is to remember that scores grouped into intervals lose their identity and represented by the midpoint of that particular interval on which they fall. Therefore we multiply the midpoint of each interval and add the *fX* and divide by the N to obtain the mean as calculated with the following formula.

$$\text{Mean} = \frac{\Sigma fX}{N} = \frac{3555}{50} = 71.10$$

Calculation of midpoint has been explained in the previous chapter.

Steps to be followed in calculating mean by Long method.

Step I. The mid point of each class interval are to be calculated.

Step II. The midpoint (X) is multiplied by the frequency of the respective class interval (fX) and entered in the last column.

Step III. The sum of these products is obtained as the total of score (ΣfX).

Step IV. The sum of scores (Σfx) is divided by the total inviduals f the group (N). The formula is

$$\text{Mean} = \frac{\Sigma fx}{N}$$

Calculation of The Mean by the Short Method or Assumed Mean Method

Long method gives undoubtedly the accurate results but often requires tedious calculation. The short method has been devised for computing the mean to avoid tediousness of calculation. However this method does not apply to the calculation of the median or the mode. The most important fact to remember in computation of mean, by the short method is that we 'assure' a mean at the outset and later apply a correction to this assumed value (AM) in order to obtain the actual mean (M). See the below Table 3.

Table–7.3

The Calculation of the Mean by the Short Method

Class Intervals	*Midpoint Scores*	*f*	*Deviation from the Mean X*	*fx*
95-99	97	1	5	5
90-94	92	2	4	8
85-89	87	4	3	12
80-84	82	6	2	12
75-79	77	6	1	6
70-74	72	11	0	43
65-69	67	6	–1	-6

(Contd.)

Class Intervals	*Midpoint Scores*	*f*	*Deviation from the Mean X*	*fx*
60-64	62	4	-2	-8
55-59	57	5	-3	-15
50-54	52	3	-4	-12
45-49	47	1	-5	-5
40-44	42	1	-6	-6
				-52
			N=50	$\Sigma fx^1 = -9$

$\Sigma fx^1 = 43 + (-52) = -9$

AM = 72

AM = Assumed mean

Now we get $AM \pm \frac{\Sigma f x^1}{N} \times ci$

Steps to be followed for its calculation

Step 1. Fill the column (4) i.e. x' where the deviation of midpoint of the different steps measured from the AM in units of class interval are entered. 72 (mid point) has been assumed as mean and midpoint (77) deviates by one interval and a '1' is placed in the 'x'' column opposite to 77, in the same manner 82 deviates two interval from 72 and a '2' goes in the 'x'' column opposite 82. In this way we find the succeeding entries to be 3, 4, and 5. The last entry '5' is the interval deviation of 97 from 72, the actual score deviation is (5 × 5) 25. The zero (0) is placed in the x' column opposite midpoint 72, all the entries below 72 are negative midpoints being less than 72. The process is the same to fill the entries in 'x'' column.

Step 2. Now we compute fx' column i.e. column 5. The fx' entries are found class interval to obtain fx'. All fx' on intervals above the AM are positive and all fx' on intervals below the AM are negative as the signs of x' depend upon the signs of the x'.

Step 3. The sum of the positive values in the fx' column is 43 and the sum of the negative values in the fx' column is 52 we get x'. Algebraic sum of the plus and minus fx' and divide this sum by N (Number of cases). This gives C the correction in units of class intenval.

(43) + (–52) = –9. The value is substituted in the formula to compute:

$$\text{Mean AM} \pm \frac{\Sigma f x^1}{N} \quad i = \text{size of interval}$$

$$\text{Mean} = \text{AM} \pm \frac{\Sigma f x^1}{N} \times i = 72 \pm \frac{9}{50} \times 5$$

$$= 75 - \frac{9}{50} \times = 72 - .9 = 71.1$$

Here AM = Assured mean (72)

x' = deviation from the assumed mean.

Σ = Sum of X = –9

N = Number of cases (50)

Example 2.

Table–7.4

A Frequency Distribution (Short method)

Class Interval	*Midpoint* *f*	*f*	*x′*	*fx′*
50-54	52	7	4	28
45-49	47	3	3	9
40-44	42	5	2	10
35-39	37	7	1	7
				54
30-34	32	10	0	0
25-29	27	8	-1	-8
20-24	22	6	-2	-12
15-19	17	5	-3	-15
10-14	12	4	-4	-16
5-9	7	5	-5	-25
				-76

$\Sigma f x = 54 + (-76)$ $\Sigma f x^1 = 22$

N = 60 $\Sigma fx' = -22$

$$M = \text{AM} \pm \frac{\Sigma f x^1}{N} x\, i = 32 - \frac{22}{60} \times 5$$

$$= 32 - \frac{110}{60} = 32 - 1.83 = 30.17 \qquad \text{Mean} = 30.17$$

The Mean from Combined Samples or Groups

Sometimes we have large sample and divide that sample into different groups and we calculate their means separately and then combined mean or general mean is also computed.

Suppose there are three groups whose means are M_1, M_2 and M_3 and their size of group is N_1, N_2 an N_3 respectively. We use the following formula to calculate combined mean:

$$M_{comb} = \frac{N_1 M_1 + N_2 M_2 + N_3 M_3 .... M_n}{N_1 + N_2 + N_3 + ... N_n}$$

(If the size of the groups is unequal)

M_{comb} = Mean combined

Example. The following are the statistics of three groups.

$M_1 = 12, N_1 = 15, M_2 = 20, N_2 = 10$

$M_3 = 27, N_3 = 20$

$$M_{comb} = \frac{15 \times 12 + 20 \times 10 + 20 \times 27}{15 + 10 + 20} = \frac{920}{45}$$

$$\frac{920}{45} = 20.44$$

When the size of the groups is equal, the combined mean is obtained from the following formula

$$M_{comb} = \frac{M_1 + M_2 + M_3 .... M_n}{n}$$

For example $M_1 = 15$, $M_2 = 20$, $M_3 = 27$ and the size of three groups is equal

$$= \frac{15 + 20 + 27}{3} = \frac{62}{3} = 20.66$$

Characteristics of Mean

1. The sum of the deviation from the mean of the scores is always zero as the mean is the central value of a distribution of scores.

   Example. A group of 10 individuals have scored.

   8, 10, 13, 15, 17, 18, 20, 22, 24, 33

$$\text{Mean} = \frac{180}{10} = 18$$

Now deviation of scores from the mean:

d = (8 – 18) (10 – 18) (13 – 18) (15 – 18) (17 – 18) (18 – 18) (20 – 18) (22 – 18) (24 – 18) (33 – 18)

$$= \frac{-10, -8, -5, -3, -1, 0}{-27} = \frac{4, 2, 6, 15}{-27}$$

$\Sigma d = -27 + 27 = 0$

2. The sum of squares of deviation from the mean is always less than the sum of the squares of deviation from any other assumed mean example from the above scores.

   d = –10, –8, –5, –3, –1, 0, 2, 4, 6, 15

   d^2 = 100, 64, 25, 9, 1, 4, 16, 36, 225

   $= \Sigma d^2 = 480$

The sum of squares of deviation from the actual mean is 480 which will be less than assumed mean i.e. if we take any other assumed mean this value will be less.

3. Since the mean is central value of a set of data. Both side from the mean, the deviations are equal.
4. If we add, subtract multiply or divide the set of scores by a constant number, the mean value will be changed.
5. The mean value is a measure of sample or group which is most accurate measure of central tendency of the scores.
6. The group performance is best indicated by this value when the distribution is normally distributed.
7. It is used for interval and ratio scale.

Advantages of the Mean

1. Its concept is familiar to most people and intuitively clear.
2. Every data set has a mean. It is a measure that can be calculated.
3. It is unique because every data set has one and only one mean.
4. The mean is useful for performing statistical procedures such as comparing the mean from several data sets.

Disadvantages of the Mean

1. Although the mean is reliable as it reflects all the values in the data set, but it may also be affected by extreme values that are not representative of the rest of the data, e.g.

A group of seven students' achievement in mathematics is as follow—25, 30, 22, 28, 32, 35, 65

$$= \frac{22 + 25 + 28 + 30 + 32 + 35 + 65}{7}$$

$$\text{Mean} = \frac{237}{7} = 33.\ 85$$

If we compute a mean for the first six students and exclude 65 score, the answer is about:

$$\frac{237}{7} = 28.66$$

The one extreme value of 65 distorts the value we get for the mean. It would be more representative to calculate the mean without including such an extreme value.

2. We are unable to compute the mean for a data set that has open-ended classes at either the high or low end of the scale. Suppose the data in table (1) had been arranged in a frequency distribution shown in table (2) we can compute a mean value for these data because open ended class of '54 and above'. We have no way of knowing whether the value of 54 near 54 or for above 54.

Table-7.5

Student	1	2	3	4	5	6	7
Scores	42	43	47	48	50	51	90

Table-7.6

Class Interval	42-45	46-49	50-54	54 and above
Frequency	2	2	2	1

When to Use the Mean

1. The computation of mean or average can be excellent measure of central tendency when the scores are normally distributed.
2. When the measure of central tendency is wanted having the greatest stability.

3. When other statistics are to be computed later such as S.D., coefficient of correlation etc as many statistics are based upon the mean.
4. When we require maximum reliability.
5. When we are supposed to calculate true mode too.
6. When we are to find out the correct centre of gravity.
7. When each score of distribution is to be given importance.

The Median (Mdn)

The median item is a single value from the data set that measures the central value in the data. This single value is the middle most or most central in the set of numbers. Half of the lie above this point and the other half lie below it.

1. Median is the point while mean is the value.
2. Median is the midpoint of the frequency distribution while mean is the mid value of the scores.

These are two situations for computing median

(i) When data are ungrouped form
(ii) Data are grouped into a frequency distribution.

Calculation of Median

When data are ungrouped

The first step is to arrange the ungrouped data either in ascending or descending order. We face two situation while computing the median from ungrouped data:

(a) *When the group size (N) is in Odd Number*—**Illustration.** Supose we have the scores of 9 students 10, 8, 12, 16, 7, 9, 5, 11, 6.

As indicated above, these scores are to be arranged in ascending or descending order to obtain median. Here we arrange above score in ascending order.

5, 6, 7, 8, 9, 10, 11, 12, 16

(below cases 4-Median-4 cases above)

The midpoint is 9 of the scores lies midway in the series i.e. 4 scores lie above and 4 scores lie below the midpoint (9).

(b) *When the group size in Even Number*—Suppose we have the scores of 10 students (even number) 8, 12, 7, 6, 11, 15, 13, 17, 16, 18.

Ascending order of the scores 6, 7, 8, 11, 12, 13, 15, 16, 17, 18

Below cases is-median above cases 5.

Median $\frac{12 + 13}{2} = 12.5.$

The midpoint 12.5 of the score lies in midway of the series.

Median = the $\frac{N + 1}{2}$ measure in order of size.

In our first (a) illustration

Median the 9 + 1 or 5th score counting in from either end of the series i.e. 9 (midpoint 8.5 to 9.5).

In our second illustration (b) the median is on the $\frac{10 + 1}{2}$ th or 5.5th score in order of size i.e. 12.5 (upper limit of score 12 or lower limit of score 13).

2. Computation of the Median when data are grouped into a Frequency Distribution.

Table-7.7

Class Interval	*f*	*cf*	*cf'*
95-99	1	50	1
90-94	2	49	3
85-89	4	47	7
80-84	6	43	13
75-79	6	37	19
70-74	11	31	30
65-69	6	20	36
60-64	4	14	40
55-59	5	10	45
50-54	3	5	48
45-49	1	2	49
40-44	1	1	50
			N = 50

To locate the median in the frequency distribution we take 50 per cent (i.e. N/2) of our score as per definition of the median and count into the distribution until the 50 per cent point is reached. There are 50 scores in the above distribution, N/2 = 25 and median is that point in our distribution which has 25 scores above this point and 25 scores below this point. Beginning from the small score end of the distribution and adding up the scores in we find that intervals 40-44 to 65-69 inclusive contain just 20 fs five scores short of the 25 necessary to locate the median.

The next interval 70-74 contains 11 scores assumed to be spread evenly over the interval. In order to get 5 scores extra needed to make exactly 25, we take 5/11 × 5 (the length of the interval) and add this increment (2.27) to 69.5, the beginning of the interval 70-74. This puts the Mdn 69.5 + 2.27 = 71.77. A formula for calculating the Mdn when the data has been classified into a frequency distribution and we prepare the cumulative frequency distribution as calculated in the above table and median is calculated using the formula.

$$\text{Mdn} = l + \frac{\frac{N}{2} - F}{fm} x\, i$$

Where l = exact lower limit of the class interval upon which the median lies.

l = size of class interval

fm = frequency within the class interval upon which the median falls

F = sum of all the frequencies below l

$\frac{N}{2}$ = One-half the total number of scores.

To illustrate the use of above formula the data of above table are

$\frac{N}{2} = 25, l = 69.5, F = 20, fm, = 11, i = 5$

using formula

$$\text{Median } 69.5 + \frac{25 - 20}{11} \times 5$$

$$= 69.5 + \frac{5 \times 5}{11}$$

$$= 69.5 + 2.27 = 71.77$$

Using upper side of the class interval we find

$\frac{N}{2} = 25, F = 19, fm, = 11, i = 5$

Formula becomes

$$\text{Median} = \mu - \left(\frac{\frac{N}{2} - F}{fm}\right) xi \tag{8}$$

μ = upper limit of the class interval where = 74.5

The median falls = 74.5

F = sum of all frequencies above *u*

$$\text{Now Mdn} = \mu - \left(\frac{\frac{N}{2} - F}{fm}\right)^{L}$$

$$\text{Mdn} = 74.5 - \frac{25 - 19}{11} \times 5$$

$$= 74.5 - \frac{6 \times 5}{11} = 74.5 - 2.73 = 74.5 - 2.73 = 71.77$$

The steps to be followed in computing the Mdn.

1. Find N/2 cases in the distribution.
2. Begin at the small score end of the distribution and count off the scores in order upto the exact lower limit (l) of the interval which contains the median. The sum of these scores is F.
3. Compute the number of scores necessary to fill out N/2 i.e., compute N/2 – F. Divide this quantity by the frequency (*fm*) on the interval which contains the median and multiply the result by the size of the class interval (*i*).
4. Apply these values in the formula.

The median may also be computed by counting off one-half of the scores from the top down in frequency distribution and apply the values in formula.

Advantags of the Median

The median has several advantages over the mean.

1. The most important is that extreme values do not affect the median as strongly as they do the mean.
2. Median is easy to understand.
3. Median can be calculated from any kind of data, even for grouped data with open ended classes.

Table–7.8

C.I.	*f*
(54 and above)	1
50-53	2
46-49	2
42-45	2
37-41	3
32-36	5

Disadvantages of the Median

1. Certain statistical procedures that use the median are more complex than those use the median.
2. When we want to use a sample statistics as an estimate of a population parameter, the mean is easier to use than the median.
3. With the values 2, 5, 6, 40, 100, 213, 414 the median is 40, which has no apparent relationship to any of the other values in the distribution.

When to use Median

1. When the exact midpoint of the distribution is required.
2. When there are extreme scores which would markedly affect the mean. Extreme scores do not disturb the median for example in the series of scores 6, 7, 8, 9 and 10 the mean and median are 8 but 10 is replaced by 41, the other scores remain the same the mdn is still 8 but the mean is 14.2.
3. Where these is no sufficient time to compute mean. When incomplete distribution is given.

The Mode

The mode is defined as the most frequently occurring score in a distributions. If there is only one value which occurs a maximum number of times, then the distribution is known to have one mode or to be unimodal. In some distributions there may be more than one mode. A two mode distribution is bimodal, more than two multimodal unless median falls in an open ended class.

Mode for Ungrouped Data

In a sample ungrouped series of measures of scores the crude or empirical mode is that single measure or score which occurs most frequently. For example, 8, 10, 11, 13, 13, 19, 21. The most often recurring measure namely, 13 is the crude or empirical mode.

When the data are grouped into a frequency distribution, crude or empirical mode is usually taken to be the midpoint of the interval which contains the largest frequency. In the table 7 the interval 70-74 contains the largest frequency and hence 72.0 is midpoint, is the crude point.

When we compute the mode from a frequency distribution. It is distinguished between true mode and crude mode. The following formula is used for approximating the true mode, when the distribution is symmetrical or atleast not badly skewed.

Mode = 3 Mdn – 2 Mean

If we apply the formula in Table 7.

where

Mdn = 71.77, Mean 71.10

Mode = 3 Mdn –2 Mean

Then Mode = 3 × 71.77 – 2 × 71.10

= 215.31 – 142.20 = 73.11

Mode = 73.11

Mode for Grouped Data

When calculating the mode from a grouped data represented in a frequency distributions we differentiate between true mode and crude mode. The true mode is the point of greatest concentration in the distribution i.e., the point at which more measures fall than at any other point. The formula for computing the true mode.

$$\text{Mode} = l + \frac{fm - fi}{2fm - f_1 - f_2} \times i$$

in which l = lower limit of modal class i.e. the class interval having maximum frequency.

fm = frequency of modal class
f_1 = frequency of class interval preceding the modal class
f_2 = frequency of class interval following the modal class
i = size of class interval

Let us illustrate the use of this formula to the data given in table 7. The maximum frequency is 11 which lies in the class interval 70-

74. Therefore modal class is 70-74. Here $fm = 11, f_1 = 6, f_2 = 6, i = 5$, l = 69.5 using the above formula, we get:

$$\text{Mode} = 69.5 + \frac{11 - 6}{2 \times 11 - 6 - 6} \times 5 = 69.5 + \frac{5}{10} \times 5$$

$$= 69.5 + 2.5 = 72$$

$$\text{Mode} = 72$$

Advantages of the Mode

1. The mode like the median can be used as a central location for qualitative as well as quantitative data.
2. Like median, the mode is not unduly affected by extreme values.
   We can use the mode no matter how large, how small or how spread out the values in the data set happen to be.
3. We can use it even when one or more of the classes are open ended.

Disadvantages of the Mode

1. The mode is not used as often to measure central tendency as are the mean and median.
2. Too often, there is no modal value because the data set contains no values that occur more than once other times every value is mode, because every value occurs the same number or times. Clearly mode is a useless measure in such cases.
3. When data set contain two, three, or many modes, they are difficult to interpret and compare.

When to use the Mode

1. When a quick and approximate measure of central tendency is required.
2. When we need the most typisal value which may interpret the current situation.

Problems

1. Calculate the mean, median and mode for the following frequency distributions. Use the short and long method in computing the mean.

(a)

Scores	*f*
40-44	2
45-49	0
50-54	5
55-59	7
60-64	9
65-69	11
70-74	6
75-79	8
80-84	4
85-89	2
90-94	2

(b)

Scores	*f*
0-9	6
10-19	8
20-29	10
30-39	15
40-49	25
50-59	25
60-69	21
70-79	19
80-89	14
90-99	9
100-109	5

(c) Find out the measures of central tendency of the following ungrouped data.

Scores	*f*
4	2
5	2
6	6
7	18

(Contd.)

Scores	*f*
8	31
9	22
10	15
11	12
12	6
13	3
14	2
15	1

3. Calculate Mean, using short method and long method.

(i)	C.I.	*f*	*(ii)*	C.I.	*f*
	90-99	1		55-59	1
	80-89	4		50-54	1
	70-79	7		45-49	3
	60-69	10		40-44	4
	50-59	9		35-39	6
	40-49	9		30-34	7
	30-39	4		25-29	12
	20-29	3		20-24	6
	10-19	3		15-19	8
	10-14	2			

QUESTIONS

A. Short Answer Type Questions

1. When do we use mean?
2. What is the meaning of central tendency?
3. Differentiate between mean and median.
4. Explain the formula of Median.
5. Explain the concept of Median.
6. When do we use 'mode'?

B. Objective Type Questions

1. Mode = 3 Mn - 2 Mdn: Trule/False
2. Median is the most accurate measure of central tendency. Trule/False

3. Median is the central location of the score. True/False

4. Most accurate measure of central tendency is:
   (*a*) Mean (*b*) Median
   (*c*) Mode (*d*) None of the above.

5. Central point of frequency distribution is:
   (*a*) Mean (*b*) Median
   (*c*) Mode (*d*) None of the above

6. The sum of deviations for the mean is equal to____________.

7. The crude measure of central tendency is the:
   (*a*) Mean (*b*) Median
   (*c*) Mode (*d*) None of the above

8. The formula mode is used:
   (*a*) 3 Mdn. - 3 Mn. (*b*) 3 Mn - 2 Mdn
   (*c*) 3 Mdn - 2 Mean (*d*) 3 Mdn - 3 Mean

9. In symmetrical distribution we use:
   (*a*) Mean (*b*) Median
   (*c*) Mode (*d*) None of these

10. The cumulative frequency is used to compute:
    (*a*) Mean (*b*) Median
    (*c*) Mode (*d*) Range

8

Measures of Variability or Dispersion

Measures of central tendency are very useful in describing the nature of a distribution of measures but do not give an investigator a complete picture of the data. The three distributor's in following figure, the mean of all three curves is the same but curve. A has less curve spread (or variability) than curve B and curve B has less variability than curve C. If we measure only the mean of three distributions we will miss an important difference among the three curves. To increase our understanding of the pattern of the data, we must also measure its dispersin, – its spread or variability.

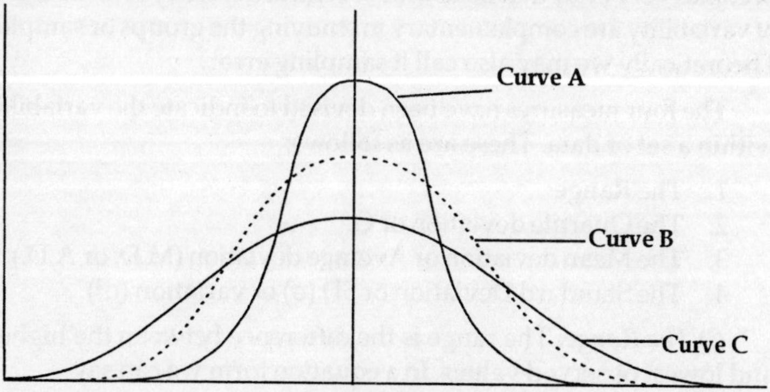

Figure 8.1 Three Curves with the Same Mean but Different Variability

The disperson of the distribution is an important characteristic to understand a measure as give us additional information that enables us to judge the reliability of our measure of the central tendency. If data are widely dispersed such as those in curve C in above figure, therefore dispersion or variability is the spread of the data in a distribution, that is the extent to which the observations are scattered. This may be noticed in above figure. The statisticians have taken keen interest to measure the variation of the distribution and to compare (1) between or among variation and variation within the group. The concept may be made clear with the help of the example or illustration.

Groups	*Data*	*Measure Mean*
A	8, 10, 12, 14, 16	M = 12
B	0, 0, 0, 0, 60	M = 12
C	12, 12, 12, 12, 12	M = 12

(i) Variation between or among groups there is no difference on the basis of mean of each group, among the three groups, but the data indicate the difference among these groups.

(ii) Variation within the group. The set of data indicate on the basis of calculated mean that there is no difference among these groups but there is a variation within the group.

The group C is homogeneous while group B is heterogeneous. It may be stated that Group C has no variation while group B has high variation. This homogeneity or heterogeneity within the group can be studied with the help of measures of variability. In the last it becomes very clear that measures of central tendency and measures of variability are complementary in studying the groups or samples. Theoretically we may also call it sampling error.

The four measures have been devised to indicate the variability within a set of data. These are as follows:

1. The Range
2. The Quartile deviation or Q.
3. The Mean deviation or Average deviation (M.D. or A.D.)
4. The Standard Deviation or SD (σ) or variation (σ^2)

(i) The Range: The range is the difference between the highest and lowest observed values. In a equation form we can say—

Range = value of highest observation or score — Value of lowest observation or score.

The range is easy to understand and to calculate but its usefulness as a measure of dispersion is limited. The range considers only the highest and lowest values of a distribution and it fails to take account of any other observation in the data set. Resultantly, it ignores the nature of variation among all other observations and it is heavily influenced by extreme values. As it measures only two values, the range is likely to change drastically from one sample to the next in a given population, even though the values that fall between the highest and lowest values may be quite similar. The range is the most general measuse of spread or scatter, and is computed when we wish to make a rough comparison of two or more groups for variability. The range is unreliable when N is small or when there are large gaps (zero 'f') in the frequency distribution.

Illustration

Suppose the scores of a group of 12 students are 100, 95, 92, 87, 85, 80, 75, 72, 70, 68, 65, 60

Range = Highest score – Lowest score = 100 – 60 = 40

Range = 40

Advantages of Range

We use Range

(i) When data are too scant or scattered to justify the computation of a more precise measure of variability.

(ii) When a knowledge of extreme scores or a total spread is all that is required.

Disadvantages or (Limitations) of Range

1. As indicated above the variability of all set of scores are not taken into consideration. The following example would illustrate it.

   1. 0, 5, 5, 5, 5, 55   2. 0, 9, 11, 29, 35, 55

   The range of these groups:

   $R_1 = 55 - 0 = 55$

   $R_2 = 55 - 0 = 55$

   The range of these groups are same but group (1) is homogeneous and group (2) is heterogenous.
2. It has least applicability in social science.
3. It is very crude measure of variability. If we change the middle scores and extreme scores are kept constant the range may not change.

The Quartile Deviation Q

According to H.E. Garrett, "The Quartile deviation or Q is one-half the scale distance between the 75th and 25th percentile in a frequency distribution."

Odell defined, "The Quartile deviation or semi-inter Quartile range is one-half of the distance between the first and third quartiles."

Skinner states "Quartiles are those three points that divide a distribution four equal parts."

The Quartile deviation is considered an improvement over the range. The 25th percentile or Q_1 is the first quartile on the score scale, the point below which lie 25 per cent of the scores. The 75th percentile or Q_3, is the third quartile on the score scale the point where lie 75 per cent of the scores when we have these two points the quartile deviation is found from the formula:

$$Q = \frac{Q_3 - Q_1}{2} \text{ or } \frac{P_{75} - P_{25}}{2} \qquad \text{.............................(1)}$$

The Q_3 (75th percentile) and Q_1 (25th percentile) are calculated exactly in the same way as was the median which is the 50th percentile or Q_2.

The point to remember is that the only difference is that ¼ of N for Q_1 and ¾ of the N for Q_3 are counted off from the low end of the distribution. The formulae are:

$$Q_1 = l + \left(\frac{\frac{N}{4} - \text{cum fi}}{\text{fq}}\right) i \qquad \text{.............................(2)}$$

$$Q_3 = l + \left(\frac{\frac{3N}{4} - \text{cum fi}}{\text{fq}}\right) i \qquad \text{.............................(3)}$$

where

l = the exact lower limit of the interval in which the quartile falls.

i = the length of the interval

cum f_1 = cumulative frequency upto the interval which contains the quartile

fq = the f on the interval containing the quartile.

Table–8.1

Class Interval	*f*	*Cf*	
C.I.	*f*	*Cf*	
40-42	5	50	
37-39	8	45	Q3 = 36.69
34-36	9	37	
31-33	10	28	
28-30	7	18	$Q_1 = 28.14$
25-27	5	11	
22-24	4	6	
19-21	2	2	
	N = 50		

We know that $Q = \dfrac{Q_3 - Q_1}{2}$

$$Q_1 = l^2 + \left(\frac{\frac{N}{4} - \text{cum } fi}{\text{fq}}\right) i$$

Here $\dfrac{N}{4} = \dfrac{50}{4} = 12.5$

$l = 27.5$, cum $f_1 = 11$

$\dfrac{N}{4} = 12.5, fq = 7, \text{i} = 3$

$$Q_1 = 27.5 + \left(\frac{12.\ 5 - 11}{7}\right) \times 3 = 27.5 + \left(\frac{1.5 \times 3}{7}\right)$$

$= 27.5 + .64 = 28.14$

$$Q_3 = l + i\left(\frac{\frac{3N}{4} - \text{cum fi}}{\text{fq}}\right)$$

$l = 36.5$, cum $f_1 = 37$, $\dfrac{3N}{4} = \dfrac{3 \times 50}{4} = 37.5$

$i = 3, fq = 8$

By substituting in the formula:

$$Q_3 = 36.5 + \left(\frac{37.5 - 37}{8}\right) \times 3$$

$$= 36.5 + \left(\frac{.5 \times 3}{8}\right) = (36.5 + \frac{1.5}{8})$$

$$= 36.5 + .187 = 36.68 \text{ or } 36.69$$

$$\text{Now } Q = \frac{Q_3 - Q_1}{2} = \frac{36.69 - 28.14}{2} = \frac{8.55}{2} = 4.275 \text{ or } 4.28$$

$$Q = 4.28$$

Advantages of Quartile Deviations

We use Q when

1. Median is the measure of central tendency.
2. There are scattered or extreme scores which would influence the SD disproportionately.
3. The concentration is around the median.

Limitations of Quartile Deviation (Q)

1. The quartile deviation does not indicate variation of total distribution.
2. It represent the variability of middle 50 percent distribution.
3. It does not consider extreme 25 per cent top and 25 per cent bottom scores.

Mean Deviation (MD) or Average Deviation

According to Garrett H.E., "The (AD) average deviation or AD (also written mean deviation or MD) is the mean of the deviations of all of the separate scores in a series taken from their mean (occasionally from the median or mode). In averaging deviations to find the AD no account is taken of signs, and all deviations whether plus or minus are treated as positive."

(1) *Computation of the AD from ungrouped scores.*

We use the following formula to compute. Average deviation (AD)

$$\text{A.D.} = \frac{\Sigma \mid d \mid}{N}$$

In which | | enclosing the d indicate that signs are disregarded in summing up. N = Number of scores, d = deviation of a score, from the mean i.e.

$$X - M = D$$

Example. Calculate mean or average deviation from the following ungrouped data.

Table–8.2

X	*Mean* *M*	*Deviation d* = *X* – *M*
10	18	8
15	18	3
10	18	8
17	18	1
19	18	1
21	18	3
27	18	9
17	18	1
23	18	5
21	18	3
$\sum X = 180$		$\sum d = 42$

$$\text{Mean} = \frac{\sum X}{N} = \frac{180}{10} = 18,\ \text{AD} = \frac{\sum d}{N} = \frac{42}{10}$$

$$\text{AD} = 4.2$$

Table–8.3
Calculation of the AD from Grouped Data

1	*2*	*3*	*4*	*5*	*6*	*7*
C.I.	*f*	*X*	*x*'	*fx*'	*d(X – M)*	*fd*
60-64	2	62	5	10	27.6	55.2
55-59	3	57	4	12	22.6	67.8
50-54	5	52	3	15	17.6	88.0
45-49	3	47	2	6	12.6	37.8
40-44	8	42	1	8	7.6	60.8
35-39	4	37	0	0 51	2.6	10.4
30-34	5	32	–1	–5	–2.4	12.0
25-29	6	27	–2	–12	–7.4	44.4
20-24	7	22	–3	–21	–12.4	86.8
15-19	7	17	–4	–28 –66	–17.4	121.8
	N = 50,	$\sum \lvert d \rvert = 130.2$		$\sum fx' = -15$		$\sum fd = 585.0$

$\Sigma fx = -66 + 49 = -15$

$M = AM \pm \left(\frac{\Sigma f x^1}{N}\right)^i, \Sigma|fd|$ 585.0

$= 37 - \frac{15}{50} \times 5 = 37 - 1.50 = 35.5$

$A.D. = \frac{\Sigma|fd|}{N} \quad \Sigma|fd| = 585.0$

$A.D. = \frac{585.0}{50}$

$AD = 11.70$

The AD is rarely used in modern statistics. The method to be followed to compute A.D. Steps:

1. Compute mean of the distribution from each class.
2. Calculate deviation from the mean $d(x - M)$ as in column 5
3. Calculate $|fd|$ i.e. multiply frequency (f) with (d) as column No. 6 of each class interval.
4. Compute $\Sigma|fd|$
5. Use formula $AD = \frac{\Sigma|fd|}{N}$

Use the AD

1. When it is desired to weight all deviations from the mean according to their size.
2. When extreme deviations would influence SD unduly.

The Standard Deviation or S.D (σ)

The standard deviation is the square root of the average of the squared distances of the observations from the mean.

In other words it may be stated that standard deviation is the square root of the variance while the average of the squared deviations of the measures or scores from their mean is known as the variance.

The standard deviation is the most stable index of variability. It differs from AD is different ways.

In computing AD, we disregard signs and treat all deviations as positive while computing the SD we square the separate deviations. One thing is to remember that the squared deviations used in computing the SD are always taken from the mean (never frm median or mode). The symbol for the SD is the Greek letter sigma (σ).

(1) Computation of the SD (σ) from the Grouped Scores

The procedure to calculate SD (σ) is illustrated with an example.

Example—A group of 10 students scored as X = 10, 12, 14, 18, 19, 21, 27, 28, 29, 32 find out the SD(σ) of this group.

$$\text{Mean} = \frac{10 + 12 + 14 + 18 + 19 + 27 + 28 + 29 + 32}{10}$$

$$\text{Mean} = \frac{210}{10} = 21$$

d = (10–21), (12–21), (14–21), (18–21), (19–21), (21–21), (27–21), (28–21), (29–21), (32–21)

d = –11, –9, –7, –3, –2, 0, 6, 7, 8, 11

d^2 = 121, 81, 49, 9, 4, 0, 36, 49, 64, 121

Now $\Sigma d^2 = 121 + 81 + 49 + 9 + 4 + 0 + 36 + 49 + 64 + 212 = 534$

$$\sigma = \sqrt{\frac{\Sigma d^2}{N}} = \text{Here } \Sigma d^2 = 534, N = 10$$

$$\text{then} = \sqrt{\frac{534}{10}} = \sqrt{53.4} = 7.30$$

σ = 7.30.

(ii) Calculation of σ from original measure or scores.

A convenient formula to compute σ from the original measures or scores

$$\sigma = \sqrt{\frac{\Sigma X^2}{N} - M^2}$$

or replacing the M^2 by $\left(\frac{\Sigma X}{N}\right)^2$

$$\text{then } \sigma = \sqrt{\frac{N \Sigma X^2 - (\Sigma x)^2}{N}}$$

This method of computing is especially useful when we have relatively few scores i.e., 50 or less and when the scores are expressed in not more than two digits so that squares may not become unmanageable.

Illustration

Table-8.4

Scores (X)	X^2
15	225
18	324
20	400
25	625
27	729
30	900
17	289
21	441
28	784
18	324

$\Sigma X = 219, N = 10$ $\Sigma X^2 = 5041$

$AM = 0$

$$M = \frac{219}{10} = 21.9$$

σ = correction

$C = 21.9 - 0 = 21.9$

$C^2 = 479.61$

$$\text{Now } \sigma = \sqrt{\frac{\Sigma x^2}{N} - c^2}$$

$$\sigma = \sqrt{\frac{5041}{10} - 479.61}$$

$$\text{or} \sqrt{504.1 - 479.61} = \sqrt{24.49}$$

$$\sigma = \sqrt{24.49}$$

σ = 4.948 or 4.95

S.D. $(\sigma) = 4.95$

Table–8.5

Calculation of SD from Grouped Data by Long Method

Class Interval	X	*f*	*x*	*fx*	fx^2
1	2	3	4	5	6
95-99	97	1	26	26	676
90-94	92	2	21	42	882
85-89	87	4	16	64	1024
80-84	82	6	11	66	726
75-79	77	6	6	36	216
70-74	72	11	1	11	11
65-69	67	6	–4	–24	96
60-64	62	4	-9	-36	324
55-59	57	5	–14	–70	980
50-54	52	3	-19	-57	1083
45-49	47	1	-24	-24	576
40-44	42	1	-29	-29	841
		N = 50			$\sum fx^{12}$ = 7435

Mean = 71.1 (from table 7.2 Chapter 7)

Here assumed 71 to avoid Last calculation

$$\sigma = \sqrt{\frac{\sum fx^2}{N}}$$

The fx^2 entries have been obtained by multiplying each x by its corresponding fx. The sum of the fx^2 column is 7435 and N = 50. Hence applying above formula we get.

$$\sigma = \sqrt{\frac{7455}{50}} \sqrt{148.7} = 12.19$$

S.D. or $(\sigma) = 12.19$

Calculation of the SD by the Short Method

(1) Calculation of σ from grouped data

The short method of computing the mean has already been outlined in the concerned chapter. This method is also used in calculating the SD.

Table–8.6

Class Interval	X *mid point*	*f*	x^1	fx^1	fx^2
95-99	97	1	5	5	25
90-94	92	2	4	8	32
85-89	87	4	3	12	36
80-84	82	6	2	12	24
75-79	77	6	1	6	6
70-74	72	11	0	0/43	0
65-69	67	6	–1	–6	6
60-64	62	4	–2	–8	16
55-59	57	5	–3	–15	45
50-54	52	3	–4	–12	48
45-49	47	1	–5	–5	25
40-44	42	1	–6	–6	36
				–52	
			$\sum fx^1 = -9$	$\sum fx^2 = 299$	

Formula for SD (σ) is $= \sqrt{\frac{\sum fx^2}{N} - \left(\frac{\sum fx}{N}\right)^2} Xi$

Here i = 5

$\sum fx^2 = 299$

$\sum fx^1 = -9$

N = 50

By substituting these values in the above formula.

$$\sigma = \sqrt{\frac{299}{50} - \left(\frac{-9}{50}\right)^2}$$

$= 5\sqrt{5.98 - (.18)^2}$

$= 5\sqrt{5.98 - .0324}$

$= 5\sqrt{5.98 - .0324} = 5\sqrt{5.9476}$

$= 5 \times 2.4387$

$= 5 \times 2.44 = 12.20$ $\qquad \sigma = 12.20$

Uses of Standard Deviation SD(σ)

1. The standard deviaton enables us to determine, with a great deal of accuracy where the values of a frequency distribution are located in relation to the mean.
2. Standard deviation (SD) is also useful in describing how far invidual scores in a distribution depart from the mean of the distribution.
3. When the statistic having the greatest stability is required.
4. When extreme deviations should exercise a proportionally greater effect upon the variability.
5. When coefficient of correlation and other statistics are subsequently to be calculated.
6. When most reliable and accurate measure of variability is wanted.
7. It is used when distribution is normal.

Effect upon σ of (adding (a) constant to each score, or (b) multiplying each score by the same number.

(a) If each score in a frequency distribution is increased by the same number, the σ be unchanged. The following illustration will make this point clear.

Table–8.7

Original			Original		
Scores	x'^2	x'^2	$x + 5$	x'	x'^2
12	2	4	17	2	4
9	–1	1	14	–1	1
11	1	1	16	1	1
10	0	0	15	0	0
8	–2	4	13	–2	4
50/5		$\Sigma x'^2 = 10$	10 + 5 = 15		$\Sigma x^2 = 10$

M = 10

$$\sigma = \sqrt{\frac{\Sigma x^2}{N}} = \sqrt{\frac{10}{5}}$$

$$\sigma = \sqrt{\frac{\Sigma x^2}{N}} = \sqrt{\frac{10}{5}} = \sqrt{2}$$

$\sigma = \sqrt{2} = 1.41$

(*b*) When constant number is multiplied in each score, what happens to the mean and σ. The following illustration gives its answer.

Table–8.8

Original	*Scores*	*Deviation*	*Scores*
x	$x \times 10$	x^1	x^2
12	120	20	400
9	90	–10	100
11	110	10	100
10	100	–0	0
8	80	–20	400
	$\sum x = 500 \div 5 = 100$		1000

$50 \div 5 = 10 \qquad \frac{500}{5} \qquad \sqrt{\frac{\sum x^2}{N}} = \sqrt{\frac{1000}{5}} = \sqrt{200}$

M = 100

σ = 14.14

The net effect of this procedure is to multiply the mean and the σ by 10.

4. The σ standard deviation from combined distribution.

When two sets of scores are combined into a single set. We can compute σ of the total distribution from the σ of the two component distribution.

The formula is:

$$\sigma_{comb} = \sqrt{\frac{N_1(\sigma_1^2 + d_1^2) + N_2(\sigma_2^2 + d_2^2)}{N}}$$

where σ_1 = SD of distribution 1

σ_2 = SD of distribution 2

$d_1 = (M_1 - M_{comb})$

$d_2 = (M_2 - M_{comb})$

$N = (N_1 + N_2)$ = Total number of cases in component distribution 1 and 2 i.e., N_1 and N_2.

	N	*M*	*SD*
Class A	15	70	12
Class B	25	60	20

$$M_{comb} = \frac{N_1 M_1 + N_2 M_2}{N} = \frac{15 \times 70 + 25 \times 60}{40}$$

$$= \frac{1050 + 1500}{40} = \frac{2550}{40} = 63.75$$

$$\text{Now } \sigma_{comb} = \sqrt{\frac{N_1(\sigma_1^2 + d_1^2) + N_2(\sigma_2^2 + d_2^2)}{N}}$$

$$\text{Now } \sigma_{comb} = \sqrt{\frac{15\,(12 \times 12) + 6.25 \times 6.25 + 25\,(20 \times 20 + 3.75 \times 3.75)}{40}}$$

$$\sigma_{comb} = \sqrt{\frac{15 \times 183 + 2.5 \times 414.06}{40}} = \sqrt{\frac{13096.5}{40}}$$

The above formula may be extended to include more than two component distribution by adding N_3, S_3, d_3 and so on.

Problems

1. Calculate mean deviation from the following ungrouped data. 10, 15, 10, 20, 25, 15, 25, 20, 17, 23
2. Calculate mean deviation from the following frequency distribution.

C.I.	*f*
55-59	1
50-54	1
45-49	3
40-44	4
35-39	6
30-35	7
25-29	12
20-24	6
15-19	8
10-14	2

3. Calculate standard deviation from the ungrouped data given on question 1.
4. Calculate standard deviation from the following frequency distribution.

C.I.	*f*
90-99	1
80-89	4
70-79	7
60-69	10
50-59	9
40-49	9
30-39	4
20-29	3
10-19	3

5. Calculate Quartile deviation from the following frequency distribution.

(i) C.I.	*f*	(ii) C.I.	*f*
40-44	3	80-89	5
35-39	3	70-79	2
30-34	5	60-69	3
25-29	7	50-59	2
20-24	5	40-49	5
15-19	3	30-39	4
10-14	2	20-29	3
		10-19	2
		0-9	4

6. Calculate quartile deviation, mean deviation, standard deviation from the following frequency distribution.

C.I.	*f*
77.83	3
70-76	13
63-69	16

(Contd.)

C.I.	*f*
56-62	13
49-55	6
42-48	22
35-41	18
28-34	6
21-27	1

QUESTIONS

A. Short Answer Type Questions.

1. What do you understand by standard deviation?
2. Explain in short types of variability.
3. When do we use quartile deviation?
4. Explain the utility of dispersion.
5. Distinguish between mean deviation and standard deviation.
6. Explain the formula for computing S. D. for grouped data (short method)

B. Objective Type Questions.

1. Variance is the square root of S.D. True/False
2. S.D. is the most sensitive measure of variability. True/False
3. Addition of constant has not effect on the measure of standard deviation. True/False
4. Subtraction of constant has an effect on the measure of S.D. True/False
5. The most accurate measure of variability is..................
6. The variance measure is the square of ....
7. The quartile deviation is used with:
   (*a*) Mean (*b*) Median
   (*c*) Mode (*d*) Range.
8. Mean and standard deviation are used simultaneously. True/False
9. Measures of variability are used for a group of:
   (*a*) Homogeneity (*b*) Heterogeneity
   (*c*) Both of the above (*d*) None of these.
10. The most crude measure of variability is:
    (*a*) Q (*b*) Range
    (*c*) Variance (*d*) S.D.

9

The Normal Probability Distribution

In the last chapter, it has been described that frequency distribution is a useful way of summerising variation in observed data.

The frequency distribution was prepared by listing all the possible outcomes of an experiment and then indicating the observed frequency of each possible outcome. The probability distributions are related to frequency distribution. In other words, it may be stated that probability distribution is a theoretical frequency distribution. A theoretical frequency distribution is a probability distribution that describes how outcomes are expected to vary. Because such distributions are dealt with expectations, they are useful models in making inferences and decisions under conditions of uncertainty. It can be illustrated with the following examples of probability distributions.

Example: Suppose we toss a fair coin twice.

The following table illustrates the possible outcomes from this two-toss experiment.

Table-9.1

X	*First Toss*	*Second Toss*	*Probability of four Possible Outcomes*
Possible outcomes	T	T	$.5 \times .5 = .25$
from two tosses	T	H	$.5 \times .5 = .25$
of a fair coin	H	H	$.5 \times .5 = .25$
	H	T	$.5 \times .5 = .25$
			1.00

Table–9.2
Probability

	Number of Tails (T)		Tosses of this outcomes (T)
Probability Distribution			
of the possible number	0	(H, H)	.25
of tails from two tosses	1	(T, H) + (H, T)	.50
of a fair coin	2	(T, T)	.25

Now suppose that we want to formulate a probability distribution of the number of tails that could possibly result when we toss the coin twice. We would begin by noting any outcome that did not contain a tail. With a fair coin, that is only one tail (the second and fourth outcomes in table-1, and finally we would note that the first outcome contains two tails. In table 2, we rearrange the outcomes of table 1 to stress the number of tails contained in each outcome. Here it is to be noted that table 2 is not the actual outcome of tossing a fair coin twice. Rather it is a theoretical outcome i.e., It represents the way in which we would expect our two-toss experiment to behave overtime. Now we are able to differentiate between frequency distributions and probability distributions.

"A frequency distribution is a listing of the observed frequencies of all the outcomes of an experiment that actually occurred when the experiment was done, whereas a probability distribution is a listing of the possibility of all the possible outcomes that could result if the experiment were done."

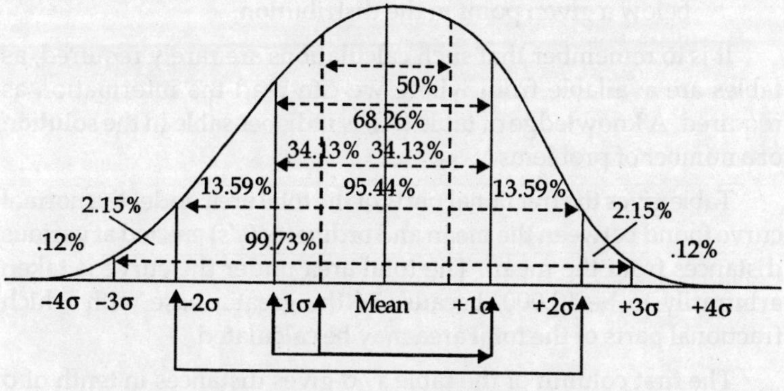

Figure 9.1 Normal Probability Curve

The two parts formed similar in shape and very nearly equ in area and exhibits almost perfect bilateral symmetry. The perfectl symmetrical curve or frequency surface as shown in the fig which is bell-shaped is called the normal probability curve or simply the normal curve. This curve has a great value in mental measurement.

J.P. Guilford defined, "Normal probability curve is a well defined, well structured mathematical curve, have a distribution of 0 scores mean and S.D. one the curve itself. It does not occur in nature, it is not biological or psychological curve.

1. ***The Equation of the Normal Curve Reads***

$$y = \frac{N}{\sigma\sqrt{2\Pi}} e \frac{-x^2}{2\sigma^2}$$

in which

x = scores expressed as deviation from the mean laid off along the horizontal axis

y = the height of the curve above the horizontal axis the frequency of a given x value.

N = number of cases in the sample of group

σ = standard deviation of the distribution

Π = 3.1416

e = 2.1783 (base of Napierian system of logarithmatic).

When N and σ are known, it is possible from this equation we can compute:

1. the frequency or (y) of a given value x
2. the number or percentage between two points i.e. above or below a given point in the distribution.

It is to remember that such calculations are rarely required, as tables are available from where we can read the information as required. A knowledge of table (A), is indispensable in the solution of a number of problems.

Table gives the fractional parts of the total area under the normal curve found between the mean and ordinates (y's) erected at various distances from the mean. The total area under the curve is taken arbitrarily to be 10,000, because of the greater ease with which fractional parts of the total area may be calculated.

The first column of the table x/σ gives distances in tenth of σ measure off on the σ base line of the normal curve from the mean as origin. We know that $x = X - M$ measures the deviation of raw score (X) from the Mean (M).

If x is divided by σ, this deviation is expressed in σ units. These deviation scores are known sigma-scores or z scores X i.e.

$$z = \frac{X - M}{\sigma} = \frac{x}{\sigma}$$

To find the number of cases in the normal distribution between the mean and the ordinate erected at a distance of 1 σ from the mean we go down x/σ column unit 1.0 is reached and the next column under .00, we take the entry opposite 1.0 viz 3413. This figure means that 3413 cases in 10000 or 34.13 per cent of the entire area of the curve lies between the mean and 1 σ. For practical purposes we take the curve to end at points -3σ and $+3\sigma$ distant from the mean as the normal curve does not actually meet the baseline.

Characteristics of Normal Probability Curve

The general characteristics of N.P.C. are:

1. It is a bell shaped curve.
2. Mean, Median and mode concentrate on one point i.e. Mean = Median = Mode. We can say that the measures of central tendency are equal.
3. The height of the curve is .3989 i.e. 39.89 percent frequencies concentrate at its centre i.e. highest frequency is at mean '0'.
4. It is an asymptotic curve. The ends of the curve never meet to the X axis.
5. For practical purposes in range of the N.P.C. is considered from -3σ to $+3\sigma$ i.e. The 50 per cent cases lie below the mean and 50 per cent cases lie above the mean.

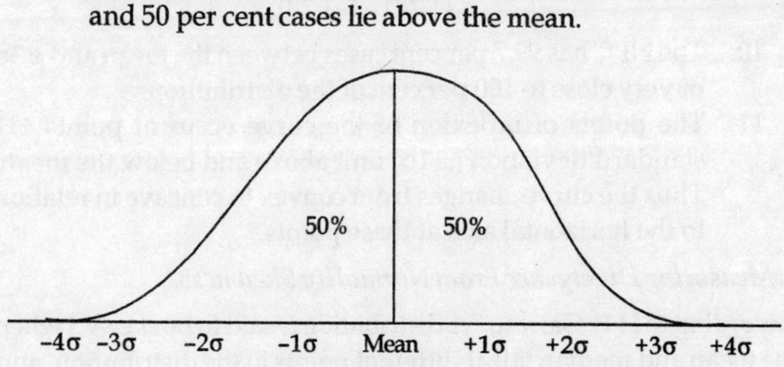

Figure 9.2

6. The distribution of frequency per cent has the definite limits. A few important limits are:
   - *(i)* The 68.26 per cent total area of the curve lies between -1σ and $+1\sigma$
   - *(ii)* The 95 per cent of the total area lies between -1.96σ and $+1.96\sigma$
   - *(iii)* The 95.44 per cent of total area of the curve falls between limits of $M \pm 2\sigma$
   - *(iv)* The 99 per cent cases lie between -2.58σ and $+2.58\sigma$
   - *(v)* 99.73 per cent of the total area of the curve falls between $M \pm. 3\sigma$
7. In the normal curve the quartile deviation (Q) is generally called the Probable error or PE. The relationship between, PE and σ are given in the following equations.

   $PE = .6745\ \sigma$

   $\sigma = 1.4826\ PE$
8. In a normal probability curve, the skewness of the curve is zero (0).

   $$SK = \frac{3\,(\text{Mean} - \text{Mdn})}{\sigma} = 0$$
9. A normal curve also called mesokurtic has the value of Kurtosis = .263

   $$K = \frac{Q}{P_{90} - P_{10}} = P_{90} = 1.28, P_{10} = -1.28$$

   $$\text{or ku} = \text{Kurtosis} = \frac{.6745}{(1.28) - (-1.28)} = .263$$
10. The NPC has 99.7 per cent cases between the mean and $\pm 3\sigma$ or very close to 100 per cent of the distribution.
11. The points of inflexion of the curve occur at points ± 1 standard deviation ($\pm 1\sigma$) unit above and below the mean. Thus the curve changes from convex to concave in relation to the horizontal axis at these points.

2. ***Measuring Divergence From Normality Skewness***

According to H.E. Garrett, "A distribution is said to be skewed when the mean and median fall at different points in the distribution, and the balance is shifted to one side or the other to left or right."

Types of Skewness

There are two types of skewness: *(1)* Negative Skewness *(2)* Positive Skewness.

1. *Negative Skewness:* Distributions are said to be skewed negatively or to the left when scores are masured at the high end of the scale (the right end) and are spread out toward the low end or left as shown in the following figure.

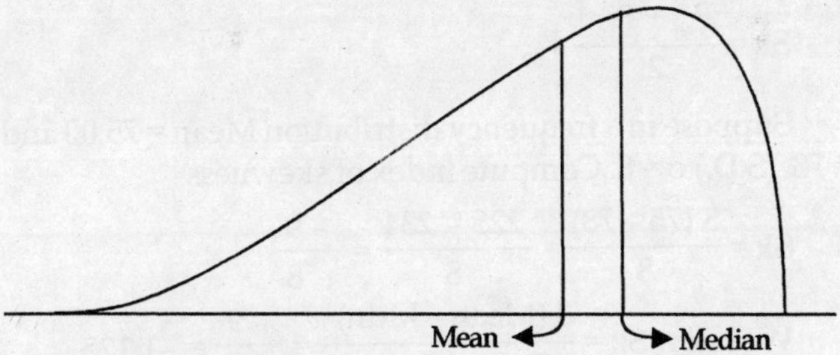

Figure: 9.3 Negative Skewness: to the Left

In negative skewness the mean lies to the left to the median. It happens generally when the test is very easy as the scores of the most student's massed right end of the curve.

2. *Positive Skewness*: Distributions are skewed positively or to the right when scores are masured at the low (or left) end of the scale and are spread out gradually toward the high right end as shown in the following figure.

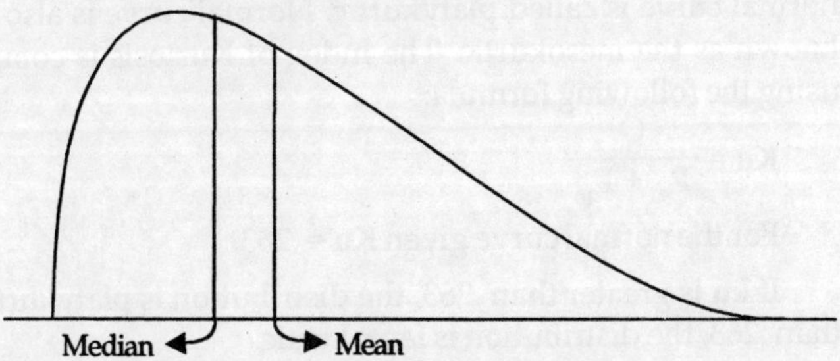

Figure: 9.4 Positive Skewness to the Right

In positive skewness, the mean lies to the right of the median. When the test is very difficult we find such type of skewness as most of the students score massed at negative end of the curve or left end of the mean.

Measurement of Skewness

Greater the gap between mean and median greater be the skewness. We can compute the index skewness with the help of the following formula.

$$Sk = \frac{3\,(\text{Mean} - \text{Median})}{\sigma}$$

A simple measure of skewness in terms of percentiles is

$$Sk = \frac{P_{90} + P_{10}}{2} - P_{50}$$

Suppose in a frequency distribution Mean = 75.00 and Median = 78. (S.D.) $\sigma = 8$. Compute index of skewness

$$Sk = \frac{3\,(75 - 78)}{8} = \frac{225 - 234}{8} = \frac{-9}{8}$$

$$\text{We know } Sk = \frac{3\,(\text{Mean} - \text{Mdn})}{\sigma} = \frac{-9}{8} = -1.125$$

SK = –1.125

Distribution is negatively skewed.

Kurtosis or Peakedness

The concept 'Kurtosis' refers to the 'peakedness' or flatness of a frequency distribution as compared with the normal curve. A frequency distribution is more peaked than the normal curve is known as leptokurtic. A frequency distribution is flatter than the normal curve is called platykurtic. Normal curve is also called or known as the mesokurtic. The index of Kurtosis is computed by using the following formula:

$$Ku = \frac{Q}{P_{90} + P_{10}}$$

For the normal curve given Ku = .263.

If ku is greater than .263, the distribution is platykurtic, if less than .263, the distribution is leptokurtic.

Application of the Normal Probability Curve

(1) To determine the percentage of cases in a normal distribution within given limits. In such cases, raw scores, or limits of standard score are given, we are asked area or number of cases or percentage of frequency is to computed.

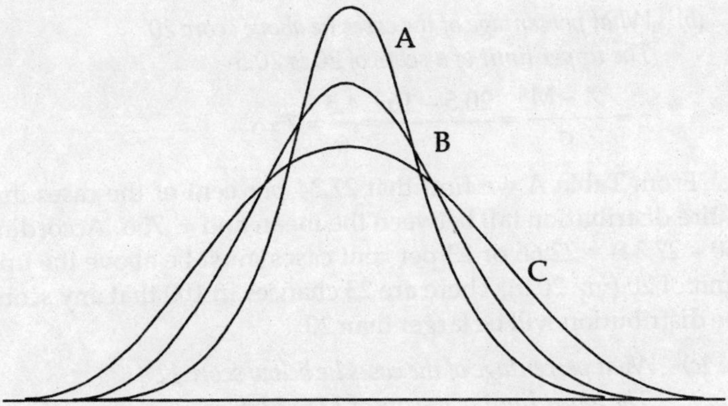

Figure: 9.5 Leptokurtic (A), Normal or Mesokurtic (B) and Platykurtic (C) Curves

Example. The mean of a frequency distribution is 16 and S.D. = 6. Assuming normality, *(a)* what percentage of the cases fall between 8 and 18 ? *(b)* What percentage of the cases lie above score 20 *(c)* below score 12.

Solution:

We know

$$z = \frac{X - M}{\sigma}$$

where X = score, M = Mean

σ = standard deviation

(a) $$z_1 = \frac{8 - 16}{\sigma} = \frac{-8}{6} = -1.33\ \sigma$$

$$z_2 = \frac{18 - 16}{\sigma} = \frac{2}{6} = .33\ \sigma$$

In the NPC table (A) the percentage of cases between Mean and 8 or –1.33σ is 42.82 per cent. Similarly the percentage of cases between mean and 18 or +.33σ are 12.93 per cent. Therefore the cases lying between 8 and 18 are 42.82 + 12.93 = 55.75 per cent.

It can also be interpreted that 55.75 per cent of the cases fall between 8 and 18. The chances are about 56 in 100 that any score in the distribution will be found between these point.

(*b*) *What percentage of the cases lie above score 20*
The upper limit of a score of 20 is 20.5

$$z = \frac{X - M}{\sigma} = \frac{20.5 - 16}{\sigma} = \frac{4.5}{6} = .75\ \sigma$$

From Table A we find that 27.34 per cent of the cases in the entire distribution fall between the mean and + .75σ. Accordingly (50 – 27.34) = 22.66 or 23 per cent cases must be above the upper limit of 20 (viz 20.5). There are 23 chances in 100 that any score in the distribution will be larger than 20.

(*c*) *What percentage of the cases lie below score 12*
The lower limit of a score of 12 is 11.5

$$z = \frac{X - M}{\sigma} = \frac{11.5 - 16}{\sigma} = \frac{4.5}{6} = -.75\ \sigma$$

From Table A we find that 27.34 per cent of the cases in the entire distribution between Mean and 11.5 (– .75σ). Hence about (50–27.34 = 22.66%) or 23 per cent cases must lie below the lower limit of 12 (11.5).

There are 23 chances in 100 that any score in the distribution will be less than 12 i.e., below the lower limit of score 12(11.5).

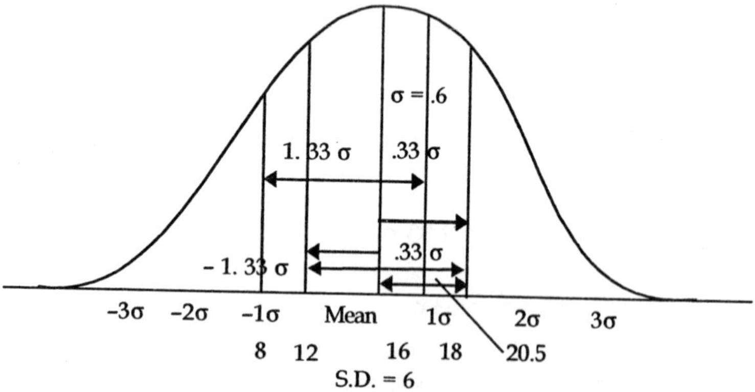

Figure 9.6

2. To find the limits in any normal distribution which include a given percentage of the cases

Example: 2 In a given distribution of scores with a mean = 16.00 and a σ of 6.00. If we assume normality, what limits will include the middle 75 per cent of the cases?

Solution: The middle 75 per cent of the cases in a normal distribution include the 37.5 per cent just above and the 37.5 per cent just below the mean (37.5% + 37.5% = 75).

From Table A 37.5 per cent of the distribution, fall between the mean and 1.15σ and similarly 37.5 per cent also falls between the mean and –1.15 σ.

The middle 75 per cent of cases lie between Mean and ± 1.15 σ.

The σ in the problem given = 6

± 1.15 × 6 = ± 6.90

Mean (given) = 16

16 ± 6.9 = 22.9 and 9.1

The middle 75 per cent cases lie between 22.9 and 9.1. See the figure.

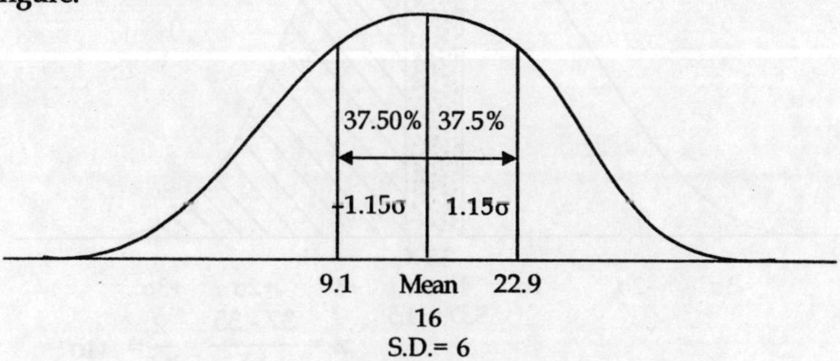

Figure 9.7

3. *To compare two distributions in terms of overlapping.*

Example 3: In a given distribution of the scores made on a rote memory test by 250 boys and 200 girls. The boys mean score is 22.00 with a σ of 3.00. The girls mean score is 24.00 with a σ of 5.00. The medians are boys 21.00 and girls 23. What percentage of boys exceed the median of the girls distribution?

Solution: On the assumption that these distributions are normal.

The girls median is 23 – 22 = 1 score unit above the boys mean

$$\text{or} = \frac{X - M}{\sigma} = \frac{23 - 22}{3} = .33\,\sigma$$

We find that the girls median is .33 σ above the mean of the boys distribution.

Table A shows that 12.93 per cent of a normal distribution lies between the mean and .33σ hence (50% –12.93%) 37.017 per cent of the boys exceed the girls median.

Example 4: A vocabulary test was administered on class IX A and IX B. The mean of the class IX A is 37.00 and S.D. is 4.00. The mean of class IX B is 35.00 and S.D. is 4.5. Find percent of cases of class IX B which is below the mean of IX A and calculate the percentage of class IX A which is above mean of class IX B.

Solution: $X_1 = 37$, $\sigma_1 = 4.00$ $X_2 = 35$, $\sigma_2 = 4.5$

(*i*) Curve of IX B

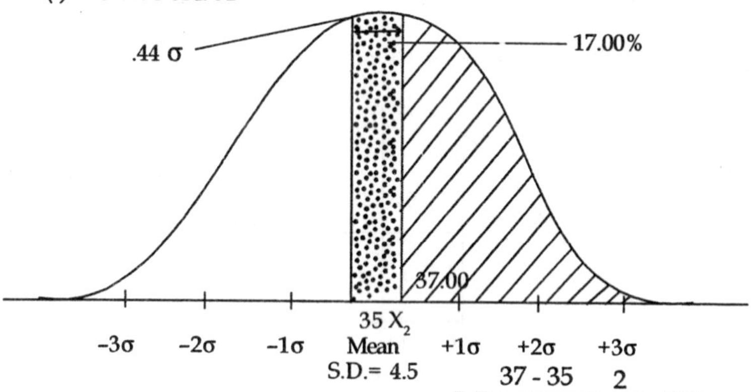

$$z_1 = \frac{37 - 35}{4.5} = \frac{2}{4.5} = .44\sigma$$

Curve of Class IX A

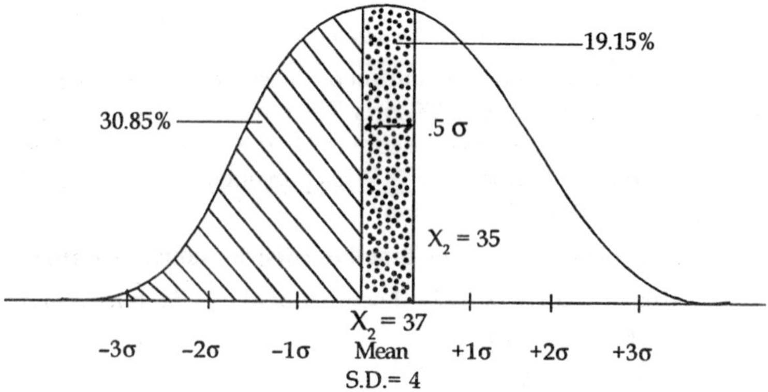

Figure 9.8

$$\frac{X_2 - M}{4} = \frac{35 - 37}{4} = \frac{2}{4} = -.5\sigma$$

(i) In the first Mean of class IX A = 37.00, σ = 4.00 and Mean of Class IX B = 35.00, σ = 4.5

$$\text{Now } z = \frac{X - M}{\sigma}$$

We are to find out the per cent of cases of class IX B which is below the mean of IX A.

$$z = \frac{\text{Mean of the IXA} - \text{Mean of the IX B}}{\sigma \text{ of IX B}}$$

$$= \frac{37 - 35}{4.5} = .44\ \sigma$$

The percentage between mean and .44 σ of class IX B distribution as shown in the figure of curve of IX B in table A is 17.00 per cent.

The total percentage above the mean 35 is 50 per cent. *The percent of cases of class IX B 17* per cent *which is the below the mean of IX A* and the percent of 50 per cent – 17.00 = 23 per cent.

(ii) Similarly—The percentage of class IX A which is above the mean of class IX B.

$$z - \frac{35 - 37}{4} - -.5\ \sigma$$

The percentage between mean and .5 σ of class is 19.15 per cent

Now the percentage of above the mean of class IX B = 50 + 19.15 = 69.15 per cent and percentage below the mean of IX B = 50 – 19.15 = 30.85 per cent.

Example 5. In an immediate memory test boys mean score is 23.68 and a σ of 6.75. The girls mean score is in the same test is 28.52 and a σ of 5.34. Calculate what percentage of boys exceed the mean of the girls distribution.

Solution. Girls mean is above 4.84 from the mean of the boys (28.52 – 23.68 = 4.84).

Now we may convert into sigma score by using the formula.

$$z = \frac{X - M}{\sigma} = \frac{28.52 - 23.68}{6.75} = .72\ \sigma$$

Girls mean falls towards the positive of .72 σ from the boys mean. By consulting Table A we find that between M and .72 σ, 26.43 per cent of individuals falls. Now the percentage boys score above the girls mean can 50 – 26.42 = 23.58.

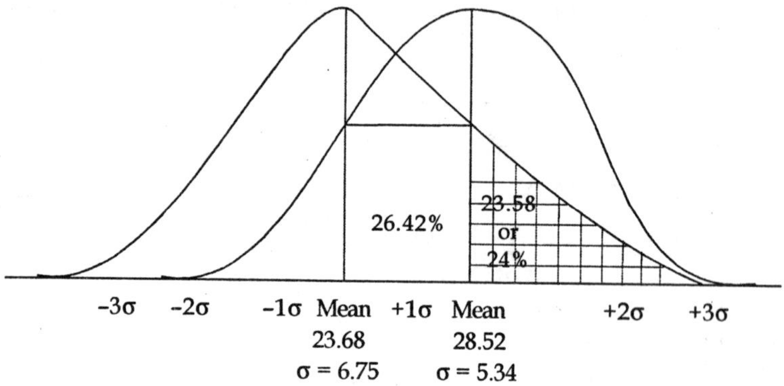

Figure 9.9

To Find the Difficulty Levels of the Items

Example 6. Given a test items 1, 2 and 3 passed by 50 per cent, 40 percent and 30 per cent respectively of a large sample. What percentage of the sample must pass item 4 in order for it to be as much more difficult than 3 as 2 is more difficult than 1?

Assuming that scores of the test are normally distributed.

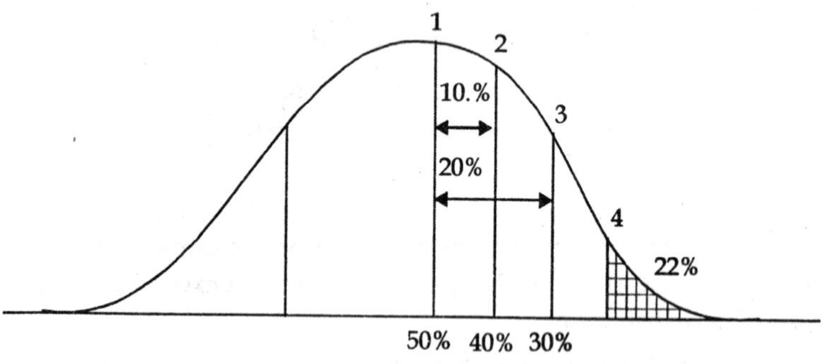

Figure 9.10

Item 1 is passed by 50 per cent, is marked at the centre of NPC. The σ score is zero (0σ). Similarly item 2 is passed by 40 per cent, the area between mean and σ is 10 per cent. The table A indicates the value .25σ.

The item 3 is passed by 30 per cent the area between mean and σ is 20 per cent its σ score is .52σ. These values are depicted in the following table.

Item	*Passed by*	*σ Score*	*Difference*
1.	50%	0σ	
2.	40%	.25σ	.25σ
3.	30%	.52σ	
4.	22%	.77σ	.25σ

The item 2 has the σ score = .25 σ which is difficult than item 1. The item 4 must be difficult more .25σ than item 3.

Therefore the limit of item 4 is: (.52σ + .25.σ = .77σ).

Now after consultation table A, we find the area between mean and .77 σ is 27.94 or 28 per cent of the distribution. The per cent above item 4 is (50 – 28 = 22), i.e. 22 per cent. Thus, the item 4 is passed by 22 per cent of the distribution.

5. To separate a given group into sub groups according to capacity, when the trait is normally distributed.

Example 7. An entrance examination test is administered on 500 fresh college students. The administrator wants to classify the group into 5 sub-groups A, B, C, D and E according to their ability, the range of ability to be equal in each category.

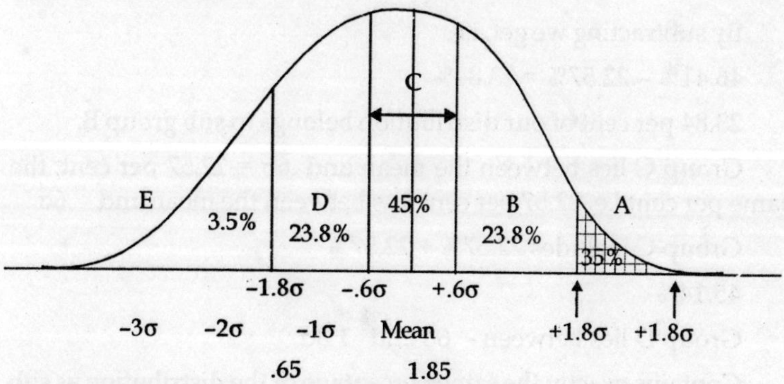

Figure 9.11

The positions of the 5 sub-groups is shown diagramatically on a normal curve as shown in the figure.

If baseline of the curve is considered to extend from – 3σ to + 3σ i.e. over a range of 6σ, dividing this range by 5 (the number of sub group) It becomes

$\frac{6}{5}\sigma = 1.2\sigma$ as the baseline extent to be allotted to each group. These five interval may be laid off on the baseline as shown in the figure. The various subgroups have been erected in the figure.

Group A covers the upper 1.2σ
Group B covers the next 1.2σ
Group C lies $.6\sigma$ to the right and
$.6\sigma$ to the left of the mean

Groups D and E occupy the same relative positons in the lower half of the curve that B and A occupy in the upper half.

Now the percentage of group A lies between 3σ (upper limit of the group A) and 1.8σ (lower limit of the group A).

From Table A between mean and $3\sigma = 49.86$ per cent and between mean and $1.8\sigma = 46.41$ per cent.

Hence total area under in normal curve = 49.86 – 46.41 = 3.45 therefore Group A comprises 3.45 per cent of the group Similarly the percentage of group B lies between 1.8σ (upper limit of the group B) and $.6\sigma$ (lower limit of the group B).

The percentage between mean and 1.86 = 46.41 per cent and between mean and $.6\sigma = 22.57$ per cent.

By subtracting we get, i.e.

46.41% – 22.57% = 23.84%

23.84 per cent of our distribution belongs to sub group B.

Group C lies between the mean and $.6\sigma = 22.57$ per cent, the same per cent i.e. 22.57 per cent less between the mean and $-.6\sigma$

Group C includes 22.57% + 22.57%

45.14%

Group D lies between $-.6\sigma$ and -1.8σ

Contains exactly the same percentage of the distribution as sub group B, i.e. 23.84 per cent. Similarly Group E lies between -1.8σ to -3σ.

Contains exactly the same percentage of whole distribution as sub group A.

Now the percentage and number of men/students in each group are given below.

	Groups				
	A	*B*	*C*	*D*	*E*
Percentage of total in each group	3.45	23.84	45.14	23.84	3.45
Number in each group	17	120	226	120	17

Limitations of Normal Curve

1. The σ values do not reveal the position or rank of an individual in his group as percentile does.
2. The σ values are also in negative which are not useful in human measurement.
3. No variable in behavioural science is normally distribution.
4. Normal Probability curve is only an assumption. Thus it involves error.

Measures of Relative Positions

As we know that a raw score is meaningless. It gets meaning only by comparing it with some reference group or groups. We can compare with the help of the following measures:

1. Sigma Scores (σ scores)
2. Standard scores (Z or T scores)
3. Percentiles
4. Percentile ranks.

Sigma Scores (σ scores)

Deviations from mean expressed in terms are called sigma scores. This is illustrated with the help of following examples. Suppose the mean of a test is 100 and S.D. = 20.

In this test Anil scores 150.

Now his deviation from the test's mean = 150 – 100 = 50

Dividing this deviation of 50 by the S.D. (σ) 20.

We provide him a score of $\frac{50}{20} = 2.5$

Now his score in sigma unit = 2.5

We can also write it as 2.5 σ

Similarly if Rakesh's scoe is 80 on this test. His deviation from the mean's test = 80 – 100 = –20 divided by S.D. = 20.

we get = –1

Now his score in sigma unit = –1

or we can say it –1σ too

The mean of a set of σ scores is always 0 (the reference point) and the standard deviation (σ) is always 1.00. A half of the score in normal distribution lies below and scores are negative and a half falls above the mean i.e. 50 per cent of sigma scores are negative and a half positive. A sigma scores makes possible a realistic comparison of scores. Sigma scores are also useful in hypothesis testing, determination of percentile ranks and probability judgements.

Standard Scores (Z and T scores)

Sigma scores are often small decimal fractions and indicated earlier a half of them are negative, hence are inconvenient to deal with in computation. Therefore σ scores are converted into a new distribution with mean and S.D. So selected as to make all scores positive and so relatively early to handle in computation such scores are called standard scores and are expressed as Z or T scores.

The raw scores are converted into standard scores with the help of a linear transformation which scores not change the shape of the distribution is anyway. We use the following formula to convert raw score into standard score.

Let X = a score in the original distribution

X^1 = a standard score in the new distribution.

M = Mean of the raw scores

M^1 = Mean of the standard scores

σ = SD of raw scores

σ^1 = SD of standard scores

$$\text{then} = \frac{X^1 - M^1}{\sigma^1} = \frac{X - M}{\sigma}$$

$$\text{or } X^1 = \frac{\sigma^1}{\sigma}(X - M) + M^1 \qquad (1)$$

When we take Mean (M^1) and standard deviation (σ^1) are taken to be 50 and 10 respectively, the standard score is called a T score

$$\text{i.e. } X^1 = \frac{10}{\sigma}(X - M) + 50 \qquad (2)$$

Illustration

In a given distribution mean = 80, σ = 15. Ram's score is 90 and Anil's 85. Express these raw scores a (1) standard scores in a distribution with mean of 500 and σ = 100 and (2) T score.

(1) By formula:

$$X^1 = \frac{\sigma^1}{\sigma}(X - M) + M^1$$

$$= \frac{100}{15}(X - 80) + 500$$

Substituting Ram's score of 90

$$X^1 = \frac{100}{15}(90 - 80) + 500$$

$$= 6.67\ (10) + 500$$

$$= 66.7 + 500 = 566.7$$

Substituting Anil's core of 85

$$X^1 = \frac{100}{15}(85 - 80) + 500$$

$$= 6.67\ (5) + 500$$

$$= 33.35 + 500 = 533.35$$

By formula (2) Ram's score—

$$T = \frac{10}{\sigma}(X - M) + 50$$

$$T = \frac{10}{15}(X - 80) + 50$$

$$T = \frac{10}{15}(90 - 80) + 50$$

$$T = .66 \times 10 + 50$$

$$T = 6.66 + 50 = 56.66$$

By Substituting Anil's score in formula 2

$$T = .66\ (85 - 80) + 50$$

$$T = .66 \times 5 + 50 = 3.30 + 50 = 53.30$$

3. Percentile

Percentiles are the points which divide the entire scale of, measurement into 100 equal parts and are denoted by P_0, P_1, P_2 ... P_{10} ... P_{50} ... P_{60} ... P_{100}.

First percentile may be defined as that point in a frequency distribution below which lie 1 percent of the total measure of scores.

Similarly Tenth percentile may be defined as that point in a frequency distribution below which lie 10 per cent of the total measure of scores.

It is evident that P_{50} is expressed as a median. It is to be noted that P_0 lies at the beginning of the distribution and P_{100} at the end of the distribution.

The method of calculating percentiles is essentially the same as that used in finding the median. The formula is:

$$P_P = l + \left(\frac{pN - F}{fp}\right)^i \quad (3)$$

in which

P_P = Percentage of the distribution wanted e.g. 5 per cent 10 etc.
l = exact lower limit of the class interval upon which P_P lies.
p^N = Part of N to be counted off in order to reach P_P
F = Sum of all scores upto intervals below l.
f_P = number of scores within the interval upon which P_P falls.
i = Size of the class interval.

The following example will illustrate method the calculation of percentiles: Calculate P_{30}, P_{60}, P_{75}.

Table–9.1

Frequency Distribution	*f*	*Cumulative (F) Frequency*	*Cu. per cent fp*
130-134	2	40	100.0
125-129	0	38	95.00
120-124	1	38	95.00
115-119	3	37	92.5
110-114	5	34 P_{75}	85.0
105-109	7	29 P_{60}	72.5
100-104	6	22	55.0
95-99	2	16	40.0
90-94	7	14 P_{30}	35.0
85-89	5	7	17.5
80-84	2	2	5.0
	N = 40		

For computing P_{30}, we have to find out first $P^N = P^N = 30$ per cent of 40 $= \frac{40 \times 30}{100} = 12$

$$P_{30} = l + \left(\frac{p^N - F}{fp}\right) x^{i}$$

$$= 89.5 + \left(\frac{12 - 7}{7}\right) \times 5$$

$$= 89.5 + \frac{5 \times 5}{7} = 89.5 + 3.57 = 93.07$$

$$P_{60} = l + \left(\frac{P^N - F}{fp}\right)^{i}$$

$$= 104.5 + 60\ \%\ \text{of}\ 40 = \frac{60 \times 40}{100} = 24$$

$$= 104.5 + \left(\frac{24 - 22}{7}\right) \times 5 = 104.5 + 1.43 = 105.93$$

$$P_{75}\ \text{of}\ 40 = \frac{75 \times 40}{100} = 30$$

$$P_{75} = 109.5 + 1/5 \times 5 = 109.5 + 1 = 110.50$$

Percentile Ranks

The percentile rank is the point in the distribution below which a given percentile of scores fall. For example if the 80th percentile rank is a score of 70, 80 per cent of the score fall below 70. The median is the 50th percentile ranks i.e., 50 per cent of the score fall below it.

In general, it may be stated that if K per cent of the members of a sample have score less than a particular point value X then X is the Kth percentile and K is the percentile rank of X.

The Calculation of Percentile Rank from Ordered Data

We are to compute ranks corresponding to particular scores. In case of individual scores, first we find out the rank of individual scores from the bottom i.e. rank in ascending order.

If R is the rank and N is the total number of cases then

$$\text{Percentile rank or } P_R = 100 - \frac{100\,R - 50}{N} \qquad (4)$$

Suppose Sheila ranks 5th in her class of 150 students. 4 students rank above her, 145 below her. Her percentile rank is:

$$P_R = 100 - \left(\frac{100 \times 5 - 50}{150}\right) = 100 - \frac{450}{150} = 97$$

Her percentile rank = 97

To calculate cumulative per cent

As shown in the above table we calculate rate which becomes

$$\text{Rate} = \frac{1}{N} \text{ i.e. } \frac{1}{40} = .025$$

Hence multiplying 2 by .025 we get .05 or .05 × 100 = 5, Similarly .05 × 7 × 100 = 17.5 see table 9.11 column (4).

To Calculate Percentile Rank from a Frequency Distribution

Calculate percentile rank of a student score whose obtained score 122.

Now score 122 falls in interval 120-124. There are 37 scores upto 119.5, i.e. exact lower limit of this interval (see table 9.11 column 4 cum *f*) and 1 score spreads over this interval. Dividing 1 by 5 (size of class ......) gives .20 per unit of interval. The score 122, which we are seeking is 2.5 score units from 119.5 i.e. exact lower limit of the interval within which the score of 122 lies. Multiplying 2.5 × .20 we get 0.50 as the score distance of 122 from 119.5 and adding .50 to 37 number of scores below 119.5 we get 37.5 as the part of N lying below 122. Dividing 37.5 by 40 gives 93.5 as that proportion of N below 122. Hence the percentile rank of score 122 is 93.75 or 94. The formula to calculate becomes like it.

$$PR = \frac{100}{N}\left(C.f + \frac{X - L \times f}{L}\right)$$

c.f. = cumulative frequency below which the score falls.
X = original score
L = lower limit of the class interval where the score falls
i = size of class interval
f = frequecny where the score falls

$$PR = \frac{100}{N}\left(C.f + \frac{X - L \times f}{L}\right)$$

$$= \frac{100}{N}\left(37 + \frac{122 - 119.5 \times f}{5}\right)$$

$$= \frac{100}{N}\left(37 + \frac{2.5 \times 1}{5}\right) = (37 + .5)$$

$= 2.5 \times 37.5 = 93.75$

$= 93.75$

Hence PR of the student is 94 whose score is 122

Problems—The Normal Probability Curve

1. What percentage of a normal distribution is included between:
   (a) mean and 1.54 σ
   (b) –3.5 PE and 1.0 PE
   (c) –1.73 σ and .56 σ
   (d) 1.8 PE and –2.5 PE
2. In a normal distribution: Find P_{25}, P_{40}, P_{54} and P_{80} in σ units.
3. In a sample of 1000 cases the mean of a certain test is 14.40 and $\sigma = 2.50$. Assuming normality of distribution.
   (a) How many individual score fall between 12 and 16.
   (b) How many score fall above 18? below 8 ?
4. In an Intelligence Test the distribution is essentially normal with a M = 100, S.D. = 20
   (a) What per cent of scores lie between 85 and 125?
   (b) The middle 60 per cent fall between what two points?
   (c) On what score does Q_3 fall ?
5. Calculate PR of the students whose scores are 34, 46, and 55 from the following frequency distributions.

C.I.	*f*
90-99	4
80-89	3
70-79	2
60-69	5
50-59	3
40-49	4
30-39	2
20-29	6
10-19	4
0-9	7

QUESTIONS

A. Short Answer Type Questions

1. What are the main general characteristics of normal probability curve?
2. Indicate use of NPC.
3. Define and explain the term NPC.
4. What is Kurtosis?
5. Explain skewness.
6. Explain the formula of Kurtosis and skewness.
7. Explain types of kurtosis.

B. Objectives Questions

1.. The NPC is mesokurtic curve. True/False
2. The NPC has the ku = .363. True/False
3. In NPC Mean and median not mode concentrate on one point. True/False
4. The X-axis of NPC indicates the z scores or s-scores. True/False
5. In the limits –1.96σ and + 1.96σ of NPC .... cases fall in between.
6. The middle 99 per cent cases of NPC fall between .... and ....
7. The ranges of NPC in terms of σ is generally considered equal to ....
8. The normal distribution curve measures:
   (*a*) Mean = 0, σ = 1 (*b*) Sk = 0
   (*c*) Ku = .263 (*d*) All the above.
9. The skewness is calculated by the formula:
   (*a*) 3 (Mdn – Mean)/σ (*b*) 3 (Mn – 3Mdn)/σ
   (*c*) 3 Mn – 2 Mdn/σ (*d*) 3 Mdn – 2 Mn/σ
10. The cases lie between + 2.58 s to –2.58s are:
    (*a*) 95 per cent (*b*) 99 per cent
    (*c*) 99.90 per cent (*d*) 68.26 per cent

10

The Coefficient of Correlation

The description of the degree of simultaneous variables of two measures for each individual is called a bivariate data. The essential characteristic of this type of data is that one measure can be paired with another measure for each member of the group. The degree of relationship between measures of bivariate data is known as correlation. It is represented quantitatively by the coefficient of correlation. Its value ranges from –1.00 to +1.00. A value of –1.00 depicts a perfect negative correlation and a value of + 1.00 describes perfect positive correlation. A zero (0) value describes complete lack of correlation between the two variables. The sign (+ or –) of the coefficient indicates the direction of the relationship of two variables X and Y). The use of the coefficient of correlation also describe how well one variable is explained by another. When we deal with samples, the sample coefficient of correlation is denoted by *r*.

If an inverse relationship exists i.e. of Y decreases as X increases then *r* will fall between 0 and – 1. Similarly if there is a direct relationship (if Y increases as X increases) there will be a value within the range of 0 to + 1.

The following figures illustrate these various characteristics of *r*.

Correlation is rarely computed when the number of cases is less than 25. H.E. Garrett cited an example to illustrate this concept of *r* which lies –10 to 1.00.

Example. Suppose that four tests A, B, C, D have been administered to a group of 5 children. The children have been arranged in order of merit as a test A and their scores have been compared separately with test B, C and D to give the following three cases.

The following figures illustrutes these various charactenstics of r.

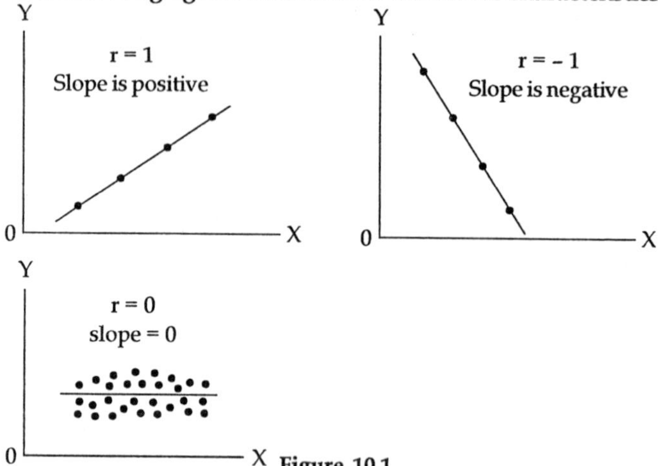

Figure 10.1

Case 1

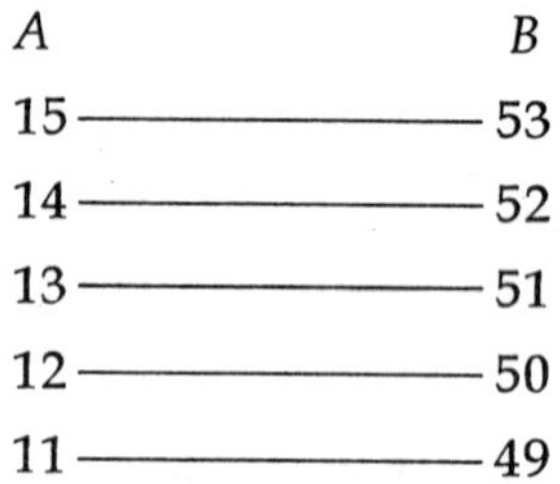

All connecting lines are horizontal and paralles and the correlation is positive and perfect $r = 1.00$

Case II

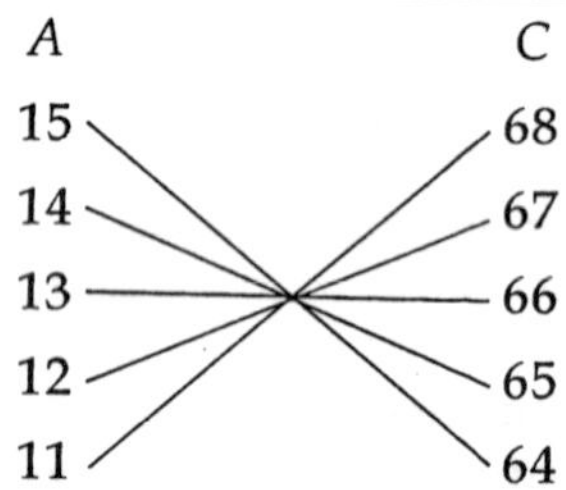

All connecting lines intersect in one point. The correlation is negative and perfect and $r = -1.00$

Case III

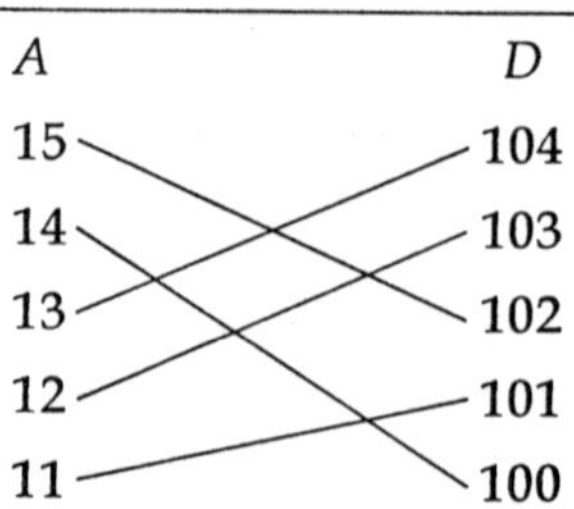

No system is exhibited by the connecting lines but the resemblance is closer to case II than to case I. Correlation low and negative.

Methods of Computing Correlation

There are various methods of calculating correlation. Their use is relative to the situation and kind of data. Some of these methods of correlation are described as under.

Product-moment correlation:

(1) The Calculation of r from ungrouped data

(a) The formula for r when deviatons are taken from the means of the two variables X and Y.

When deviations are taken from the actual means of the two variables, we use the following formula

$$r = \frac{\Sigma xy}{\sqrt{\Sigma x^2 \times \Sigma y^2}}$$

Where x and y are deviations from actual means

Σx^2 = The sum of the squared deviation in x

Σy^2 = The sum of the squared deviation in y.

r = Coefficient of Correlation

To illustrate the calculation of r from ungrouped scores when deviations are taken from the means of the series.

Table–10.1

Subject	*Test I*	*Test II*					
	X	Y	x	y	x^2	y^2	xy
1.	45	26	–2.4	.7	5.76	.49	–1.68
2.	50	29	2.6	3.7	6.76	13.69	9.62
3.	47	35	–.4	9.7	.16	94.03	–3.88
4.	35	28	–12.4	2.7	153.76	7.29	–33.48
5.	48	20	.6	–5.3	.36	28.09	–3.18
6.	52	15	4.6	–10.3	21.16	106.09	–47.38
7.	61	17	13.6	–8.3	184.96	68.89	112.88

(Contd.)

	X	Y	x	y	x^2	y^2	xy
8.	59	30	11.6	4.7	134.56	22.09	54.52
9.	40	22	-7.4	-3.3	54.76	10.89	24.42
10.	37	31	10.4	5.7	108.16	32.49	-59.28
	474	253			$\Sigma x^2 = 670.4$	$\Sigma y^2 =$ 384	$\Sigma xy =$ -173.2

$M_X = 47.4, M_Y = 25.3$

We know that $r = \dfrac{\Sigma xy}{\sqrt{\Sigma x^2 \times \Sigma y^2}}$

By substituting calculated values in the formula. We get

$$r = \frac{-173.2}{\sqrt{670.4 \times 384}} = \frac{-173.2}{\sqrt{257433.6}}$$

$$r = \frac{-173.2}{507.37} = -0.341$$

We may outline the steps in computing.

Step 1. Find the mean of Test I (X) and the mean of test II (Y). The means in table are $M_x = 47.4$ and $M_y = 25.3$.

Step 2. Find the deviation of each score on test from its mean 47.4 and enter it in the column X, similarly find the deviation of each score on test II (A) from its mean 25.3 and enter it in the column Y.

Step 3. Square all of the x's and all of the y's and enter these squares in column x^2 and y^2 respectively. We obtain total of x^2 i.e. Σx^2 and of y^2 i.e. Σy^2.

Step 4. Multiply the x's and y's in the same rows and enter these products (with due regard for sign) in the xy column. Now total the xy column, taking account of sign to get Σxy.

These value have been substituted in the formula and calculated accordingly in which is $r = -0.34$.

Illustration of the calculation of r from ungrouped scores when deviations are taken from the assumed mean of the series.

Table–10.2

Subject	*Test I*	*Test II*					
	X	Y	*x*	*y*	x^2	y^2	$x'y'$
1	45	26	–7	6	49	36	–42
2	50	29	–2	9	04	81	–18
3	47	35	–5	15	25	225	–75
4	35	28	–17	8	289	64	–136
5	48	[20]	–4	0	16	0	0
6	[52]	15	0	–5	0	25	0
7	61	17	9	–3	81	09	–27
8	59	30	7	10	49	100	70
9	40	22	–12	2	144	04	–24
10	37	31	–15	11	225	121	–165
			$C_x^1 =$ –4.6	$\sum y' = \frac{53}{10} = 5.3$	$\sum x^2 =$ 882	$\sum y^2 = 665$	$\sum x'y' =$ –417

$AM_X = 52$ $\quad AM_Y = 20$ $\quad \sum x^2 = 882$

$M_X = 47.4$ $\quad M_Y = 25.3$ $\quad \sum y'^2 = 665$

$C_x' = -4.6$ $\quad C_y' = 5.3$ $\quad \sum x'y' = 417$

$C^2_x = 21.16$ $\quad c_y^2 = 28.09$

$$\sigma x = \sqrt{\frac{\sum x^2}{N} - C_x^2} \qquad \sigma y = \sqrt{\frac{\sum y^2}{N} - C_y^2} = \sqrt{\frac{665}{10} - 28.09}$$

$$= \sqrt{\frac{882 - 21.16}{10}} \qquad \sigma y = \sqrt{66.5 - 28.09} = \sqrt{38.41}$$

$$= \sqrt{\frac{882 - 21.16}{67.04}} \qquad = \sqrt{38.41} = 6.19$$

$$\sigma_y = 6.19$$

$\sigma x = 8.18,$

$$= \frac{\frac{\sum x^1 y^1}{N} - C_x C_y}{\sigma x \, \sigma y} \qquad \frac{\frac{-417}{10} - (-4.6 \times 5.3)}{8.18 \times 6.19}$$

$$r = \frac{-17.32}{50.63} = -.34$$

$r = -.34$

Table-10.3

Subject	*X*	*Y*	*Sub.*	*X*	*Y*	*Subject*	*X*	*Y*
1.	38	35	26	8	7	51	23	17
2.	32	37	27	12	9	52	21	16
3.	30	39	28	10	6	53	22	18
4.	33	30	29	14	9	54	24	19
5.	27	31	30	4	12	55	20	15
6.	37	28	31	6	13	56	39	24
7.	32	26	32	12	10	57	34	30
8.	33	28	33	14	13	58	38	24
9.	27	28	34	10	12	59	32	22
10.	25	29	35	16	14	60	29	19
11.	26	25	36	18	10	61	20	24
12.	32	22	37	22	12	62	17	10
13.	38	23	38	13	18	63	24	9
14.	29	24	39	15	17	64	16	23
15.	25	20	40	19	15	65	7	6
16.	20	22	41	16	18	66	23	38
17.	23	21	42	17	15	67	27	14
18.	24	23	43	15	19	68	35	27
19.	19	24	44	18	16	69	22	10
20.	16	20	45	19	15	70	15	22
21.	2	4	46	16	17			
22.	2	3	47	19	18			
23.	3	8	48	24	19			
24.	7	8	49	20	15			
25.	9	6	50	20	22			

Bivariate Frequency Distribution Using Scatter Diagram

A frequency distribution involving two variables is known as a bivariate frequency distribution or scatter diagram. It is a table form comprises of a number of rows and columns. The columns correspond to class interval of the x variable and the rows to class interval of the y variable. Each pair of observations or score is marked as one tally in its concern cell.

The calculation of *r* from a scatter diagram

Step 1. A scatter diagram for the two variable to be correlated is constructed and from it correlation table is drawn as below from the data.

Table-10.4

Marks in History (X Variable)

Marks in English Y Variable — Y \ X	0–4	5–9	10–14	15–19	20–25	25–29	30–35	35–39	*fy*
35–39					I 1		II 2	I 1	4
30–34						I 1	II 2	I 1	4
25–29						III 3	II 2	II 2	7
20–24				IIII 4	III 3	III 3	II 2	II 2	14
15–19			I 1	IIII IIII 9	IIII III 8	I 1			19
10–14	I 1	I 1	III 3	III 3	II 2	I 1			11
5–9	I 1	IIII 4	III 3		I 1				9
0–4	I 1	I 1							2
fx	3	6	7	16	15	9	8	6	70

Step 2. The distribution of marks of English for 70 students falls in the *fy* column at right of the diagram. The mean at the class interval of 15-19 has been assumed as per rules prescribed and has been taken at the said interval i.e. (mid point of interval 15-19 which is 17. The procedure to calculate mean and S.D. has been adopted (short method), (See the chapter of central tendency and standard deviation). Now the fy^1 and fy^2 columns have been filled in. From the first column *cy*, the correction in units of interval is obtained and this correction together with the sum of the fy'^2 gives the σ of distributions of marks in English as shown by the calculation in the above table, the value of $\sigma_y = 1.69$ in unit of C.I. or 8.45.

The distribution of the marks in history of the 70 students is found in the f_x row at the bottom of the diagram. The same method of calculation has been adopted as mentioned above. The mean for the marks of history is taken at 15-19, the midpoint is 17 and the x's are taken from this point. The fx' and fx'^2 rows were filled in from the first we calculated C_x, the correction in unit of interval, and from the second the σ_x was calculated, the σ of the entire marks in English distribution. The value of σ_x is found 1.84 in the unit of C.I. and 9.20.

Step 3. Calculation of the entries in the $\Sigma x'y'$ column may be illustrated by considering.

The single entry in the only occupied cell in the top most row. The deviation of this cell from the AM of the marks is history that is, its x' is four intervals and its deviation from distribution of marks in English that its y' is also four intervals. Hence the product of the deviation of this cell from the two AM's is 4 × 4 or 16 and a small score 16 is placed in the upper right hand corner of the cell. The 'product deviation' of the one entry in this cell is 1 (3 × 4) or 12 also hence score 12 is placed in the lower left hand corner of the cell. This cell shows the product of the deviations of this single entry from the AM's of the two distribution similarly the same procedure for other 3 cells of x' and y' cells in X variable deviation i.e. x' deviation is four interval and its deviation from y' is 3 intervals. Hence the product of this cell is 4 × 3 or 12 and a score of 12 is placed and the product deviation of entry of this cell is (4 × 3) or 12, hence score 12 is placed in the lower left corner. The total of each entries of the left corner of the cell is calculated of this row, 52 is placed at once under the + sign in the $\Sigma x'y'$ column. Now we may total up the plus and minus entries in row and column and enter the results in the $\Sigma x'y'$ column and row under the appropriate signs.

Step 4. The sum of the $x'y'$ computed from the rows should be checked the sum of the $x'y'$ computed from the column which should be equal if the procedure has correctly been adopted as the table indicates. Two other useful checks have also been shown in the table. The fy' will equal the $\Sigma y'$ and fx' will equal the $\Sigma x'$ if no error has been made.

Step 5. After completing all the entries in the $\Sigma x'y'$ column and column totaled the coefficient of correlation is computed by the formula:

$$r = \frac{\frac{\Sigma x^1 y^1}{N} - cx\ cy}{\sigma x\ \sigma y}$$

It is important to note that c_x, c_y, $\sigma' x$, $\sigma' y$ are all in units of class interval in the above formula.

$$Cy = \frac{21}{70} = .3$$

$$Cy^2 = 0.09$$

$$CX = \frac{53}{70} = .75$$

$$CX^2 = .56$$

$$\sigma\, Y = 5\sqrt{\frac{207}{70} - 0.9}$$

$$= 5\sqrt{2.87}$$

$$\sigma\, y = 1.69$$

$$= 5 \times 1.69 = 8.45$$

$$\sigma\, x = i\sqrt{\frac{\Sigma fx^2}{N} - c^2 x}$$

$$= \sqrt{\frac{277}{70} - .56}$$

$$= 5\sqrt{3.96 - .56} \qquad = 5\sqrt{3.40}$$

$$\sigma\, x = 1.84 \qquad = 5 \times 1.84 = 9.20$$

$$r = \frac{\frac{\Sigma x^1 y^1}{N} - cx\ cy}{\sigma x\ \sigma y}$$

$$= \frac{\frac{188}{70} - .75 \times .3}{1.69 \times 1.84} \qquad = \frac{2.68 - .225}{3.606}$$

$$= \frac{2.455}{3.606} \qquad = .68$$

$$r = .68$$

Table-10.5

Marks in Histroy 'X' Variable

Marks in English 'Y' Variable

Y \ X	0-4	5-9	10-14	15-19	20-24	25-29	30-34	35-39	f	y^1	fy^1	fy^{12}	Σx^1y^1 (a)	Σx^1y^1 (b)	Σx^1	Σx^1y^1
35-39					4 1 4		24 2 12	16 1 16	4	4	16	64	44	×	11	44
30-34						6 1 6	18 2 9	12 2 12	4	3	12	36	36	×	12	36
25-29						12 3 4	12 2 6	16 2 8	7	2	14	28	40	×	20	40
20-24				0 4 0	3 3 1	6 3 2	6 2 3	8 2 4	14	1	14/56	14	23	×	23	23
15-19			0 1 0	0 9 0	0 8 0	0 1 0			19	0	0	0	0	0	9/75	0
10-14	3 1 3	2 1 2	3 3 1	0 3 0	-2 2 -1	-2 1 -2			11	-1	-11	11	8	4	-4	4
5-9	6 1 6	6 1 4	6 3 2		-2 1 -2				9	-2	-18	36	28	2	-13	26
0-4	9 1 9	6 1 6							2	-3	-6/-35	18	15	×	-5/-22	15
fx	3	6	7	16	15	9	8	6	70		Σfy^1=21	Σfy^{12} = 207			Σx^1=53	Σx^1y^1 =188
X	-3	-2	-1	0	1	2	3	4								
FX^1	-9	-12	-7/-28	0	15	18	24	24/81	Σyx^1 = 53							
FX^2	27	24	7	0	15	36	72	96	277							
Σx^1y^1 +	18	24	9	0	7	24	60	52								
−					4	2										
Σy^1	-6	-12	-9/-27	1	3	11	20	13/48	Σy^1 = 21							
Σx^1y^2	18	24	9	0	3	22	60	52	Σx^1y^1 = 188							

Calculation of the Product Moment Coefficient of Correlation between Marks in English and History of 70 Students.

Correlation From Ranks or Rank Order Correlation

The rank order correlation is the simplest method of correlation. It is also known as the Spearman rank order coefficient of correlation and is denoted by p (*r*ho). This method is used when the data are available only in ordinal form of measurement (ranked) rather than in interval or ratio form or if the number of paired variables is more than 9 or fewer than 30. To compute the Spearman rank order coefficient of correlation, the following formula is used

$$\rho = 1 - \frac{6 \Sigma D^2}{N(N^2 - 1)}$$

D = the difference between paired ranks

D^2 = The sum of the squared differences between ranks.

N = number of paired ranks.

This method is considered non-parametric of free distribution statistics of correlation.

Illustration

To illustrate the calculation of rank difference correlation coefficient two judges X and Y ranked 12 students in a declamation contest the ranks given by the two judges are given in the following table.

Table–10.6

Students	*Rank assigned by X*	*Rank Assigned by Y*	*D*	D^2
A	1	2	-1	1
B	5	3	2	4
C	4	5	-1	1
D	6	4	2	4
E	3	6	-3	9
F	2	1	1	1
G	7	7	0	0
H	9	8	1	1
I	10	9	1	1
J	8	10	-2	4
K	11	12	-1	1
L	12	11	1	1
N = 12				$\Sigma D^2 = 28$

Using formula:

$$P\,rho = 1 - \frac{6\,\Sigma D^2}{N\,(N^2 - 1)} = 1 - \frac{6 \times 28}{12 \times 143} = 1 - .098 = .90$$

$P\,rho = .90$

The *P*(*rho*) correlation is + .90 which shows very high and positive correlation between the judgement of two judges.

Interpretation of Coefficient of Rho-correlation

The interpretation is usually done on the basis of size of sample or after testing the significance of coefficient or correlation. J.P. Guilford has given a guideline for the interpretation of coefficient of correlation.

Correlation coefficient	Interpretation
.20 and below	Almost negligible relationship
.21 to .40	Low correlation, definite but small relation
.41 to .90	High correlation marked relationship
.91 and above	Very high correlation very dependable relationship

The above interpretation of correlation coefficient is made for both positive as well as negative correlation

The rank-difference method when there are tied ranks.

The relationship between the marks in Maths and in English of 10 students is almost negligible.

In column (4) the studetns have been (R_m) ranked in mathematics in order of merit in accordance to the marks obtained student No. (8) ranked first (1) in maths according to marks obtained. Student No. (3) is ranked 2 and so on down the list. Note that student no. 5, 6 and 7 have the same marks in maths and that each is ranked 6 (5 + 6 + 7)/3 = 6. Similarly each student has been ranked in English also. The procedure is the same. The difference between each pair of ranks is entered in column (6) and in column (7) each D is squared. The sum of the column (7) is 197.50. Substituting for ΣD^2 and for N, we have that *P*(rho) = .196 or –.20 which is negligible as interpreted earlier.

Advantages of Pearson's Correlation (Product-moment method)

The Pearson's product moment correlation is widely used in measurement. The following are main uses.

Table–10.7

Sl. No. (1)	*Marks in Maths* (2)	*Marks in English* (3)	*Rm* (4)	*Re* (5)	*D* (6)	*D^2* (7)
1.	5	8	8	1	7	49
2.	2	7	9.5	2	7.5	56.25
3.	10	2	2	9.5	-7.5	56.25
4.	8	6	3	3.5	.5	.25
5.	6	3	6	8	-2	4.0
6.	6	5	6	5	1	1
7.	6	4	6	6.5	–.5	.25
8.	12	4	1	6.5	–5.5	30.25
9.	2	2	9.5	9.5	0	0
10.	7	6	4	3.5	.5	.25
						$\Sigma D^2 = 197.50$

$$P = 1 - \frac{6\Sigma D^2}{N(N^2-1)} = 1 - \frac{6 \times 197.50}{10(100-1)}$$

$$\rho = 1 - \frac{1185}{99 \times 10} = 1 - \frac{1185}{990}$$

$$P = 1 - 1.196 = -.196 \text{ or } -.20$$

(i) The reliability and validity of the test are computed and estimated with the coefficient of correlation (r).

(ii) The cut of score is determined with the help of scatter plot of Pearson's (r)

(iii) Item discrimination power is computed by using Pearson's (r).

(iv) Multiple r correlation. Partial correlation and factor analysis technique use the Pearson's (r).

(v) Pearson's correlation is used in regression equation specially for prediction.

(vi) Theories of intelligence have been developed by using the Pearson's (r).

(vii) Most of the personality theories have also been developed by using the coefficient of correlation of Pearson's (r).

Limitations

1. It is linear correlation when the two variables have the linear distribution would yield accurate coefficient of correlation.

If it is not so, r Pearson's (r) is not dependable.

2. The distributions of scores of the two variable should be normal. If the distribution is skewed, it would not yield dependable correlation. However this assumption is rarely observed.

Problems

1. Calculate the coefficient of correlation between Maths and English scores as given below.

Subject	A	B	C	D	E	F	G	H
English	41	42	40	42	50	46	43	45
Maths	21	16	15	18	22	20	19	17

2. Prepare bivariate frequency distributions table (scatter diagram) of 40 students whose scores on two variable A and B are given below:

A	*B*	*A*	*B*
32	28	21	17
26	26	25	26
19	31	26	45
17	18	19	30
14	12	18	28
45	36	21	23
10	12	19	17
26	16	18	28
35	47	46	21
49	22	19	35
19	25	18	32
17	36	40	37
16	27	27	18
46	45	35	41
21	28	26	44

(Contd...)

A	*B*	*A*	*B*
27	18	15	13
19	37	24	18
36	42	19	30
25	20	21	27
19	12	42	36

Calculate Pearson's (r) organizing data in grouped form.

3. Calculate the Spearman's *P* (rho) correlation coefficient for the following data:

Subject	A	B	C	D	E	F	G	H	I	J
X	5	10	5	11	12	4	3	2	7	1
Y	1	6	2	8	5	1	4	6	5	2

QUESTIONS

A. Short Answer Type Questions

1. Explain the term correlation.
2. Compare Spearman's and Pearson's correlation.
3. Write the uses of Pearson's (r).
4. When do we use (ρ).
5. Explain the formula that we use in computing Pearson's (r) when the data is in bivariate frequency distribution.

B. Objective Questions

1. Correlation indicates cause and effect relationship. True/False
2. Spearman's method of correlation is used for large sample. True/False
3. Spearman's correlation has no assumption. True/False
4. Pearson's correlation is .... correlation.
5. Pearson's (r) is used in regression and prediction. True/False
6. Pearson's correlation indicates:
   (*a*) Ratio correlation (*b*) Curvilinear correlation
   (*c*) Linear correlation (*d*) All the above
7. Pearson's (r) technique is used in:
   (*a*) Ordinal data (*b*) Discrete data
   (*c*) Continuous data (*d*) All the above.

8. Frequency distribution table is used is:
   (*a*) Spearman's (ρ) (*b*) Pearson's (r)
   (*c*) Rank difference method (*d*) All the above
9. Pearson's (r) method is used for small as well as large sample. True/False
10. Correlation is not a ....

11
Individual Differences

No two individuals are alike. They differ in mental abilities, in physique and traits of personality. The differences among individuals are also marked when we consider their cognitive abilities, interests, aptitudes and other behavioural characteristics. Thus it aptly may be stated that each individual is unique in himself. The differences may be slight, moderate or extreme. It indicates that individual cannot be classified either of two extremes however it does not mean that there are no persons at either extreme in the measuring abilities and personality traits. This only shows that when individuals in general are studies, it is found that instead of two opposed direction, there is a continuous gradation from one extreme to the other which shows concentration of individuals about a central point with the frequency of occurrence decreasing as the duration from the central tendency increases. Individuals differ from one another only in degree. Such variations in degree among individuals are always within certain limits and are distributed along a continuum. These variations in physical as well as psychological characteristics of the individuals do not start from an absolute zero nor do they go up to infinity.

Normal Probability Curve or Normal Curve

Differences are normally distributed. If we select a large number of individuals at random from the general population and measure any of their Physical or Psychological characteristics or attributes. We find that the attribute is distributed in special manner. Majority of the people's score are found around the average, with a few people who scored very high and a few scored very low. When we plot these scores graphically a bell-shaped curve is obtained which is called the normal distribution curve or normal probability curve or normal curve. (See figure and its more description in chapter 9).

Individual difference indicates that two individual of the world do not equal with each other even two brother are not similar to each other. This lack of similarity is called individual difference. According to John P. Dececco, "The psychology of individual differences is largely the study of group differences. This study classifies individuals by age, trait, sex, race, social class and so on and observe the differences within and between those groups."

R.S. Woodworth and D.G. Marquis state, "Individual differences are found in all psychological characteristics physical abilities, mental abilities, knowledge, habits, personality and character traits.' We find:

1. Physical differences;
2. Mental differences;
3. Emotional differences;
4. Difference in learning;
5. Differences in special qualities;
6. Differences in interest;
7. Differences in personality traits;
8. Differences in values;
9. Social differences;
10. Differences in character.

Determinants of Individual Differences

There are various factors which cause the individual differences. Following are the important factors that lead to individual differences. The determinants of individual differences are usually divided into two categories viz;

1. Heredity.
2. Environment.

Supporters of heredity view point claim that genetic inheritance determines the differences in individuals, while there are others who advocate that environmental factors like family, school, society and culture influences are the major determinants of individual differences.

Contributions of Heredity

Mechanism of Heredity

It is essential to understand the mechanism of heredity before going to study its contributions in individual differences.

Heredity unquestionably has a significant and considerable influence on individual differences. Individual's height, size of his bones, the complexion and texture of his hair, shape of his face, nose and other parts of the body even the nature of his entire physical and mental structure are largely determined by his inheritance. There are general laws of heredity which explain something about heredity. These laws are:

1. Like begets like;
2. Law of variation;
3. Law of regression.

The general principle of heredity is that children resemble their parents and that 'like' tends to 'beget like' (1st law). The children resemble with both of their parents.

Children differ even within the same family because they do not develop out of the same combination of genes. That is why even in large families complete similar abilities are absent (2nd law).

Third law of regression states that children of bright parents tend to be less bright and the children of very inferior parents are often are less inferior. This law indicates to move towards the average. The heredity of a child is not solely determined by his immediate parents. He inherits from all his forefathers and ancestors also. Reputed psychologist McDougall, is of the opinion that heredity is the main cause of individual differences. It is said that genes are responsible for these differences among individuals.

Contributions of Environments

There are a number of environmental factors that influences the individual throughout his life. We may divide them into four groups.

1. Physical factors;
2. Socio-cultural factor;
3. Economic factors;
4. Psychological factors.

1. *Physical factors:* Physical factors include climate and natural resources. People who live in extreme climatic conditions

undergo a lot of adaptive physiological changes. People living in extreme cold and hot regions, deserts, hilly areas and plains have differences in their height, body built, skin colour, habits and style of living. It has also been observed that the inhabitants of warm countries are lethargic and are not able to have a good health for a long time. On the other hand, people of cold climate are hard working and intelligent.

2. *Socio-cultural factors:* We include in this category family, neighbourhood, school and other social groups, transmission of socio-cultural values, attitudes, prejudices and language etc., the family plays a significant and important role in determining the personality of an individual in particular manner. Child develops interests, attitudes, emotional reaction, moral and ethical values, aspirations, stereotypes and so on while interacting with his parents and other members of the family as well as neighbours. The school has significant role on the development of personality of the child. In the school, teacher serves as substitute for the parents to the satisfaction of all his psychological, sociological and emotional needs. The association and interaction with teachers, students learn a lot from them. It has a great importance in social learning. Teachers serve as role models for their students. All these factors in different interaction and combinations have an influence in producing variations in the personality of individuals.

   In every society, the cultural heritage is passed on from generation to generation by their inhabitants. New invention of that time facilitate the impact of a particular culture on its individuals. The mass media plays an important role in this direction. The impact involves values, ideas, customs, beliefs and faiths through the process of observational learning. The socialization of each individual takes place in different ways. In this ways socio-cultural factors have different influence on individuals in the same society and culture.

3. *Economic factors:* Economic conditions of person influence different aspects of his development viz., physical, mental, social, motivational, cognition language and personality. It also affect school achievement and cognitive development.

It has been found that poverty and malnutrition affect adversely on the development of the children. It also may lead children towards delinquent behaviour. Not only delinquent behaviour pervades in them but other forms of abnormal behaviour such as feeling of alienation, frustration, anxiety and aggression have been marked among the children who live in poor economic status.

4. *Psychological factors:* The personality of an individual is a dynamic organization that determines his unique adjustment with his environment. The abilities to perceive, to think, to imagine, to judge, the reason and to learn all sort of skills are different in each individual which make him unique. His interest are varied. His attitudes, values and ideals are the outcomes of his interaction with his family members and his group members. The differences in psychological factors are important in determining individual differences.

Individual Differences are the Product of Interaction Between Nature of Nurture

The development of personality cannot be solely attributed either to heredity or environment exclusively. It may be stated that individual differences among individual are determined partly heredity and partly environment conditions of the individual to which he is exposed. Individual differences are the product of interaction between nature and nurture. The nature provides the potential or talent and the nurture provides the opportunities for the unfolding of potentialities. It may be stated mathematically like it.

Area of rectangle = base × height or $b \times h$

If we assume that:

Area of rectangle = Development of personality
Base = Heredity
Height = Environment

Therefore, Development of personality = Heredity × Environment.

As a human organism an individual emerges as the product of both biological (heredity) and the socio-cultural environment. There are some important variables which cause differences in two individuals viz., intelligence, aptitude, school achievement and interest. We would like to throw a light on these variables separately:

Intelligence

It has been acknowledged by the educationists, psychologists and teachers that the most important variable that affects academic achievement is intelligence. A lot of studies conducted by the researchers who found that there is a high positive coefficient of correlation between intelligence and school achievement. Not only in school achievements but also in other fields or spheres of human life, intelligence seems to be dominant factor in influencing the success and competence of people. Psychologists have defined intelligence in different ways. Some psychologists interpret intelligence as a general ability or a kind of energy which affects a person's thinking, reasoning, learning and on other psycho-motor activities. Some other psychologists are of the view that it is a composite ability made up of different types of abilities. It may be stated that intelligence is the capacity to acquire and apply knowledge.

The Intelligence Quotient (I.Q.) is accepted to be the measure of intelligence. Alfred Binet introduced the concept of mental age to calculate intelligence quotient.

(i) *Mental age (M.A.):* It is defined as the level of development in mental ability which is characterized to the chronological age at which the individuals on the average reach that level. For example, child of the mental age of 10 reaches the mental level of the group of ten years old on the average. By applying tests of intelligence, the mental age of an individual is estimated.

(ii) *Intelligence Quotient (I.Q.):* It is the indicator of degree of brightness or ability of an individual.

Chronological Age

It is calculated from the date of birth of the individual. We can calculate the I.Q. with this formula:

$$\text{I.Q.} = \frac{\text{M.A.}}{\text{C.A.}} \times 100$$

C.A. = Chronological Age

M.A. = Mental Age

Suppose a child whose C.A. is 15, M.A. is 15, his

$$\text{I.Q.} \ \frac{\text{M.A.}}{\text{C.A.}} \times 100 = \frac{15}{15} \times 100 = 100$$

I.Q. = 100 (average).

Characteristics of I.Q.

1. Generally the mental age differs from the chronological age.
2. Mental age of a person increases with his chronological age but upto certain period of development.
3. I.Q. is expressed as the ratio of the mental age (M.A.) and chronological age (C.A.) multiplied by 100 (for the convenience of calculation).
4. I.Q. indicates the degree of brightness of an individual.
5. I.Q. remains more or less stable throughout one's life with minor fluctuations.
6. I.Q. is considered to be a reliable measure of human intelligence.
7. The I.Q.level of average intelligence has been accepted to be 100. This means when the mental age equals with the chronological age, it indicates average intelligence.
8. The development of intelligence partly depends on genetic constitution and partly on the environmental conditions and the contribution of both is significant.
9. Distribution of I.Q. in the general population confirms the normal probability distribution.
10. Individual differences in intelligence is quantitative rather than qualitative.

Aptitude

It is difficult to define aptitude like intelligence as there are different view points regarding the concept of aptitude. There are psychologists who believe that aptitude refers to one's inherited capacity while others say that aptitude means an individual's present ability for acquisition of some psycho-motor activity. Some psychologists are of the opinion that aptitude means not only one's potentiality, but also refers to the individual's preparedness and suitability for acquiring some skill or occupation.

F.N. Freeman defined, "An aptitude is a combination of characteristics indicative of an individual's capacity to acquire (with training) some specific knowledge, skill or set of organized responses such as ability to speak a language, to become a musician, or to do a mechanical work.

It may be stated that an individuals's aptitude for a particular type of psycho-motor activity indicates the capacity to acquire proficiency under appropriate conditions. It also refers to his potentialities at present as revealed by his performance which too predicts his performance for the future.

Characteristics of Aptitude

1. Aptitude is an inborn capacity affected by the environment of the individual.
2. An aptitude in particular ability facilitates the learning in that ability.
3. Aptitudes are regarded as stable however variations occur within the framework of environmental factors.
4. Aptitudes are pluralistic and not unitary.
5. Individuals differ one from another in their potentialities.
6. An aptitude identified early in life may disappear for the lack of favourable opportunities and the required type of amount of training.

Aptitude Testing

The aptitude of an individual is tested with a view to measure the individual differences in aptitudes. It measures an individual's potential ability in a specialized kind of activities it is revealed by his performances on appropriate standardized tests which have predictive value. According to Freeman, "an aptitude test is given to an individual in order to obtain a measure of his promise or essential teachability in a given area. Now-a-days we have ample of aptitude tests developed by psychologists which are standardized and predict the success of an individual in almost any work or profession in the field of academics, business, industry or any other vocation."

Preparation of Aptitude Tests

There are two methods of preparing aptitude tests:

1. In this method, a particular profession or occupation is studied and analysed with a view to prepare an aptitude test. Thus this analysis enables the test makers to have a list

of items which refers to the various aspects of abilities needed for an occupation. On the basis of this list the aptitude test for that occupation is prepared. This type of test is generally used to select workers in the industry.

2. In this method, the aptitude test maker takes into account the important factors necessary for success in an occupation. The efforts are made to measure the important components of an occupation. It may be stated that independent test are prepared of each important factor involved in a particular occupation. This method has widely been used for the preparation of aptitude tests.

There has been developed various types of aptitude tests to measure the different abilities of the individual.

1. *Aptitude tests of vision and hearing:* Such tests have been prepared to measure the visual and hearing abilities of the individual as these are needed in industrial occupations. Such tests have not so much importance in the field of education.
2. *Motor and manual aptitude test:* This tests measure the individual's motor strength and manual dexterity.
3. *Mechanical aptitude tests:* Mechanical aptitude tests are designed to measure capacity and performance on a higher level of organization than those of sensory motor capacity and dexterity.
4. Musical aptitude tests.
5. Aptitude tests for medicine.
6. Aptitude tests for engineering.
7. Aptitude tests for science.
8. Aptitude tests for numerical ability.

First, the Aptitude tests are used in admitting students in different types of courses or training programmes. Secondly, individuals can be selected for different jobs by administering appropriate tests on them.

Teaching Aptitude Tests

As regards, teaching aptitude test, Freeman is of the opinion that such tests can not be easily devised due to differences in the contents of courses. According to him, "of equal importance with general mental ability and competence in subject-matter to be taught are the personality traits essential in successful teaching." Although the general and professional information and judgements being evaluated are essential for successful teaching.

According to Freeman "A test of aptitude for teaching should include items pertaining to motives for teaching emotional stability, social values, ability to communicate and ability to an establish rapport."

Aptitude tests can also be used to provide guidance to students in choosing their subjects of study and selecting their career in life.

School Achievement

By school achievement we generally means grades, rank of the student in the evaluation of academic subjects. Parents and teachers are always concerned about the achievement of their wards and students at school. In the class there are some high achievers, some low achievers and most of the students are average in their achievement. In other words, it may be stated that there are individual differences in school achievements. This is the reason that the teacher faces problems in maintaining the difficulty level of subject content which is appropriate to meet the ability of everyone in the class.

Achievement of a student is considered to be an outcome or the consequences of individual differences. The difference in ability and performance of the students lead to different levels of achievement. The achievement of the student is the result of the interactions:

(1) Intelligence, (2) Aptitude, (3) Interest, (4) Environment impacts, (5) Miscellaneous factors, (6) Motivation. The environmental factors includes—*(i)* Social status, *(ii)* Economical conditions, and *(iii)* Educational opportunities. The impact of the varied environmental conditions affect the school achievement thereby resulting in varying level of achievements.

Motivation is an important factor, the achievement is directly related with it. Motivation is the heart of learning. It impels the students to work hard to achieve their goals. We may say that:

Performance or achievement $= M \times A \times E$

Here,

M = Motivation

A = Ability

E = Environmental opportunities.

Interest

Interest are those important aspects of personality which affects on the achievement and on efficiency of the students. Most of the psychologists defined interests as pre-occupations, objective, likes and dislikes and motives.

According to William James, "Interest is a form of selective awareness or attention that produces meaning out of the mass of one's experiences."

Berdie defined, "Interests are factors that attract an individual to or repel him from objects, persons and activities."

The operational or experimental approach we most frequently use in the assessment of interests involves a study of the individual's likes and dislikes.

Strong speaks of interest as likes and labels, dislikes as aversions. It is a determinate indicator of success.

From operational view point, it is sufficient to look upon as interests are organism conditions that result in a desire for further stimulation from a particular type of object, idea or experience. It may be expressed that what one enjoys doing indicates one's interest.

Characteristics of Interests

1. Interests are not super final transitory.
2. Interests are being manifested in hobbies.
3. Interests consistently show themselves in the activities of individuals.
4. Interest are deeper traits.
5. Individuals differ among themselves with regard to their interests.
6. The motivation of an individual is influenced by his interest over and above his aptitude and abilities.
7. Interest plays an important role in determining the selection of a career.
8. Interest can be measured.

Measurement of Interests

There are individual difference about what a person enjoys by way of activities and it is very useful in educational and vocational guidance to have the knowledge of the interest of the students. The school counseller may help the student in selecting a career by knowing his/her interests alongwith other abilities. The study of interests was initiated in the area of educational counselling in the 1920's , with the development of strong vocational interest blank by E.K. Strong. Due to pressing needs of vocational selection and classification, several tests of interest have been developed. The measurement of interest is considered to be a great practical significance because a student's or worker's achievement or performance or production depends not only on his/her abilties but also on his/her interest. There are a few interest inventories which have been designed to measure interests of the school students.

1. *Kuder's preference record:* It measures interest in ten general areas.
2. *Stewart and Brainard's specific interest inventories:* There are four forms available, one each for men, boys, women and girls.
3. *Cleeton's vocational interest inventory:* This inventory contains separate forms for men and women.
4. *Strong's vocational interest blank:* It is usually used for individuals who are above 17 years. According to Strong, interests stabilise at this stage.

Factors Influencing Interests

Interest to some extent are innate as well as acquired. The following factors play their role in its development.

1. Physical development.
2. Mental health.
3. Age.
4. Sex.
5. Socio-economic status of the family.
6. Type of rearing practices in the family.
7. Education and training.
8. Opportunities provided for exploring interests.
9. Intelligence.
10. Values and ideals.

A teacher should know the interests of each of his learner early in the school year and teaching–learning process should begin at the point of interest of the child, this can never be accomplished unless their interest are known.

Educational Implications

We have seen how children differ in different aspects. A successful teacher needs to understand that there are inter and intra individual differences. Inter individual differences are differences between two individuals, on the other hand, intra-individual difference deal with the differences within an individual. Besides this as it has been discussed earlier that there are different kinds of individual differences such as physical and physiological differences, differences in ability, aptitudes, interests, personlity traits and emotions. It becomes responsibility of the teacher to understand a child's these different aspects before imparting him educational instructions.

Charles, E. Skinner is of the opinion, "by the time children enter the first grade, differences in abilities are already marked, and absolute variations become more pronounced as they progress. Whatever, the reasons for these diversities, the fact is that the school should deal with them by means of differentiated curricula and individualized instruction as far as possible."

He further states that the provision for individual differences does not end here but there are appreciable differences in aptitude. Here role of the teacher becomes more important, he is to provide means of instruction that will meet pupils special needs. It is a major task of the schools to discern and cultivate superior and creative intellects and to bring the subnormal to their maximum levels of effectiveness. This indicates that educational instructions should differ according to various age levels. This means that due emphasis should be given on human variability i.e., in the content and methods of teaching–learning process.

Ability Differences and Teaching

Tracking

When whole classes are formed based on ability, the process is called between-class ability grouping or tracking. This system of grouping in which students are assigned to classes based on their measured ability or their achievements. This seems to be an efficient way to teach. Researches have shown that segregation by ability may benefit high achieving students, but causes problems for low achieving students (Garm & Nystrand, 1995).

Drawbacks

1. Low-ability class tend to get lower-quality instruction in general.

2. Teachers stress lower-level objectives and routine procedure with less academic focus.
3. There are more student behaviour problems.
4. Students problems increase, teacher stress and decrease enthusiasm.

Untracking

There has been a movement for untracking. It means redesigning schools to teach students in classes that are not grouped by ability i.e., teaching all students in mixed ability groups but providing extra help for those who struggle and enrichment for those who learn quickly (Corno, 1995). Jeannic Oakes and Army Wells (2002) described several different ways to teach effectively in secondary schools withcut tracking.

1. Eliminate remedial courses and have one regular and one advanced track.
2. Often honours assignment options or challenge pull-out activities within each course.
3. Require all students to take a common core of classes, then allow self–selection into advanced classess after the core.
4. Encourage minority group students to enroll advanced placement courses.
5. Provide additional times during inter-cessions when struggling students can get extra help.
6. Providing tutoring before and after school.
7. Staff a homework help centre with teachers, parents and community volunteers.
8. Instead of 'dumbing down' content, teach students learning strategies for dealing with difficult material.

Not everyone agrees that untracking is a good idea. This movement has been more successful at the elementary than secondary level.

Non-Graded Elementary School/The Joplin Plan

In the Joplin plan, students stay in their regular mixed ability grade level classes but are regrouped across grade levels for reading. Here the arrangements wherein students are grouped by ability in particular subjects regardless of their ages or grades.

Within-Class Ability Grouping

Many elementary school classes are grouped for reading and same are grouped for maths, even though there is no clear evidence that this grouping is superior to other approaches. However, thoughtfully constructed and well taught ability groups can be effective. But other approaches such as co-operative learning may also be available too. Many psychologists and even people are strongly against ability grouping of any kind. But its success depends upon the resourcefulness of the teachers.

Attention Towards the Special Aptitude and Interest of the Children

Teachers should pay their attention towards the aptitude and interest of their pupils. They should provide opportunities and congenial environment to their children so that their aptitude may come up and interest may develop accordingly.

Socio-economic Status

SES plays significant role and this factor can never be ignored while educating the children. Each student irrespective of his SES should be provided opportunities for his development.

New Teaching Methods

Various studies have been conducted in the field of teaching methods keeping in view of the individual differences. There are several techniques which have been used to make the learner understand the contents of the subject. These plans or approaches are:

1. *Winnetka plan:* This plan was introduced by Washburne in the school of Winnetka.
2. *Dalton plan:* It was introduced by Miss Helen Parkhurst at Dalton. The main principles underlying plan are—freedom, co-operation and allocation of time.
3. *Morrison plan:* It was devised by H.C. Morrison of Chicago University is based on direct guidance and stresses unit assignment.
4. *Project method:* This method was devised by Kilpatrick in this method few problem are given to solve on their own.

QUESTIONS

A. Long Answer Type Questions

1. Explain the concept of individual differences. State their educational implications.
2. Discuss the cause of individual differences. Describe its dimensions.

3. Suggest suitable guidelines for meeting the needs of individual differences.
4. What do you understand by individual differences? What are the factors responsible for them? Why do we study individual differences in education?

B. Short Answer Type Questions

1. Individual differences in intelligence.
2. Heredity and intelligence.
3. Ability grouping.
4. The Japlin plan.
5. Tracking and untracking.

C. Objective Questions

1. Environment + Heredity play important role in individual differences. True/False
2. Heredity is not the cause of individual difference. True/False
3. Environment is only the determinant of individual differences. True/False
4. Individual differences in intelligence are normally distributed. True/False
5. No two individual are alike. True/False

SUGGESTED READINGS

1. Anastasi Anne, "Individual Differences" John Wiley & Sons, Inc., 1965.
2. Anastasi and Foley, "Differential Psychology."
3. Freeman F.S., "Individual Differences", New York, Henry Holt & Company Inc., 1934.
4. Freeman, F.S. "Theory and Practice of Psychological Testing", Rev. ed., New York, Henry Holt & Company, Inc., 1955.
5. Skinner, C.E., "Educational Psychology", 4th ed., Prentice Hall Inc., New Jersey, 1959.
6. Tyler, L.E., "The Psychology of Human Differences", rev. ed, New York, Appleton Century Craft Inc., 1956.

12

Intelligence and Aptitude

Everybody is interested to know about the meaning, definition and concept of intelligence. Several attempts have been made in the past to define intelligence as it is an ambiguous and controversial concept. Undoubtedly intelligence is the capacity of the individual to solve problems, to adjust to new situations, and think rationally etc. However, in this connection, psychologists may be categorized in three groups according to their viewpoints. Psychologists who believe in: (1) Intelligence is the ability to adjust, (2) Intelligence is the ability to learn and (3) Intelligence is the ability of abstract thinking.

Intelligence is the Ability to Adjust

One group of psychologists emphasises on adjustment or adaptation of the individual to his total environment, or to some limited aspects of it. Accordingly intelligence is general mental adaptability to new problems and new situations of life. Or, otherwise stated, it is the capacity to reorganise one's behaviour patterns so as to act more effectively and more appropriately in novel situations. Thus, the more intelligent person is one who can more easily and more extensively vary his behaviour as changing conditions demand.

Some of the definitions of the psychologists who belong to this category are as follow:

Cyril Burt, "Intelligence is the capacity for flexible adjustment."

Pintner, "Intelligence is the ability of the individual to adapt himself adequately to relatively new situations in life."

Stern, "Intelligence is a general capacity of an individual consciously to adjust his thinking to new requirements."

Wells, "Intelligence is the power of recombining our behaviour patterns as to act better in novel situations."

Intelligence is the Ability to Learn

A second type of definition states that intelligence is the ability to learn. Accordingly, a more intelligent individual who readily and extensively is able to learn more easily, readily and extensively as compared to the others.

Ebbinghaus, "Intelligence is the ability to continue the element of experience or it is the integrative ability."

Buckingham, "Intelligence is the ability to learn."

Intelligence as the Ability to Carry on Abstruct Thinking

This indicates the effective use of concepts and symbols in dealing with situations especially those problems to be solved through the use of verbal and numercial symbols.

Terman, "Intelligence is the ability to think in terms of abstract ideas."

Ryburn, "Intelligence is the power which enables to solve problems and to achieve purposes."

Munn, "Intelligence is the flexibility on versatility in the use of symbolic processes."

Binet, "Intelligence is the ability to judge well, to comprehend well, and to reason well. These three are the essential qualities of intelligence."

Two Comprehensive Definitions (Wechsler and Stoddard)

1. *David Wechsler,* "Intelligence is the aggregate or global capacity of the individual to act purposefully, to think rationally and to deal effectively with his environment."
   If we analyse this definition, we find that it encompasses all the definitions. (Three types of definitions defined by the different group of psychologists as mentioned above.)

This definition states that an individual's intelligence is revealed by his behaviour as a whole (global) and that intelligence involves behaviour towards a goal, which may be more or less immediate (purposefully). The second aspect includes the effective dealing with the environment. This shows, more the individual is intelligent the more his/her behaviour shall be adjusting with the environment.

Third category is included in this definition that the intelligent behaviour of the individual is based on rational thinking.

2. *Stoddard defines intelligence as,* "The intelligence is the ability to undertake activities that are characterised by (1) difficulty, (2) complexity, (3) abstractness, (4) economy, (5) adaptiveness to a goal, (6) social value and (7) emergence of originals and to maintain such activities under conditions that demand a concentration of energy and a resistance to emotional forces.

This definition in fact also includes the first three types of definitions presented earlier but it goes more than them in several respects. The author specifies several attributes of intelligence.

Kinds of Intelligence

E.L.Thorndike has divided intelligent activity into three types:

1. *Social intelligence:* Ability to understand and deal with persons.
2. *Concrete intelligence:* Ability to understand and deal with things as in skilled trades and scientific appliances.
3. *Abstract intelligence:* Ability to understand and deal with verbal and mathematical symbols.

Of the three kinds of abilities enumerated above, abstract intelligence is one that receives greatest weight and is the most pronounced in current test of intelligence.

Theories of Intelligence or Analysis of Mental Ability

The definitions of intelligence are functional in character i.e., how intelligence operates. But in addition, psychologists have been concerned to know the structure of intelligence. They have analysed intelligence to determine its underlying factors.

The Multifactor Theory

This theory was propounded by E.L. Thorndike. According to him intelligence is a magnitude of atoms of mental ability. This theory is also called atomistic. Any mental act involves a number of these minute elements operating together. Any other mental act also involves a number of elements in combination. Hence, if performances on these two mental tasks are positively correlated, the degree of correlation is due to the number of common elements or atoms involved in the two acts.

Thorndike distinguished four attributres of intelligence.

(a) *Level* : This attribute refers to the difficulty of a task that can be solved. Tests items are arranged in sequential order of increasing difficulty. To what extent we solve the difficulty level of items determine our level of intelligence.

(b) *Range:* It refers to the number of tasks at any given degree of difficulty that we can solve. In intelligence tests, range is represented by items of equal difficulty we cannot measure level without range.

(c) *Area:* It means the total number of situations at each level to which an individual is able to respond. Area is the summation of all ranges at each level of intelligence processed by an individual.

(d) *Speed:* This refers to the rapidity with which we can respond to test items. Speed and level are positively correlated.

According to this theory, there is no such factor as general intelligence, there are only many highly specific acts. Thorndike adds that certain mental activities have so many of their elements in common that it is useful to classify these tasks into separate groups to which special names are given e.g. (1) Verbal meaning, (2) Arithmetical reasoning, (3) Comprehension, and (4) Visual perception of relationship. Thorndike designed a test to measure intelligence with is composed of four parts. Sentence Completion (c), Arthmetic reasoning (A), Vocabulary (V) and Following Directions (D). This instrument is known as the CAVD test. However, it has not been claimed that these four sets of items encompass the entire range of abstract intelligence.

The Two Factors Theory

Spearman is the author of this theory. It is opposed to Thorndike's theory of the nature of intelligence which stands at the other extreme of interpretation. In 1904, Spearman published his theory of general intelligence. He described general intelligence which he called 'g', as a kind of well or spring of mental energy that flows into everything that the individual does. After establishing the foundation of general intelligence 'g', he turned to the question of special abilities. Spearman hypothesized that 'g' factor is found into various activities in different degrees. The different manifestations of the general intelligence of specific activities are called 'S' factor. We may say that general intelligence 'g' is the fountain of a spring from which specific abilites flow like stream of water into different thought processes.

Thus, the two factors theory states that all mental activities have in common some of the general factors, each mental activity might also be a member of a group and each has also its own specific factor. The practical implications of this theory is clear so far as test construction is concerned. A test conforming to this theory would be one whose materials and several parts are saturated with the general factors, so that measurement thereby would cause other testee's level and quality of 'g' to emerge, while the specific factor (s) would be cancelled out. His logic was (see Figure 12.1).

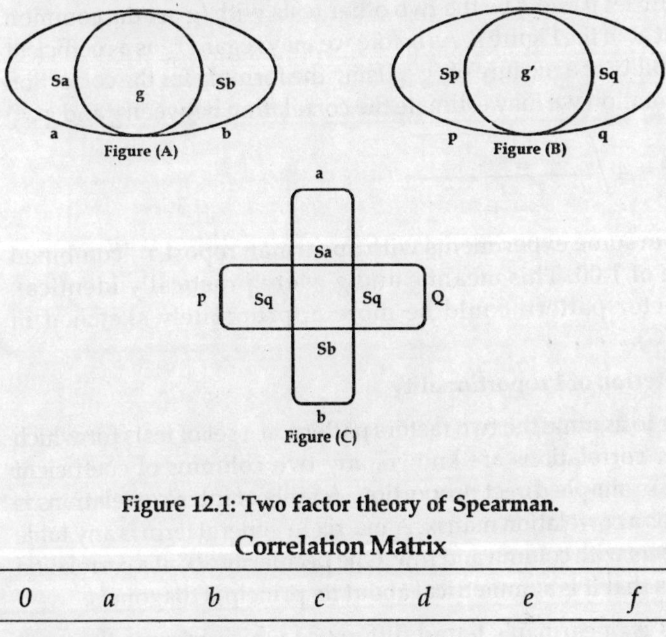

Figure 12.1: Two factor theory of Spearman.

Correlation Matrix

0	*a*	*b*	*c*	*d*	*e*	*f*
Zero		.40	.10	.45	.30	.35
B	.40		.16	.72	.48	.56
C	.10	.16		.18	.12	.14
D	.45	.72	.18		.54	.53
E	.30	.48	.12	.54		.42
F	.35	.56	.14	.63	.42	

The criteria of proportionality require.

First we may assumme that any correlation between two tests implies a factor common to both plus two specific factors as indicated in the Figure 'A'.

Let the two tests be called *a* and *b*, the common factor 'g' and the two specific factors S_a and S_b as shown in the diagram, we may then regard test *a* and *b* as two measures of the common element 'g' with the two remainders S_a and S_b. Since *a* and *b* are measures of the same ability we may look upon the r_{ab} as a coefficient of reliability.

Now let *p* and *q* be the two other tests with 'g' as the common element as in the Figure B. As before we may regard r_{pq} as a coefficient of reliability of a meaure of 'g'. Using the formula for the correction of attenuation we may estimate the correlation between *g* and *g'*.

$$r_{gg'}^{\ 2} = \sqrt[4]{\frac{r_{ap}\, r_{aq}\, r_{bp}\, r_{bq}}{r_{ab}\, r_{pq}}}$$

From some experiments with Spearman report r_{gg} 'combined a value of 1.00. This meant *g* and *g'* were practically identical. This factor pattern could be more appropriately sketched in Figure (C).

The Criterion of Proportionality

In order to assume the two factors pattern in a set of tests for which the inter correlations are known, any two columns of coefficient must be in simple direct proportion. A table of inter-correlations is known as a correlation matrix. A matrix in general term is any table of numbers with column and row. One pecularity about a correlation matrix is that it is symmetrical about its principal diagonals.

This is Spearman's tetrad difference which became the most acceptable criterion of the two factors pattern. If it is computed for other it will be noted that all the tetrad differences are zero.

The criteria of proportionality require:

$$\frac{r_{ac}}{r_{bc}} = \frac{r_{ad}}{r_{bd}} = \frac{r_{ac}}{r_{be}} = \frac{r_{af}}{r_{bf}}$$

$$\frac{r_{ac}}{r_{bc}} \times \frac{r_{ad}}{r_{bd}} = \frac{.10}{16} \times \frac{.45}{.72} = r_{ac} \cdot r_{bd} = r_{bc} \cdot r_{ad}$$

$$=.\,10 \times .72 = .16 \times .45 = .072 = 0.72 - .072 = 0$$

Characteristics of 'g' Factor

Spearman was of the opinion that 'g' factor which is present in all the mental or intellectual activities. Followings are its characteristic:

1. The 'g' factor is ominipresent.
2. This is hereditary.
3. It varies from individual to individual.
4. It is gifted and remain constant.
5. It is a kind of energy of the individual which may be transferred from one mental operations to the other and plays an important role in a variety of performances.
6. It is intelligence or mental energy which the intelligence tests measure.
7. High degree of 'g' factor guarantees a good quality and quantity of performance and success.

Characteristics of 'S' Factor

1. It is present in special activities only.
2. It also varies in the individuals.
3. A person would be expert according to the properties of specific factor in him.
4. A high degree of 'S' factor guarantees a high degree of performancc and success in that very activity.
5. There are a large numbers of specific abilities such as verbal, numerical, perceptional and memory etc.
6. All these abilities presuppose a general ability without which they cannot function.
7. An individual may have any number of these specific abilities although it may vary.

Spearman himself modified his theory by adding to it certain group factors, less general widely spread and homogenous than 'G' and 'S' factors which he called it later group factor theory of intelligence.

Sampling Theory of Mental Ability

The two factors theory has been criticized by some psychologists notably G.H. Thomson and L.L.Thurstone. Thomson offers a sampling theory to explain the same tables of inter-correlations. His view is that the coefficients of correlations are the results of common sampling and combinations of independent factors. The number of common independent factors utilized by two tests will determine the coefficient of correlation between these two. This theory is the

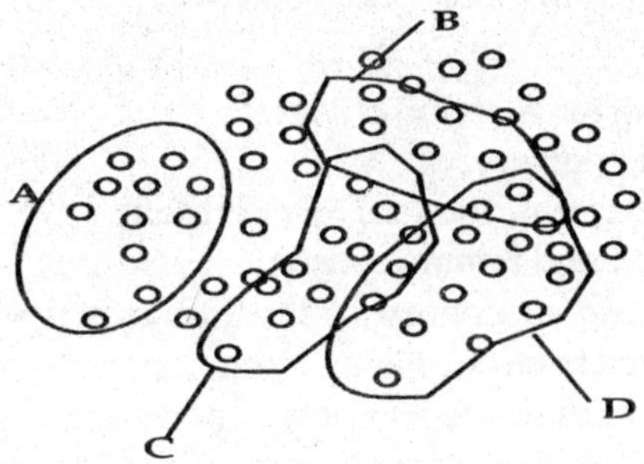

Figure 16.2 : Thomson's Sampling Theory.

same as that of Thorndike except that Thomson concedes the practical usefulness of a concept like 'g'. This theory is shown graphically.

Each small circle represents a unit of ability which through very limited in scope may enter into a great variety of performances. He believes in a general ability like Spearman but it is not basic entity. Both theories (Spearman and Thomson) require that a scale measuring general mental ability should pool a variety of tests that differ in content and mental processes employed. The two factors theory requires subtests (part of the scale) that have high inter correlations. The sampling theory requires subtests having low inter correlations among themselves but high correlation with the criterion of validity.

Group Factor Theory

Intermediate between theories of Thorndike and Spearman are group factor theories. Prominent among them is that of Thurstone. His work resulted in the construction of a set of measures called *Tests of Primary Mental Abilities.*

According to the group factor theory, intelligent activity is not an expression of immediate highly specific factors as Thorndike claimed nor is it the expression of primarily of a general factor that pervades in all mental activities and is the essence of intelligence as Spearman held. According to Thurstone certain mental operations have in common a primary factor that gives them psychological and functional unity which differentiates them from other mental operations.

There are a number of groups of mental abilities, each of which has its own primary factor, giving the group a functional unity and cohesiveness. Thurstone and his collaborator concluded that seven primary factors emerged clearly enough for identification and use in test design and constructions.

1. *The number factor (N):* Ability to do numericals rapidly and accurately.
2. *The verbal factor (V):* Found in verbal comprehension.
3. *The space factor (S):* Any task in which the subject manipulates an object imaginally in space.
4. *The word fluency factor (W):* To think of isolated words at a rapid rate.
5. *The reasoning factor (R):* The subject puts his ideas and expression with a reason.
6. *The rote memory (M):* The ability to memorise quickly.
7. *The perceptual speed (P):* The subject keenly and quickly observe the hidden ideas in a situation.

Thurstone devised a battery of tests to measure each of these abilities called *Test of Primary Mental Abilities.*

Hierarchical Theory of Intelligence

(i) C. Burt propounded a theory of intelligence which emphasises that there is a kind of hierarchy between various types of mental abilities. This theory assumes that there are four levels of mental processes:

1. *Sensory motor level (SM):* This is the lowest level of mental process and possesses sensations and simple movements.
2. Perceptions (P) and coordinated movement (C) are at second level in their hierarchy.
3. The third level is known as the associative level and it is connected with the functions of memory (M) and habit formation (H).
4. That fourth and the highest level refers to cognitive and aesthetic aspect of intelligence. It contains: (1) Relations finding and (2) Applying. Burt regards intelligence as the integrative capacity of the mind and state that is to be found at all the four levels.

(ii) Vernon also believes in hierarchical theory but in a different way. He proposed that elements of 'G' factor theory and the multifactor theories be combined to form a hierarchical

theory. In such a theory, intelligence is pictured as sort of Pyramid. At the top of the pyramid is 'G' (general intelligence) which shows up in virtually all kinds of intellectual activity. Underneath it, are several moderately specific ability factors like Thurstone's primary mental abilities. At the bottom of the pyramid are a larger number of highly specific abilities, similar to Spearman's 'S' factor abilities that may come into play on one particular task. This hierarchical theory borrows from several factor theories to form a multilayered view of intelligence.

Cattell's Theory of Intelligence

The factor analytic approach to the study of individual differences in intelligence and personality is R.B. Cattel who is considered as the leading American exponent. Cattel believes that his modification of the Spearman and Thurstone techniques provides evidence for two fundamental types of intelligence. Both of which are underlying general order factors. These are: (1) Crystallized intelligence and (2) Fluid intelligence.

Fluid intelligence is the capacity for insight into complex relationships. In other words, it may be stated that it is the capacity for acquiring new concepts and demonstrating general brightness and adaptability in novel situations. Resultantly Fluid intelligence is relatively independent of education and test that measure it minimize scholastic training and cultural factors. Crystallized intelligence is a combination of acquired knowledge and developed intellectual skills. In Cattell's own terminology it is the investment of Fluid intelligence in the higher level skills of the culture in which the individual is exposed. Cattell and his associates developed a culture fair test of intelligence that show high positive loadings (-0.48 to + 0.78) on the fluid intelligence dimension in factor analysis studies and low negative loading (-0.02 to -0.11) on the Crystallized intelligence dimension. The culture fair test makes use of perceptual relations items consisting of geometric forms in which the testee's answer must be developed as a logical deduction or correlate from given relationship. Theoretically tests of this kind are culture fair in the sense that they do not draw upon educational achievement and minimize difference in performance that are the result of culture factors.

Jenson's Two Level Theory of Intelligence

Arthur Jenson (1969-1970) has suggested that intellectual functioning consists of—(1) associative abilities and cognitive abilities, both are largely hereditary. Associative abilities are those that associate certain stimuli and events. The short-term memory and information task on I.Q.tests are associative. Cognitive abilities are those that deal with reasoning and problem solving. Jenson claims that these two abilities are inherited.

Intelligence as a Process

An alternative approach has been taken by several influential theorists who focus on intellectual processes, the patterns of thinking that people use when they reason and solve problems. They used somewhat different vocabulary and often spoke of cognition and cognitive processes rather than intelligence. They are often more interested in how people go about solving problems and figuring out answers than in how many right answers people get. They also tend to focus on the development of intellectual processes.

(i) *Piaget's theory:* Jean Piaget is a particularly prominent process theorist. In his view, intelligence is an adaptive process that involves an interplay of biological maturation and interaction with the environment. He views intellectual development as an evolution of cognitive process such as understanding the laws of nature, the principles of grammar and mathematical rules.

(ii) *Bruner's theory:* Jerome Bruner is also a process theorist who seeks intellectual development partly as a growing reliance an internal representation. Babies have a highly action oriented form of intelligence, they know an object only to the extent that they can act on it. Young children know things through perception and are influenced by their vivid perceptual characteristics of objects and events. Older children and adolescents know things internally. Conceptually and symbolically. Bruner was interested in how these growing abilities are influenced by the environment, especially by the rewards and punishments people receive for using particular intellectual skills in particular ways.

Theories of Spearman and Cattell tend to describe how individual differ in content of intelligence and in different abilities.

Recent work in cognitive psychology has emphasised, how do humans gather and use information to solve problems and behave intelligently. Robert Sternberg's (1985-1990) *Triarchic theory of intelligence* is a cognitive process approach to understand intelligence. This theory has three parts – analytic, creative and practical.

1. *Analytic/componential intelligence:* Involves the mental processes of the individual that lead to more or less intelligent behaviour. These processes are defined in terms of components – elementary information processes that are classified by the functions they serve and by how general they are: Meta components perform higher-order functions such as planning, strategy, selection and monitoring. Executing the strategies selected is handled by performance components. Gaining new knowledge is performed by knowledge acquisition components.
2. *The second part of Sternberg's Triarchic theory creative/ experimental intelligence:* Involves coping with new experiences. Intelligence behaviour is marked by two characteristics: (1) *Insight:* or the ability to deal effectively with novel situations and (2) *Automaticity:* It is the ability to become efficient and automatic in thinking and problem solving.
3. *The third part of Triarchic theory is practical/contextual intelligence:* Highlights the importance of choosing to live and work in a context where success is likely adapting to the context and reshaping it if necessary.

Practical intelligence is made up mostly of action–oriented tacit knowledge. This type of knowledge is learned during everyday life than through formal schooling.

Guilford's Structure of Intellect Model (S-I Model)

J.P. Guilford founded that both Spearman an Thurstone's model of intelligence are imcomplete. He suggested that in any intelligent act there are three elements, viz: 1. Contents, 2. Operations, and 3. Products. The individual is first presented with the content of a problem, which become in subject of his mental operations and then in turn, produce certain products. Guilford recognizes four sub-categories under the content category, five under the operations category and six under that of products. These sub-categories are given below:

Contents	*Operations*	*Products*
1. Figural	1. Cognition	1. Units
2. Semantic	2. Memory	2. Classes
3. Symbolic	3. Divergent thinking	3. Relations
4. Behavioural	4. Convergent thinking	4. Systems
	5. Evaluations	5. Transformations
	6. Implications.	

Contents

1. *Figural* content refers to the utilization of pictures or images.
2. *Symbolic*-content is largely mediated through numbers and letters.
3. *Semantic* content is referred through verbal meaning.
4. *Behavioural* content is meant by interpreting anothers behaviour (Social intelligence).

Operations

1. *Cognitions* refers to the awareness of the meaning of words or concepts.
2. *Memory:* It refers to the ability to retain information.
3. *Convergent thinking:* It is the ability to come to valid or logical conclusion on the basis of given pieces of information.
4. Divergent thinking is essentially a creativity.
5. *Evaluation:* It is a judgement of the behaviour.

Products

1. *Units:* Units are single products such as word or number.
2. *Classes:* Refers to a class of unit such as noun, a species.
3. *Relations* are relationship between units such as similarities or difference.
4. *Systems* refer to plan or systems for actions.
5. *Transformation* involves a change.
6. *Implications* involves making a prediction.

Since there are 4 contents, 5 operation and 6 products, the resulting combinations involve total of 120 ($4 \times 5 \times 6 = 120$), as shown in Figure 12.3. All these mental elements (120) can all interact with each other.

For the teacher, the importance of this model lies in the fact that where a child fails to solve a particular item, the failure can be ascribed to one or other of the sub-categories or to the interaction between them. The child might be unable to cope with the symbols or the semantics involved in the contents of with the memory task or the evaluation involved in the operation, or with the units or the systems in the products. Obviously, a teacher cannot spend time to diagnose the failure of each student in his class, but this model has the virtue of directing the attention of the teacher towards the likely variables creating difficulty and therefore he can help or assist to solve an intellectual problem.

Guilford's concept of intelligence means convergent thinking which is involved in solving problems with a single correct answer as opposed to divergent thinking which is closely related to creative or original problem solving.

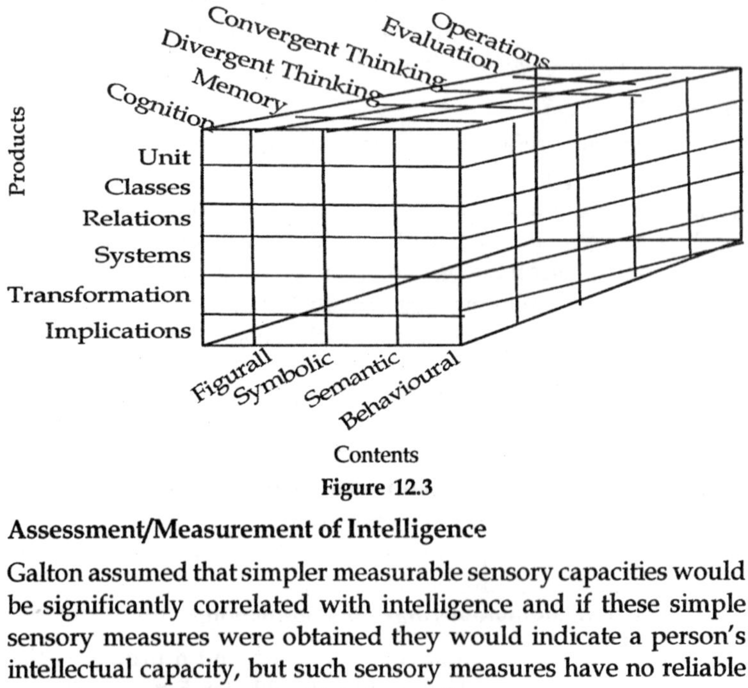

Figure 12.3

Assessment/Measurement of Intelligence

Galton assumed that simpler measurable sensory capacities would be significantly correlated with intelligence and if these simple sensory measures were obtained they would indicate a person's intellectual capacity, but such sensory measures have no reliable value for evaluation of the higher complex processes.

The relatively simple tests have low inter-correlations ranging generally from zero to 20 as such they have no predictive value with academic performance. In Binet's early work, he used tests of tactual discrimination, reaction time, visual discrimination and so on.

Classification of Test

Intelligence test are of two kinds – 1. Verbal and 2. Non-verbal or we may also call them as (1) Linguistic or Non-linguistic. The verbal or linguistic tests require the knowledge and use of language while the non-verbal or non-linguistic test do not require the knowledge or use of language and subjects are asked to perform something only through the manipulation.

We can also classify intelligence tests in the following ways:

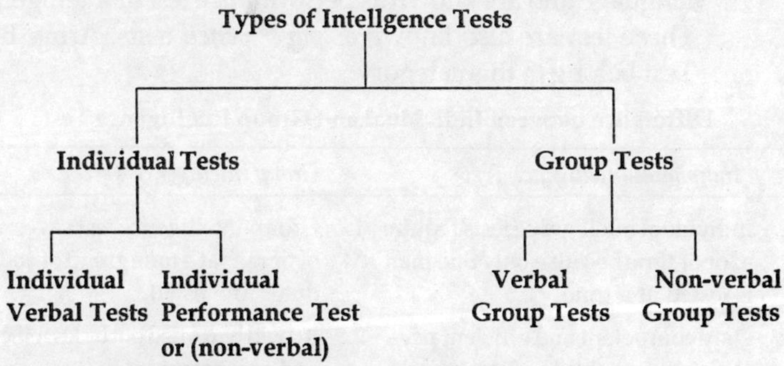

Individual Test (Verbal or Linginstic Tests)

As explained above, such tests require the knowledge and use of language. Individual (Non-verbal or Non-linguistic test) such tests do not require the knowledge or use of language, subjects are asked to perform something only through manipulation.

(i) *Individual test:* These tests are given to one invidual at a time. The Binet-Simon tests of Intelligence belongs to this category. The tests were revised by Terman and Merrill in America and Cyril Burt revised them in England.

(ii) *Individual performance:* Individual is instructed to perform test of non-verbal activity.

Group Intelligence Tests

In 1914, during the First World War, group intelligence test was introduced in America. An able minded and intelligent soldiers were required. In order to find such persons Psychologists constructed intelligent tests which may measure the level of intelligence. Two types of group intelligence tests were constructed:

(a) *Army alpha intelligence test:* This test was intended for the persons who knew English.

(b) *Army beta intelligence test:* This test was meant for those who were foreigner or not knowing English. He could not read or write English. It is consisted of a variety of diagram and pictures.

Group Test

When a group of subjects are tested at the same time. It is a groupt test.

(i) *Verbal group tests:* These type of test involve the use of language. Such as Army Alpha test.

(ii) *Non-verbal group tests:* These tests do not involve the use of language and are known as performance test of intelligence. These test are also known as *paper pencil* tests. Army Beta Test belong to this category.

Difference between Individual and Group Intelligence Test

Individual Intelligence Test	*Group Intelligence Test*
1. Individual intelligence tests require a lot of time because only one man is tested at a time.	1. Group intelligence test saves a lot of time as at a time group of individuals are tested.
2. Only competent and efficient psychologists are able to administer the test.	2. It could be carried out by less efficient and competent.
3. Language, knowledge and practical aspect play a vital role.	3. In Group tests such situations do not crop up.
4. It is costly to apply.	4. It is economical.
5. It requires a lot of rapport to establish.	5. It does not require so much rapport.
6. Construction of individual Intelligence Test is difficult.	6. It is a bit easy to construct.
7. Result are more reliable and valid.	7. It is not so to that extent.

Performance Tests

These tests are useful in asertaining and judging intelligence of illiterate deaf, dumb and blind people. These test may also conducted on other people too.

Early Work of Binet–Simon Scales

The Binet–Simon Scale of 1905

The first scale was devised to identify mentally deficient children in a school in Paris. The principle is that we may identify mental differences in degree of brightness or dullness with differences in levels of development as represented by the average capacities of children of various ages. Thirty items in order of increasing difficulty were included in this scale. This set of lists was not separated into age groups. The children were regarded as normal on the basis of the fact that they were in grades just right for their ages. The scale enabled Binet and Simon to classify idiots, imbeciles and morons in a more objective manner than it had been possible earlier.

The Binet-Simon Scale of 1908

The defects of the above scale were recognised and it was thought that an improved scale would have to be provided more valid norms, based upon a larger and more representative sampling of children at each age. Consequently in this scale the items were grouped at the appropriate age levels from 3 years to 13 years. This test contained 59 items.

The 1911 Revision of the Binet-Simon Scale

The major changes incorporated in the 1911 scale were the following:

1. Four of the tests at the 11 year-level were raised to the 12-year level.
2. All 12-year tests were raised to the 15 year level.
3. The three tests of years 13, plus two new ones constituted the new adult level.

Some of the test were omitted because they seemed to depend too much on school learning or an incidental information.

Early Revisions of Binet-Simon Scale

The two most widely known and used adaptations of the Binet scale in the United States were the stanford revision of 1916 and 1937.

The Stanford Revision of 1916

The Stanford Revision of the Binet-Simon Intelligence Scale is derived from the fact that the revision was made at Stanford University under the direction of L.M. Terman. This was standardized and adapted adequately for use in U.S. The 1916 scale includes 90 test items, covering an age range from 3-14 years, with a group of test items added at the average adult level and another at the superior adult level.

Scoring Method

Each age level, from 3 years through 10, has six items (plus the alternate which may replace one of the six). Each of these carries credit of two months so that the test in each of the age level provides an year's increment in mental age.

There are no tests at the 11 years level, the reason being that the authors of the scale were unable to devise test that would indicate a one year difference at this stage of mental development since the eight test items at age 12 cover a span of two years each and carries a credit of three months in order to yield an average mental age of 12, when added to the 10 years level.The same explanation applied to the six test items at the age 14, each of which gives a credit of four months towards mental age score as there is no test at the 13 years level.

The method of scoring the 1916 scale is as follows: The examiner goes downwards in the test until the level is reached where the subject passes all items. This is called 'Basal age' or 'basal year'. The examiner then proceeds upward in the scale until the level is reached where the subject fails all items. This level is called the 'terminal year' or 'ceiling age'. Each listed item carries specified credit in terms of months, contributing to the mental age score. These credits are added to the age value of the basal year/basal age and the total obtained in the mental age.

Classification of IQs: Stanford Binet Scale 1916

IQ	*Classification*
Above 140	'Near' genius or genius
120–140	Very superior intelligence
110–119	Superior intelligence
90–109	Normal or average intelligence
80–89	Dullness
70–79	Borderline deficiency
Below 70	Definite feeble mindedness

Adult Mental Age and Adult IQ

1916 Stanford Binet scale includes test at the levels of average adult and superior adult. It was mandatory to make provisions for computing adult mental ages and intelligence quotient. Terman's reasons is for locating average adult performance in the mental age ranges of 15 to 17 with the assumed mid-point at 16 years. It indicates that the test performance of the average adult is equal to that of the average old individual until the process of decline sets in the average adult continues to have a mental age of 16, according to the 1916 Stanford Binet. On the basis of this assumption then, in the computation of an I.Q. for a person who is 16 years of age or older the denomination in the formula is as follows:

Here $IQ = \frac{MA}{CA}$

M.A. = Mental Age

C.A. = Chronological age or actual age.

By taking his Mental Age (M.A.) always as 16, if his Actual Age (C.A.) was used, he would appear to be getting less and less intelligent with the succeeding years.

The Standard Binet Scale 1937 and 1960 Rivision

The 1937 Scale

This scale is different from that of 1916 in many details, but it doesn't differ in its essential and basic conceptions. The principal differences and modifications are as stated below:

1. The 1937 scale has two equivalent form (L & M), each of this contains 129 test items as compared to the 90 items in the first Stanford Binet.
2. The 1937 scale extends downward to the level of age 2, and upward through three levels of superior adult (known as superior Adult I, II, III thus increasing its usefulness.
3. The levels below age 5 and those above age 14 have been more carefully and validly standardized.
4. Scoring standards and instructions for administering the test are improved.
5. Group of tests are provided at age 11 and 13.

Mental Age and Intelligence Quotient

The scoring method is the same as that used with the 1916 scales. A few differences.

1. Whereas the maximum mental age attainable on the 1916 Stanford Binet was 19 years, 6 months, the maximum on the 1937 revision was 22 years and 1 month.
2. In the 1937 scale the maximum C.A. in the denominator was 15 as compared to 1916 scale in which is was altogether 16.

The 1960 Revision

The 1960 revision was an improved version of the 1937 scales (L & M) with the introduction of an important innovation i.e., deviation intelligence quotient. Second innovation was that the I.Q. labels were extended to include chronological age 17 and 18.

Basically the deviation I.Q. of the 1960 scale is a standard score derived from a mean of 100 and a standard deviation of 16. The deviation I.Q. is calculated by the use of the following formula:

$$DIQ = (IQ\times - IQm)\,K + 100$$

Where $K = 16/SD$

IQ × is the conventional i.e. $\frac{MA}{CA} \times 100$

IQm is the mean I.Q. at the age in question.

Deviation I.Q. (DIQ) = A standard IQ test score that has the same mean and standard deviation at all ages. The deviation I.Q. replaced the traditional MA/CA formula and it is a type of standard score i.e. an I.Q. expressed in standard deviation units.

Calculation of DIQ = The first step is to calculate, in actual raw scores, how far an individual's score deviates from the average. We can express this score through a formula:

$$\text{Standard Score} = \frac{X - M}{SD}$$

Where X = The individual's score, M = mean, S.D. = Standard deviation.

Wechsler Test

David Wechsler developed a family of tests for people at various age levels.

1. Wechsler Adult Intelligence Scale (Revised WAIS-R 1981).
2. The Wechsler Preschool and Primary Scale of Intelligence (WPPS, 1967).

Wechsler Intelligence Scale for Children

These are all individual tests made up of variety of tasks. They don't have separate levels for different ages. Instead, all the tasks of a single kind are grouped together in a sub-test. Wechsler hypothesized that adult intelligence consists more of the ability to handle the environment than of skill in solving verbal and abstract problems.

The sub-tests can be grouped into two categories, verbal and performance. This feature is often helpful in testing people with limited verbal skills. The instrument has six sub-tests of verbal scale and 5 sub-tests in the performance.

Verbal Sub-test	*Performance Sub-test*
1. Information	1. Picture arrangement
2. Comprehension	2. Picture completion
3. Memory Span	3. Block design
4. Arithmetic	4. Object assembly
5. Similarities	5. Digit symbol
6. Vocabulary	

We have three IQs in the test.

1. Verbal scale IQ
2. Performance scale IQ
3. A full scale IQ

The Intelligence Scale for Children

This scale for children from 5 through 15 years of age (WISC) is developed on the same principles and in the same form as the WAIS: verbal sub-test, performance sub-test and have three IQS as in WAIS a verbal IQ, a performance IQ and a full scale IQ.

The Kaufman Assessment Battery for Children (K-ABC)

Psychologists Alan and Nadeen Kaufman have developed a test with the belief that they could eliminate bias that was present in other popular IQ tests. In their view, the Kaufman Assessment Battery for Children (K-ABC) uses tasks that tap the experience of all people, regardless of their background. The K-ABC is an individually administered measure of intelligence and achievement that assesses styles of information processing and problem solving. It was designed especially for assessment, intervention and remediation and was standardized on a large representative sample of both normal and exceptional children, ages two and a half through twelve and a half. The means score on the K-ABC is 100 and SD is 15 points.

Kaufman and Kaufman define intelligence in terms of an individual's level of mental processing and is measured in terms of an individual's ability to process information effectively in solving novel problems. The K-ABC comprises of four global scales, three measure mental processing abilities (sequential processing, simultaneous processing and a composite of two) and the fourth assesses achievement.

Individual Performance Scale

A performance scale is one in which language is used only in the instruction or not at all when directions are given in pantomime. The task to be performed needs an overt motion response other than verbal. The principal characteristic of the performance test is that a response to, or a solution of the action/task does not require the use of language or number. It is also known as the non-verbal test.

The Represenative Scales

1. The Pintner -Paterson Scale
2. The Arthur Point Scale
3. The Ferguson Formboards
4. The Kent -Shakow Formboard series
5. The Carl Hollow -Square Scale
6. The Good Endough Drawing Test.
7. The Columbia Mental Maturity Scale.

Group Scale of Intelligence

1. The California Test of Mental Maturity
2. Henman-Nelson Test of Mental Ability
3. Kuhlmann-Anderson Test
4. The Lorge-Thorndike Intelligence Test
5. Terman -McNemer test of Mental Ability

Culture-fair Intelligence Tests

Culture-fair tests attempt to measure the intelligence of individuals who are outside the culture in which the test was devised. These tests are language free and attempt to eliminate skill and feelings. A classic example of this is the good enough Draw-a-person-Test, which requires only knowledge of the human body.

Cattell's culture-fair Intelligence Test is based on a distinction between two different kinds of general intelligence. According to Cattell crystallized general ability is what we use when we are required to apply prior knowledge to new information, as in taking an achievement test. Fluid general ability comes into play when we have to adopt to new situation, where crystallized abilities are not very helpful. A test if it is a culture-fair has to measure fluid general ability, which is largely innate.

Important Test of Intelligence (Indian Adaptations)

Verbal (Group Tests)

1. Group Test of General Mental Ability (1972), S. Jalota (Hindi) for 11 to 16 years.
2. Verbal Intelligence Test (VIT), Ojha and Chaudhary (Hindi) for 13 to 20 years.
3. General Intelligence Test (Hindi), S.M. Mohsin. It is meant for children from 9 to 15 years.
4. Group Test of Intelligence, (English), G.C. Ahuja for 13 to 17 years.

Non-Verbal (Paper-Pencil)

1. Bicycle Drawing for Measuring Intelligence T.R. Sharma (English for 6 to 12 years Children).
2. Draw a Man Test for Indian Children, Hindi/English. It is meant for children from 2½ to 16 years.
3. Human Figure Draw a Man Test, A. N. Mishra for 6 to 12 years children.

Non-Verval (Performance)

1. Indian Adaptation of Wechsler Adult Performance Intelligence Scale (WAPIS), P. Ramalingaswami.
2. Bhatia's Performance Battery of Intelligence Test by C.M. Bhatia.

Process-oriented Assessment of Intellectual Development

Process--oriented theorists have now begun to develop assessment method of their own though they are still in their infancy. Inauzagin and Hunt developed a set of six development scales intended to measure "progressive levels of cognitive organization" in the first 2 years of life. These scales are based on cognitive theory of Piaget. Because this theory deals with stages of intellectual development, the scales developed by them are stage like. They are designed to indicate where a particular baby is at a given time within a particular sequence of developmental stages. The scales are not useful as are traditional IQ tests.

Multifactor Test Batteries

Multifactor batteries are those scales that are intended for the independent measurement of each of several kinds of mental operations and that provide a separate score for each and also known as multiple-aptitude and differential-aptitude tests. These instruments stand in contrast to other tests of mental abilities. In the multifactor batteries, the objective is to obtain a number of separate scores in order to differentiate among the several abilities within each individual since most of multifactor-test batteries aim to measure relatively independent factors. Each part of the battery can provide its own norms and can be validated for each of varieties of occupation and curricula. Thus an individual's potentiality in a number of academic and vocational areas can be analyzed and appraised by means of a series of relatively brief tests.

Important Multifactor Test Batteries

1. Tests of Primary Mental Abilities: Thurstone published a series of multifactor tests originally known as the Chicago Test of Primary Mental Abilities. Later editions are named the SRA (Science Research Associates) Primary Mental abilities.
2. Differential Aptitude Tests (DAT).
3. Flanagon Aptitude Classification Test (FACT).
4. General Aptitude Test Battery (GATB).
5. Multiple Apptitude Test (MAT) by D. Segal and E. Raskin.

Emotional Intelligence

Emotional Intelligence is the ability to sense, understand and effectively apply the power and acumen of emotions as a source of human energy, information and influence of others. The concept of emotional intelligence is a kind of umbrella term that captures a broad collection of individual skills and disposition, usually referred as soft skill or inter or intra personal skills that are outside the traditional areas of general intelligence, the technical or professional skills.

According to Deniel Goleman, "Emotional Intelligence is the ability to motivate oneself and persist in the face of frustration of control impulse and delay gratification to regulate one's mood and keep distress from swamping the ability to think, to emphasize and to hope."

This view fits well with the commonly held notion that it takes more than just brains to succeed in life. It is appropriate here to state that one should also be able to adjust by having healthy interpersonal relations with others. Salovey and Nayor coined the term 'emotional intelligence' in 1990. They described emotional intelligence as a form of social intelligence that involves the ability to monitor one's own and others' feelings and emotions, discriminate among them and to use this information to guide one's thinking and action.

IQ may be very good predictor of scholastic achievements but not to that extent of job performance. Hunter and Hunter estimated that at best IQ accounted for about 25 per cent of the variances. IQ is not the only factor for the success in life. It is effective at entry level but it is the social and emotional intelligence which to a greater extent affects future success than IQ.

It is true, 'proper emotion at proper time in proper quantity' is key for the success at every stage i.e., emotional stability is an important trait to prove oneself effective. Emotions associated with low stability include anxiety, depression, anger, embarrassment and worry. It has been experienced that emotionally surcharged leaders embrace emotionally surcharged decisions and get failures. The following components of emotional intelligence have been identified:

1. *Self-consciousness:* The ability to understand one's own moods, needs, drives strength and weaknesses as well as their effect on others. It also extends to person's understanding of his/her values, goodness and goals.
2. *Self-regularization:* It is the ability to control or redirect destructive impulses and moods, i.e., to think calmly before acting. This demands high degree of tolerance to other's views before considering decisions.
3. *Motivation:* It is a keen desire to work for reasons beyond only calculation of money or power to pursue goals with energy and persistence. People with high motivation remain optimistic even when the score is against them. It has been found that self-motivated achiever is a person who is more successful than the one who depends on external rewards.
4. *Empathy:* It is the ability to understand the emotional make up of other and the skill in treating them in accordance with their emotional reactions.
5. *Social skills:* There are the abilities that establish rapport with

various sections of society and form cohesiveness among the people.

Artifical Intelligence

Problem solving programmes like the logic theorist and the General Problem Solver (GPS) were among the first artificial-intelligence programmes, or a computer programme developed by Newell Shaw and Sincon. One of the most sophisticated examples of machine thinking is the General Problem Solver (GPS).The GPS and a human subject are given the task of providing a mathematical theorem. Both receive a set of axioms for developing their proofs. The humans think aloud, giving the experimenter a record of the order in which he tries the rules and his reasons for accepting or rejecting his results. Both computer and humans try and reject the rules in the same order. The one difference seems to be found that the humans can correct their mistakes by changing a previous decision where as a computer cannot. Computers have also been programmed to play chess and checkers, the way people do. Like people, computers also use heuristics-rules of thumb that enable them to limit the search for solutions by ignoring blind alleys. Heuristics for making decisions are generated by analysing the ways in which experts solve problems in their domain of knowledge.

Artificial intelligence has come in for a great deal of criticism. We should not dignify what computers do with the term intelligence. Skeptics say that computers have only some of the hallmarks of human intelligence as they lack creativity. Other critics convinced of the power and possibilities of artificial intelligence are anxious about the unforeseen consequences of creating an 'alien intelligence' with which they will have to share the world.

Aptitude

Students have different abilities and their talents are to be recognized in schools by the teachers who encourage them in developing special abilities or aptitudes.

F.N. Freeman described, "An aptitude is a combination of characteristics indicative of an individual's capacity to acquire (with training) some specific knowledge skill, or set of organized response, such as the ability to speak a language, to become a musician or to do a mechanical work. An aptitude test, therefore, is designed to measure person's potential ability in an activity of a specialized kind within a restricted range."

It may be referred as the potentialities present in an individual as are revealed by his performance to predict for the future. Aptitude is different from skill and proficiency.

Skill

It means the ability to perform a given act with ease and precision. Proficiency has the same meaning except that it is more comprehensive as it includes not only skill but also other types of activities as shown in one's competence in language, history and mathematics.

Aptitude includes capacity to acquire proficiency under appropriate conditions i.e., one's potentialities as revealed by his performance on selected tests that have predictive value. It is an innate capacity affected by the environment in which the individual lives. An aptitude in a particular ability facilities learning, consequently the ability gets full expressions of that innate potentiality.

Hence, it may be stated that an aptitude depends on the one hand, as the inherent potentiality for its emergence and on the other hand, as the favourable environment for its manifestation. Aptitudes are relatively stable in life. It is also to be kept in mind that any aptitude recognized early in life may disappear if favourable and suitable environment and opportunities are not provided to develop it.

Testing for Special Aptitudes

There is no clear dividing line between intelligence tests and aptitude tests. Only difference seems that intelligence tests provide us a broad assessment of intellectual capacity while aptitude tests help us to measure the more specialized abilities required in specific occupations and activities.

Scholastic Aptitudes

If we want to predict success in academic training, we speak of scholastic aptitude.

1. *Scholastic Aptitude Test (SAT):* It is for those students who want to enter arts college.
2. *Graduate Record Examination (GRE):* This test has been designed for students who plan to do graduate in a number of fields in arts and sciences.
3. *Miller Analogies Test (MAT):* It also predicts success in graduate school.

Vocational Aptitudes

Psychomotor tests are a second general class of vocational aptitudes tests. They involve such psychomotor tasks as manual dexterity, steadiness, muscular strength, speed of response to a signal and co-ordination of many movements into a unified whole. Vocational aptitude tests are used both by employers to select employees and by vocational counsellors to assist persons to assess their aptitudes for different types of work.

Mechanical Aptitude Tests

An individual having mechanical aptitude should have sensory and motor capacities as well as perceptual and spatial abilities. Hence, mechanical aptitude tests are constructed to measure capacity and performance on a higher level of organization than those of sensory motor capacity and dexterity.

Some Misconceptions About Intelligence Test and Testing

Sl. No.	*Misconception*	*Reality*
1.	Intelligence test measure innate intelligence	I.Q. scores measure some of an individual interaction with the environment, they never solely measure intelligence.
2.	I.Q. are fixed and never change	People's I.Q. change throughout life, but specially from birth through age seven. Even after this age, significant change can occur.
3.	Intelligence test provide perfectly reliable scores	Test scores are only estimates.
4.	Intelligence test measure all we need to know about a person's intelligence	Most intelligence test do not measure the entire spectrum of abilities related to intellectual behaviour.
5.	A battery of tests can tell us everything that we need to know in making judgements about a person's competence.	No battery of tests can give a complete picture of any person. A battery can only illuminate various areas of functioning.

I.Q.: It indicates the degree of brightness of an individual.

Age Changes and Intelligence

Intelligence test performance develop with the years so that a mental age score remains appropriate at least throughout childhood. The I.Q. was based on the pre-assumption that the mental age for a bright child would grow more rapidly than for a dull one so that there would be found some degree of constancy for the ratio of M.A. to C.A. Both these conjectures were found to be approximately true. Jenson (1973) disclosed this fact. The following table indicates a true picture:

		Retest Age (in Year)			
		7	10	14	18
Test Age in Year	2	.46	.37	.28	.31
	7		.77	.75	.71
	10			.86	.73
	14				.76

Questions

A. Long Answer Type Questions

1. Discuss the nature of intelligence in the light of different types of definitions.
2. Critically examine any three theories of intelligence. Which of these theories you consider as the best? Give reasons in support of your answer.
3. Is intelligence innate or acquired. How is it measured? Explain its relation with classroom work.
4. Distinguish between various types of intelligence test by citing examples of each.

B. Short Answer Type Questions

1. Give the chief characteristics of intelligence.
2. Mention some intelligence tests used in India.
3. What is I.Q. and calculate with the following data and also interpret.
   (*i*) M.A. = 16 and C.A. = 10
   (*ii*) M.A. = 10 and C.A. = 12
4. Describe in brief any intelligence test.
5. Is intelligent constant? Explain.

C. Objective Types Questions

1. Intelligence is defined as the ability to:
   (1) Learn (2) Carry on abstract thinking
   (3) Adjust
   (*a*) 1 and 2 are correct (*b*) All are correct
   (*c*) 1 and 3 are correct (*d*) Only 2 is correct

2. "Intelligence is the aggregate or global capacity of the individual ., ..." It has been defined by
   (*a*) L.M. Terman (*b*) Stoddard
   (*c*) Spearman (*d*) Wechsler
3. The concept of Tetrad difference was propounded by
   (*a*) Spearman (*b*) Thurstone
   (*c*) Thorndike (*d*) Thomson
4. Match List I with List II and select answer using codes given below the lests:

List I	*List II*
A. The Multifactor theory	1. Spearman
B. The Group factor theory	2. Thurstone
C. The Two factor theory	3. Thorndike
D. Sampling theory	4. Thomson

Codes

	A	B	C	D
(*a*)	1	2	3	4
(*b*)	3	2	1	4
(*c*)	2	1	4	1
(*d*)	4	3	2	1

5. Army alpha test was constructed for the group of individuals who were
   (*a*) Illiterate (*b*) Literate
   (*c*) For both a and b (*d*) Well educated
6. CAVD test was constructed by:
   (*a*) Spearman (*b*) Binet and Simon
   (*c*) Wechsler (*d*) Thorndike
7. Most intelligence tests measure:
   (1) Convergents thinking (2) Divergent thinking
   (*a*) Both are true (*b*) 2 is true 1 is false
   (*c*) 1 is true 2 is false (*d*) Both are false

SUGGESTED READINGS

1. Anstasi, Anne, "Psychological Testing" (5th edition) Macmillan Publishing Co. NY. 1962.
2. Freeman, Frank S., "Theory and Practice of Psychological Testing". New Delhi, Oxford and IBH Publishing Co, 1962.
3. Freeman, F.S., "Individual Differences," New York, Henry Holt and Company Inc., 1934.

4. Galton, F., "Heredity Genius", MacMillan, London, 1925.
5. Wingfield, A.H., "Twins and Orphans: The Inheritance of Intelligence", London Deut, 1928.
6. Flavell, J.H., "The Developmental Psychology of Jean Piaget", New York, Van Norstrand, 1963.
7. Charles, E., Skinner, "Educational Psychology" (4th edition) Prentice-Hall, Inc, New Jersey, U.S.A., 1959.

13

Personality and its Measurement

The word ' Personality' comes from the Latin word 'Persona', which means mask worn by actors to signify their role in the drama. Today the word, however, refers to more enduring personal qualities. The personality is a typical way of reacting to the world and relating to the people around us. Personality characteristics describe consistencies both at different times and at different situations. Seeming and being are different. The 'self' that we present to the world is often false, a personal construction behind which we conceal our real selves. Infact an individual have three different faces: a social face, a personal face and a real face.

Social Face

A social face represents how a person acts in public. This face may have several interchangeable styles, depending upon whom a person wishes to impress. In public we wear a kind of false face, a mask in order to present ourselves at best. We use superficial aspects (clothes, cosmetics) to create for ourselves a public image, a social face.

Personal Face

Personal face represents our self-concept or the way we see ourselves. The feelings we have about ourselves are reflected in this private vision. Our self-concept can be positive or negative. If positive concept one has, one may think oneself as competent, worthy, and likeable and intelligent and if a negative self-concept one has, one may think oneself as inadequate, inferior and worthless. Our idea about ourselves and the impressions others have about us is often different.

Real Face

Real face represents what we are in reality. This is how we would appear if we could see ourselves clearly. If we could be peeled like an onion, with our outer shell of pretence and pride removed, our naked core of real self would be exposed.

Psychological Meanings of Personality

It is rare to find a psychologist who will accept another's definition even though both agrees that personality is a biophysical event. Inspite of multiplicity of definitions it is possible to categorize them into five basic classes as stated by Allport:

1. *Omnibus definition:* This is a commonest type of definition that states, "Personality is the sum total ......" One of the best known definitions is that of Morton Prince. "Personality is the sum total of all the biological innate dispositions, impulses, tendencies of the individual and the acquired dispositions and tendencies acquired by experience."
   This type of definition has been criticized by saying that such omnibus definition renders absolutely no service to science.
2. *Integrative and configurational definition:* A simple formulation of this type is that of Warren and Carmichael: "The entire organization of a human being at any stage of his development."
3. *Hierarchical definition:* First is the material self where one possesses one's family and friends whom one cherishes. There is next social self determined by the recognition one obtains from one's associates. James made his famous statement that a man "has as many different social selves as there are distinct group of persons about whose opinion he cares." Third is the spiritual self that unifies so far as is possible man's discordant tendencies. A fourth level, the Pure Ego (the known the self or selves) is required by certain philosophical system but according to Ames not distinguishable from the third level Mc Dougall and others offer the term levels or layers of dispositions, usually with a unifying or integrative principle at the top.
4. *Definitions in terms of adjustment:* Personality is the whole organism in action. This point of view is most fully developed by Kempf. According to him Personality is defined as: "The integration of those systems of habits that represent an individual's characteristic adjustment to his environment."

5. *Definition in terms of distinctiveness:* Schoen writes, "If all the members of any social group acted alike, thought alike, and felt alike personality would not exist." Hence he proposes personality as the organized system, the functioning whole or unity of habits, dispositions and sentiments that mark off anyone member of a group as being different from any other member of the group.

Allport defines personality taking all the above views in the following words: "Personality is the dynamic organization within the individual of those psycho-physical systems that determine his unique adjustment to his environment." Each portion of the definition is chosen for a particular reason and must be made clear if the definition is to be accurately understood.

Dynamic Organization

There must be mental organization (association), yet this organization must be regarded as constantly evolving and changing, as motivational and as self-regarding and hence "Dynamic".

Psycho-physical Systems

Habits, specific and general attitudes, sentiments and dispositions of other orders are all psycho-physical systems. The term 'system' refers to trait or groups of traits in latent or active condition.

Determine

The systems that constitute personality are in every sense determining tendencies and when aroused by suitable stimuli provoke those adjustive and expressive acts by which the personality comes to be known.

Unique

Every adjustment of every person is unique in time and place and in quality.

Adjustments to His Environment

The adjustments of men contain a great amount of spontaneous, creative behaviour towards the environment.

Some other Definitions of Personality

Cattell R.B., "Personality is that which permits a prediction of what a person will do in a given situation."

Eyesenck, H.J., "Personality is a stable and enduring combination of a person's various physical and mental aspects."

Guilford J.P., "An individual's personality is his unique pattern of traits. A trait is any distinguishable relatively enduring way in which one individual differs from another."

McDougall, J.W. defines, "Personality is a synthetic unity of all mental features and functions in their interplay."

Murphy, H.A., "Personality is a unitary mode of adjustment in relation to which each pacific activity must be taken into consideration."

All the above definitions reveal the fact that personality building is not mere collection of different aspects or features but it is an interaction or interplay which affects one another. Personality is formed because of the special and healthy relationship among its parts. It has integrated structure and functions. Any change in any one part of the structure influences other parts.

Important characteristics of personality:

1. Personality of each individual is unique.
2. Personality is dynamic and not static.
3. Personality functions in integration.
4. Personality is the product of both heredity and environment.
5. Personality in rare cases influences the environment
6. Personality is an adjustment with the environment.
7. Personality always strives for certain goal.

Important components of personality:

1. Physique
2. Emotionality
3. Intelligence
4. Social behaviour
5. Character

Determinants of Personality

There are several factors within the individual and outside that influence and shape the personality. We can classify these factors into two categories; (1) Biological factors and (2) Psycho-social factor

Biological Factors

(a) *Heredity:* Heredity is one of the major determinants of personality. Heredity is popularly employed to describe the 'innate' equipment of the individual at the time of conception. Heritage is the sum of all those qualities which are determined or caused by germinal organization. The way diverse individuals develop the peculiarities that they show, so-called laws of heredity, the extraordinary resemblances and differences between parents and off-springs, all these things depend largely on the arrangement and behaviour of genes. The physical characteristics exhibited by an individual are the result of the combination of genes from which his development has taken place. This biological fact is essential to understand the physical aspects of personality. Studies conducted on fraternal twins and identical twins who have a similar genetic make up showed similarity on psychological characteristics such as response style; intelligence, stress, tolerance and so on. However, the distinction between heredity and environment is being minimized. Nature and nurture are increasingly being looked upon as the two interlocked aspects of the process of human growth and development. The physical appearance, body-build, strength and bodily proportions may not have value as clear indicators of what an individual's personality is, but all of them have indirect influence on the development of personality. Actual deformity handicaps the child both physically as well as psychologically. The feelings of inferiority may develop if physically an individual is unsound and having good physique one develops confidence in oneself.

(b) *Nervous system:* The human nervous system consists of two major but functionally interrelated divisions: the central and the autonomic. The fetal development of the autonomic nervous system; proceeds that of the central nervous system both structurally and functionally and is of considerable significance in projecting future behaviour. Psychologists believe that perceptual conditioning (prior to the point where analytical or conceptual thinking on the part of the child is possible) may be related to the appearance of anxiety syndromes, tension state, now recognized as being of primary significance in psychological disturbances. The relationship between ANS activity (SNS & PSNS) and the phenomena of emotion and motivation has been established.

It has been found in a study that persons who have strong reactions of SNS were dependent, suggestible and idealistic and those in which parasympathetic dominated were judged cool, evasive, opportunistic and independent.

(c) *Endocrine System and Hormonal Control of Behaviour*: The human body is a complex system of interrelated organs and tissues, all of which must work together if it is to function properly. A wide variety of physiological processes have to be continuously monitored and controlled. Both monitoring and control have to take place without conscious intervention, and these are achieved by the endocrine system which carries them out with the help of a highly ingenious array of chemical messengers called hormones. In other words, we can say that there are two types of glands in the human body: glands with ducts (such as the tear and sweat glands) and glands without ducts. Psychologists are interested primarily in the ductless glands or endocrine glands. These glands secrete chemicals called hormones directly into the blood stream and can influence a person's behaviour dramatically.

1. *Pituitary gland (master gland)*: The most important endocrine gland is the pituitary, the body's master gland. It is located below the brain stem and is about the size of a pea. It secretes nine hormones which regulate the other endocrine gland and body functions.

Recently, it has been suggested that the endocrine system in general, and the pituitary system in particular, may be crucially involved in depression. Depressed patients often show abnormalities in their hormonal levels, particularly in those controlled by pituitary. Because pituitary is controlled by the brain, changes in a person's emotional state often affect the pituitary. The pituitary, in turn, affects other glands and ultimately behaviour. The pituitary gland is divided into two lobes:

(i) The anterior (Adrenohypophysis).
(ii) The posterior (Neurohypophysis).

The anterior lobe produces hormone that stimulate the thyroid and adrenal glands, which control specific behaviour and growth hormone called *somatotrophics* (STH). Too little STH creates 3 or 4 feet tall pituitary dwarf, too much STH creates a pituitary giant 8 or 9 feet tall. It produces five hormones that trigger the action of other endocrine glands. Thyrotropin hormone a (TTH) which activates the thyroid gland, adrenocorticotrophic hormone (ACTH) which triggers the reactions of the adrenal cortex and three other hormones that control the gonades, the sex glands.

The posterior (Neurohypophysis) lobe of the pituitary stores and secretes two major hormones *(i)* antidiuretic (ADH) and *(ii)* Oxytocin. ADH acts on the kidneys to increase fluid absorption and decreases the amount of urine. Oxytocin stimulates uterine contractions and causes labour to begin. It also causes the release of milk in nursing mothers.

2. *Pancreas:* This gland is situated in the middle part of the body. It is both exocrine and endocrine in its secretery functions. The exocrine cells of the pancreas are responsible for the enzymes rich pancreatic secretion. The endocrine part secretes insulin which regulates the blood sugar by increasing the deposition of glucose in liver and muscles as glycogen.
   The islets of langerhans in the pancreas control the production of insulin which facilitates the transportation of sugar into the cells, where it is metabolized. When an insufficient amount of insulin is produced, resulting in the presence of too much sugar in the blood, diabetes mellitus occurs and this condition is known as *hyperglycemia,* and if untreated it can lead to coma and death. If the pancreas produces too much insluin, the result is hypoglycemia or very low blood sugar. Such patients have no energy and often faint.
3. *Thyroid gland:* Thyroid gland is located just below the larynx, or voice box. It produces one primary hormone, *Thyroxine* which regulates the body's rate of metabolism i.e., it determines how fast or slowly the energy we need to function normally. Differences in the metabolic rate determine how alert and energetic people are, how fat or thin they tend to be. Early deprivation of thyroxine leads to cretinism or a type of feeblemindedness. Over secretion of this hormone leads to restlessness and tension and increase in appetite tempting to eat everything in sight, and a person may still remain very much an underweight. Thyroid deficiency in adulthood

leads to a condition known as *myxedema* which is characterized by overweight general sluggishness.

4. *Parathyroid glands:* Embedded in the thyriod gland are the parathyroids, four tiny pea shaped organs. They secrete parathormone which controls and balances the level of calcium and phosphate in the blood and tissue fluids. The level of calcium in the blood has a direct effect on the excitability of the nervous system. A person will be hyper sensitive with too little parathormone and may suffer from muscle spasms and twitches and too much may lead to lethargy and poor physical coordination.
   The main symptom is uncontrolled twitching and the spasms of body muscle, a condition known as *tetany*, with muscle cramps typifying less severe cases. We rely on Vitamin D to get the calcium from food which is processed in the lever and kidneys to make the hormone calcitriol. Output of calcitriol is stimulated by increase in the level of parathormone and decrease in the blood phosphate.
5. *Adrenal glands:* Adrenal Glands are located in the mid-region of the body above the kidneys and have two main parts. The outer part is called 'adrenal cortex' and the inner part is known as 'adrenal medulla'. The adrenal medulla secretes two hormones: *(i)* adrenaline (epinephrine) and *(ii)* noradrenaline (norepinephrine). These hormones are produced primarily during the times of stress and strain resulting due to fear, anger and aggression. Insufficient secretion of these hormones results in fatigue, loss of appetite, anaemia, weaknesses, sleeplessness and darkening of skin. This is popularly known as Addition's disease.
   Adrenal cortex secretes various hormones viz., steroids, corticoids and sex hormones. Over secretion in adults causes Cushing's syndrome which is characterized be obesity, excessive hair growth, diabetes and hypogonadism.
   In woman excessive androgens may cause masculinisation (virilism). In children excessive sex hormone causes precocious puberty i.e., early sexual maturity.
   In many cases Cushing's syndrome comes about because of problems with the pituitary gland. A tumour may cause to secrets excess ACTH and this stimulates the adrenal cortex to manufacture excess cortico steroids.

6. *Gonads (The Sex Glands):* The glands that produce sex hormones are the ovaries in the famales and the testes in males. Together they are called gonads. The important male sex hormones are called androgens or testosterone which are responsible for the maturation of male sex characteristics such as growth of facial hair and change of voice at puberty. Androgen is responsible for physiological changes related to sex drive.

   Ovaries secrete two important hormones *(i)* estrogen and *(ii)* progesterone. The estrogen is responsible for the maturation of female internal reproductive structure and the emergence and growth of secondary sex characteristics such as breasts and pubic hair. This hormone also plays an important role in the regulation of the menstrual cycle. Progesterone also prepares the uterus for implantation of the fertilised egg and nourishes the embryo during the early stages of prenatal development.
7. *Pineal gland:* This gland is located inside the brain. It is about the size of a pea. The main hormone secreted by this gland is melatonin. This hormone regulates the growth of the body and reproductive functions.

   The above description of endocrine glands clearly shows its role and significance in behaviour at different stages of a person's life.

   It should always be kept in mind that endocrine glands do not function independently but are interrelated and controlled and regulated by various centres of the brain.

Table–13.1

S.No.	Glands	Hormone secreted	Effect in body and on behaviour
1.	Pituitary		
	(i) Adenolhy-pophysis (anterior pituitary)	*(i)* Somatotrophic	Controls rate of protein synthesis. Promotes release of fat from fat stores.
		(ii) Adrenocorticotrophic Hormone (ACTH)	Regulates cortex of adrenal gland.
		(iii) Thyrotrophin	Regulates thyroid gland.
		(iv) Follicle stimulating Hormone	Regulates sex organ.

(Contd.)

S.No.	*Glands*	*Hormone secreted*	*Effect in body and on behaviour*
		(v) Luteinizing hormone	Promotes secretion of sex hormones.
		(vi) Prolactin	Controls with production.
	Neurohypophysis (Posterior Pituitary)	*(i)* Antidiuretic Hormone	Controls retention of fluids
		(ii) Oxytocin	Stimulates uterine contractions, Stimulates lactation.
2.	Pancreas	*(i)* Insulin	Regulates use of sugar; Regulates storage of carbohydrates.
		(ii) Glycogen	Acts synergistically with insulin.
3.	Thyroid	Thyroxin	Regulates metabolic rate.
4.	Parathyroid	Parathyroid hormone	Regulates calcium levels.
5.	*(i)* Adrenal (cortex)	Steroids	Controls resistance to stress.
	(ii) Medulla		Regulates carbohydrates metabolism.
		Adrenalin (Epinephrine	Changes metabolic activity
		Noradrenalin Norepinephrine	Generally inhibits central nervous system.
6.	Reproductive Glands		
	(a) Famale	*(i)* Estrogens	Controls menstrual cycle
		(ii) Progestins	MaintainBBs pregnancy.
	(b) Male	Adrogens	Promotes male sex characteristics and growth.
7.	Pineal	Melatonin	Regulates reproduction and growth.

Eucational Implication of Endocrine Glands

It is very important of teacher to understand the functioning of endocrine glands as it has direct affect on the growth and development of children's personality. The endocrine glands secrete hormones that are carried throughout the body the blood stream. Teachers must know that these chemicals are as essential as the nervous system to the integration of the individuals activities and to the maintenance of homeostasis and the functioning of the nervous system too depends upon the proper secretion of hormones of each gland. Any dysfunctioning of any endocrine gland will distroy the emotional intellectual, social and other development aspects of personality of the individual as the endocrine glands are responsible for growth, sexual and maternal behaviour, the children's characteristic level of energy and mood and reaction to stress. Some of the endocrine glands are controlled by the nervous system, whereas other respond directly to the internal state of the body.

An endocrine gland viz., thyroid gland produces hormones thyroxin when it becomes overactive it results in nervousness, dizziness and difficulty in sleeping. Similarly sex glands or gonads are responsible for the sex urge which effects on emotions especially on the development of personality and become significant as the child reaches to the stage of adolescene. As discussed above, the dysfunction of any these of glands, the children/individuals never be happy or well adjusted. They may suffer from apathy, anxiety, restlessness, fatigue, and irsitiability etc.

The teachers should be very cautious in this regard and spot out such children where they observe any dysfunctioning of any endocrine gland.

It is also the responsibility of the teachers to provide correct information to the adolescents regarding the functioning of sex glands. It would help the adolescents to maintain their mental health. Teachers should send such children for periodical medical checkup such facilities are available in the school, if not patients should be informed, assisted guided for medical checkup by a qualified Doctor.

Normal functioning of the these glands give rise to integrated personality but underactive or overactive functioning may lead to personality problems and even abnormalities.

Psycho-social Factors

Some of the important psycho-social determinants of personality are as follow:

Family

One of the major factors influencing personality is experience in the early years of life. Among the several conditions that influence personality development, relationship between the individual and the members of his family is ranked first i.e., the manner in which child is handed by his parents and other during his formative years.

It is generally agreed that over protection should be avoided. Most boys hold that physical affection intelligently expressed by the mother is essential to satisfactory personality development. Langford and Wickman write on the basis of their studies conducted on the aspect of parent child relationship. Most faulty parents child relationship are not due to stupidity, ignorance or a perverseness, but are related to the parents' own personality structure, emotional conflicts, biases and prejudices and past experiences. M.J. Radke conducted a study on the relation of parental authority to children's a behaviour and attitude and found the following relationship:

	Type of Home	*Type associated with Child's Behaviour*
1.	Rejective	Submissive, aggressive child of insecurity; sadistic
2.	Over protecting	Infantile and withdrawing; feeling of insecurity; jealous, submissive
3.	Dominating parents	Dependable, self-conscious; tense; hold, quarrelsome and shy.
4.	Submissive parents	Aggressive, careless; disobedient
5.	Child accepted	Socially acceptable; faces future
6.	Defective discipline	Poor adjustment; rebellious

School

Next to home and parents the school and teachers have the greatest influence on personality development. During early years children spend more time in school than in any other place except the home. Various factors in the school have their own impact on the development of personality of the children—such as curriculum, method of teaching adopted by the teacher, performance of curricular activities in the school, type of discipline adopted in the school and class teacher's personality and their relationship with the students and stress to be given on the peer group relationship.

It may be stated that a pleasant emotional environment of the school makes children to work hard and provide an atmosphere to develop their capacity in the best ways. If the atmosphere of the school is not up to the mark or if there is aversion for school it may lead to truancy or dropping out of school. Academic success is often highly valued and it depends upon the atmosphere of the school. The degree of success affects on the personality of children with regard to his positive self concept and seeking opportunities to achieve higher goals.

Emotional Factors

Emotions are important personality determinants because of their influence on adjustment. They are very much related to a person's attitudes and values. Emotional balance in which the pleasant emotions such as love, affections and happiness outweigh the negative emotions is essential to good adjustment. It is also essential for the parents to provide such a congenial atmosphere so that a child may develop tolerance and ability to cope with unpleasant experiences arising out of emotions such as anger, fear and envy etc. The studies conducted by psychologists reveal that emotional deprivation has unfavourable effects on personality. (See role of family).

Social Environment

Environmental factors constitute an integral relationship between the organization and the physical and social milieu. According the Haldane, 'personality is not something confined and complete in itself separately from an environment in space and time, but extends over that environment.' In other words, there is an abiding relationship between the individual and his environment. The individuals pass their life in a society and satisfy their needs and desires. Relations between two are reciprocal. Recent studies have shown that there is a significant positive relationship between the social environment and the development of personality. Studies have also shown that the amount of social and emotional integration within a society is related to the extent of favourable conditions for personality development. If the family and social environment is not upto the mark, it will create tension, anxiety and stress. Consequently a person may develop deviant behaviour pattern.

Educational Implications

Role of the Teacher in the Personality Development of the Children/Students

Teacher plays an important and significant role in the formation of child's personality. He is considered as a communicater, learning facilitator, manager and provider of knowledge. Teacher acts as a model for the students. They identify with the teacher and learn whatever he communicates. Character and personality of the pupils would develop as the teacher who is the model for them. Teacher and parents should also remember, 'example is better than precept', children are imitative and suggestive by nature.

They are in the plastic period of their life and easily influenced by their teachers. Ryburn is right when he put, "self analysis on the part of a teacher is necessary equipment." Prof. Raymont too urges that the teacher must avoid everything that is petty and mean. Teacher must develop the following characteristics in his personality which would be constructive for his development of children's personality.

1. *Nature for the profession:* The teacher must respect and feel the importance and significance of his profession. He should consider himself to be a teacher first.
2. *Love for children:* A teacher must be sure and feel that some time with energy is constantly supplied by the young. He always should remember, "Love the child and the child will love you, hate the child and the child will hate you, is a famous maximum."
3. *Respect individuality of each child:* Sense of respect of the child should never be injured. Emerson has rightly stated, 'the secret of education lies in respecting the pupil.'

Teacher is a Guide

Child is the hero in the field of education, he must be allowed to express his feelings and cmotions and he play an active role in teaching-learning process. The teacher is here considered as a sincere guide for him.

Teacher and parents should follow some important steps for the harmonious development of personality. Following points are helpful for the teachers and parents.

1. Recognition from the parents and teachers.
2. Sincere affection.
3. Feeling of security must be satisfied while he/she is in the class and school.
4. Feeling of curiosity; if children ask a question, the teacher and parent should try to answer with his satisfaction immediately.
5. Pay due attention – It should be kept in mind that quality of attention counts.
6. Democratic discipline.
7. Teacher should inspire the children to do some thing special.
8. If a child lives with criticism, he learns to condemn. If he lives with praise he works hard with his top capacity.

9. Teacher should always be eager to understand his ability, capacity, interest and aptitude for the effective guidance.

Measurement/Assessment of Personality

Psychologists use four basic types of tools to assess/measure personality:

(*i*) Subjective methods.
(*ii*) Objective methods.
(*iii*) Projective method.
(*iv*) Sociometric method.

Projective Tests or Techniques

The psycho-analytic approach to understand an individual's personality requires finding out about his unconscious conflicts and motives. A large part of the personality is unconscious. The projective tests have been devised as one method to uncover unconscious motives. A projective test presents an ambiguous stimulus to which the individual may respond as he desires. The individual projects his personality through his responses, the tests tap the subject's imagination and it is assumed that he reveals something about himself. According to Freeman projection is an unconscious process whereby an individual:

(*i*) Attributes certain thoughts, attitudes, emotions or characteristics to other persons or objects in his environment.
(*ii*) Attributes his own needs to others in his environment; or
(*iii*) Draws incorrect inferences from an experience.

Projection is not recognized as being of personal organ, with the result that the content of the process is experienced as an outer perception and external origin. The following are the important projective techniques which are used to assess personality.

1. The Rorschach Ink Blot Test.
2. Thematic Apperception Test (TAT).
3. Word-Association Test.
4. Sentence-Completion Test.
5. Rosenzweig Picture–Frustration Test.

The Rorschach Ink Blot Test

This is a well-known and widely used projective personality test, named after Herman Rorschach, a Swiss Psychiatrist, who began his experimentation with ink blots as a means of stimulating and testing imagination.

The Rorschach Test consists of ten cards, five are in black and white with differently shaded areas, two contain black, white and colour in varying amounts, three are in various colours (Chromatics). The cards are presented to the subject one at a time and in prescribed sequences.

Instructions: According to Rorschach's own formula:

"What does it look like?"

"What could this be?"

Several clinicians have somewhat modified the original instructions. "People see all sorts of things in these ink blots, now tell me what you see, what it might be for you. What it makes you think of."

Time: There is no time limit and there is not any fixed number of responses for each card.

Inquiry: After all ten cards have been presented for response, the inquiry follows. There are two main purposes of the inquiry.

1. To learn which aspects of the blot initiated and sustained the association process of the response to wholes, parts, small details, location, colour shading and apparent movement.
2. The inquiry gives the subjects an opportunity to add to, or clarify his original responses.

   There should be no suggestion from the examiner.

   Scoring: The scoring is based upon four major aspects;

   (i) *Location:* The first is the location which has been perceived as the basis of each response. Location of the responses is the basis of obtaining scores for wholes called (W) large usual details (D), small usual details (d) , unusual details Dd, the white spaces (S). Additional symbols are used to designate other aspects of location but these five are the major categories.

   It reveals extent of the subject's perceptual organization or disorganization and ability to analyze the whole and synthesize the parts.

   (ii) *Determinant:* What qualities of the blot determined the response – the shape, the colour, the shading? Did the response indicate motion?

Forms may be perceived with ordinary accuracy (F) or they may be unusual and clear percepts (F+), or poor percepts (F–). With regard to colour, pure colour without form being involved C, responses to a combination of form and colour in which form is dominant (FC) and in which colour is dominant (CF). Movements-human movements (M), an animal movement (FM) and inanimate movement (m) perspective or depth (FK).

The determinant of the concept of the whole (W) indicates ability to perceive "new and meaningful relations between portion of the figure are usually so organized." Organization is said to be related to level of intelligence.

3. *Contents:* Subject's responses are classified into several more common groups such as plants, animals, humans, landscapes, man-made objects etc. These items are used as a source of ascertaining the subject's personal meanings, attitudes, interest and even complexes.
4. *Originals and populars:* The forth category is originality also known as popularity. Originality was the response, a common one often cited by other persons taking the test or it was strikingly original.

The Rorschach test is believed to be useful in uncovering information about a person's general intellectual and emotional processes as well as complexes.

Thematic Apperception Test (TAT)

Another popular projective test is Thematic Apperception Test (TAT) developed at Harvard University by Henry Murray during 1930s. This test consists of thirty pictures plus one blank card. The cards are used in various combinations depending upon sex and age. Some are used with all subjects while others are used with only one sex group or age group. The maximum number of pictures used with any subject is twenty, usually administered in two sessions, ten in each one of the sessions.

Instructions

The person being examined is told that this is a test of imagination, that he is to make up stories to suit himself/her and there are no right or wrong responses. The pictures are shown one at a time. The subject is informed that each card shows a scene. He is asked (1) to tell what he thinks led up to the scene, how it came about, (2) to give an account of what is happening and the feelings of the characters in the picture and (3) to tell what the outcome will be. There is no time limit for any of the responses.

There is a basic difference between (TAT) and the Rorschach. The latter is intended to reveal the structure and organization of an individual's personality, the former is devised to bring out primarily the content of one's personality, the drives, needs, sentiments, conflicts, complexes and fantasies. The test is based upon the principle that when a person interprets an ambiguous situation, he is acting to reveal aspects of his own personality which he otherwise will not admit or of which he is not aware. The test is intended to reveal the basic themes that recur in a person's imaginative productions. Apperception means a readiness to perceive in certain ways, based on prior individual experience.

Analysis of Stories

Murray recommends that the content of stories be analyzed into: (1) the forces emanating from the 'hero' (2) the forces emanating from the environment. These two divisions are analyzed under the following six categories:

1. *The hero with whom the subject identifies*, in whom the subject is most interested, whose point of view, feelings and motives have been most intimately portrayed.
2. *Motives, trends and feelings of the heroes:* Analysis of everything each of the heroes feels, thinks and does, nothing especially the unusual.
3. *Forces in the hero's environment.* The nature and details of the situations, especially human, nothing uniqueness, intensity and frequency, as well as objects and persons not in the picture but invented by the subject.
4. *Outcomes:* The comparative strengths of the forces emanating from the hero and those from the environment, the amount of hardship and frustration experienced; relative degree of success and failure, happy and unhappy endings.
5. *Themes:* Interaction of a hero's needs with environmental forces, together with successful or unsuccessful outcome of the hero, constitute a simple theme. Combinations or sequences of these are called complex themes.
6. *Interest and sentiments:* Choice of topics and manner of dealing

with them, displayed by the positive and negative appeal of various elements in the pictures.

Word-Association Test

The word-association method received increased attention as a clinical technique. Jung and other clinicians, beginning about 1906 made extensive use of the technique as a quick means of detecting "complexes." Jung's list of one hundred words was selected to represent common emotional 'complexes'.

Instructions

The subject is told that the examiner will speak a series of words, one at a time: after each word, the subject is to reply as quickly as possible with the first word that comes to mind; there is no right or wrong response.

Procedure

The examiner records the replies to each stimulus word, the reaction time and any unusual speech or behaviour manifestation accompanying a given response. Replies to stimulus words that are emotionally toned for the subject generally have a larger or lesser reaction time as compared to mean reaction time and may also evoke physiological changes. The best known of the word association test is the one devised by Kent and Romanoff to differentiate between mentally ill and the normal.

A modification of the word-association technique is the homographic free association test. A homograph is a word spelled exactly like another but with a different meaning and different derivation. Thurston's homographic test uses a list of words each of which has two frequent associations; a social interpersonal one and a literal, physical one.

Sentence-Completion Test

There are tests that present the individual with a series of incomplete sentences, generally open at the end, to be completed by him/her in one or more words. This type of tests is regarded as superior to word-association because the subject may respond with more than one word. A greater flexibility and variety of response is possible and more areas of personality and experience may be tapped. Two fully described and frequently used instruments are:

1. Rhode's sentence completion test.

2. The Rotter incomplete sentence blank.

Rosenzweig Picture-Frustration Test

Picture-Frustration Test of Saul Rosenszweig was devised to assess to degree of frustration, guilt feeling and punishment for something going wrong by presenting to children certain frustrating situations through pictures. The full name of this test is, " Picture-Association Study for assessing reactions to frustration" consisting of twenty four cartoon like pictures, the test is intended to serve as a projective method to reveal the subject's characteristic patterns of response to common stress-producing situations regarded as important in normal and abnormal adjustment. Two forms are available, one for children of ages from 4 to 14 years and one for persons older than 14.

Each picture shows two persons involved in a frustrating situation of common occurrence. The task of the subject is to examine each picture and to write in the blank box the first response that occurs to him.

Assumption

Assumption is that the subject identifies himself, consciously or unconsciously, with the frustrated individual in each situation and his replies are projections of his own ways of acting. The situation presented is of two kinds (1) Ego-blocking and (2) Superego blocking.

Scoring

Scoring of responses is based upon (1) direction of aggression (2) reaction type:

1. *Direction of aggression:* It consists of three forms of expression:
   - *(i)* Extrapunitiveness, in which aggression is turned on to the environment.
   - *(ii)* *Intrapunitiveness:* whereby the subject turns the aggression upon himself.
   - *(iii)* *Impunitiveness:* In which aggression is evaded in an effort to gloss over the Frustration.
2. *Reaction type:* Each type of reaction also has three classes:
   - *(i)* Obstacle dominance, in which barrier occasioning the frustration stands out in the response;
   - *(ii)* Ego-defense, in which the ego of the respondent predominates, and

(iii) Need persistence, in which the subject emphasizes the solution of the frustrating problem.

The responses to the frustration pictures are intended to show the individual's frustration tolerance, which signifies the relative absence of observable disorganization in response to frustrating situations.

The Indian Adaptation of Rosenzweig picture frustration test. Devised by Dr. Udai Pareek (Children's form) is also available which has been standardized an Indian conditions:

The Subjective Method

In such methods, individual is asked to reveal what he known about himself as an object of observation. Subject has to express about his traits, attitudes, personal experiences, aims, needs and interest. Some of the important subjective methods are: (1) the autobiography, (2) The case history, (3) interview, and (4) the questionnaire or the inventory.

1. *The autobiography:* It is a narration or expression given by the individual himself either freely or according to certain subject headings provided by the examiner or tester, of his experiences throughout life. The subjest has freedom to select experiences which are significant to home and these reveal his personality traits.
2. *The case history:* It is dependent to a great extent upon the autobiography. In a case history, we integrate the information that is obtained from various sources about the individual. This method is more useful in understanding the personality pattern of an individual who has problem or is maladjusted.
3. *The interview:* It is a most common method of judging personality of an individual. The interviewer question so as to get a clear picture of individual's traits of his personality. The chief dimension in respect to which the interview may vary is the rigidity or flexibility with which the interviewer holds to a predicated outline or schedule of questions or topics. It is useful to have a definite list of points to be covered consecutively. Creater skill is required in free interviews which are not restricted by a list of definite points or questions. The interviewer evaluates personality traits not only from the content of answers to questions asked but also from the views expressed by the individual.

The limitation of the method is that it is subjective and is less valid and reliable than one believes it to be.

4. *Questionnaires:* Questionnaires are a series of printed or written questions which the individual is supposed to answer. The questions or statements describe certain traits, emotions, attitudes or behaviours in situations that reveal personality traits.

The limitation is that the subject may not be willing to disclose facts about him or may not be in conscious possession of these facts.

Pencil Paper Tests

In an attempt to devise measuring instruments that do not depend upon the skill of interviewer of the abilities of an observer, psychologists have constructed objective tests or personality inventories. There are generally paper and pencil tests that are administered and scored according to a standard procedure. Personality inventories are self-rating questionnaires that deal not only with overt behaviour but also with the person's own feelings about himself. Inventories actually evaluate aspects of personality that are beyond impression made upon observers. Personality inventories can be categorized into five types.

1. Assess specified traits.
2. Evaluate adjustment to serial aspects of the environment.
3. Classify into clinical groups.
4. Screen persons into two or three groups.
5. Evaluate interest, values and attitudes.

Representative Inventories or Some Important Inventories

1. *The bell adjustment inventory:* The inventory consists of questions intended to evaluate the subject's adjustment in respect to home, health, social, emotional and occupational. There are two forms one for students (grade 9 through college) and one for adults.
2. The Bernreuter personality inventory is a questionnaire which assesses six traits: (1) neurotic tendency, (2) self-sufficiency, (3) introversion-extroversion, (4) dominance-submission, (5) confidence, and (6) sociability.
3. *The Minnesota Multiphasic Personality Inventory (MMPI):* The inventory consists of 550 items or statements each of which is printed on a separate card. The cards are sorted by the

subject into three groups—true, false or cannot say. The items have been classified under twenty-six heading (MMPI) was originally concerned exclusively with the clinical problems. The following two instruments are based in part upon the MMPI.

(i) The Minnesota counselling inventory for use at the high school level has 355 true or false items many of which are stimuli those in the MMPL.

(ii) The California psychological inventory meant for ages 13 and older, has 480 true false items. It is devised for use with the normal, no clinical populations.

4. The Minnesota personality scale which has separate forms for men and for women. It is intended to rate the aspects of personality—moral, social adjustment, family relations, emotionality, economic conservatism.
5. *The California test of personality:* It has five scales—Primary, elementary, intermediate, secondary and adult.
   The questions answered either yes or no are grouped under the categories of personal adjustment and social adjustment.
6. *The Guilford-Zimmerman temperament survey:* This inventory based upon factor analysis is intended for use with individuals in grade 9 through 16 and with adults.
7. *The IPAT high school personality questionnaires (R.B. Cattell et al.):* The authors state that it covers all major dimensions in any comprehensive view and description of individual differences in personality. Fourteen dimensions of personality are measured.
8. The sixteen factor personality questionnaire is based on factor analysis. The author of the questionnaire isolated 16 factors as the basic personality traits. He then designed questions to measure each one of them. This inventory was prepared by R.B. Cattell.

Objective Methods

Observation Method

The Rating Scales

This type of scale is useful for learning what impression an individual has made on persons with whom he has come in contact, in respect to some specified traits or attitudes. Rating scale reflects the impression the subject has made upon the persons who do the ratings. To make the rating scales more useful and meaningful, it is necessary to observe certain established principles. The following are the major aspects to be considered in their construction and use.

Characteristics

1. Each trait should be clearly defined.
2. The degree of the trait should be defined; each trait is rated on a scale, most frequently of five or seven intervals.
3. Reliability depends upon extent of variation of judges rating; judges rating an individual on a specified trait will not always agree as to his score or rank therefore, it is good to take the median or mean of all the judgments. Reliability of ratings is usually dependent upon having a sufficient number of qualified judges, five to seven being the number frequently recommended.
4. Determination of validity is difficult.
5. Overt traits are more reliably rated than covert traits.
6. Degree of certainty of rating should be stated with each rating, it is desirable to have the respondent state his degree of certainty (i.e., very strong, strong, moderate)

Types of Rating Scales

There are two most common forms of rating scales – (1) Scoring type and (2) Ranking type.

1. In scoring type rating scale, the subject is rated at a point or level, on the scale without direct reference to or comparison with other person in his group. Each point or level on the scale carries as specific score on a scale of five e.g., the average person is scored 0, the deviated are scored +2, +1, –1 or –2 or the scores can all be positive, 1 being the lowest, 3 the average, 5 the highest.
2. The ranking scale is used with persons who are associated within a single group and who are to be rated relative to one another. This method is used with a single group of subjects when intragroup comparisons are desired.

Evaluation of Rating Scales

Rating scales are not tests, nor are they precise or objective measures; hence their reliability cannot be as high as that found for other types of psychological instruments. Rating scales do provide a means of obtaining organized description of behavioural traits from judges who have had ample opportunity to make the necessary observations.

Inspite of carefully defined traits and degrees thereof, ratings are always subject to the judge's biases, values and standards of performance and behaviour. Behaviour of the person being rated may be and at time is variable in different types of situations.

Sociometric Method

This method is credited to J.L. Moreno as the innovator. It may be defined as a technique for revealing and evaluating the social structure of a group through the measurement of the frequency of acceptance or no acceptance amount the individual who constitute the group. Learning in classroom depends upon the pattern and structure of inter-personal relationship existing at a given point of time within the group. Learning is a function of classroom situation, most of the successful teacher realize and visualize the importance of individual's personal and academic growth which virtually affect adversely or favourably by his position in the group as pupils of the group stimulate, motivate or thought one another in different ways.

Nature and Definition of Sociometry

According to Jennings, "Sociometry as a device for a graphic and straight forward portrayal of the total configuration of relations among the members of a group at a glance."

J.W. Best defines, " Sociometry is a technique for describing social relationship that exists between individual in a group."

J.L. Moreno explains, "Sociometry is a particular way of measuring social behaviour that test to study the structure and development of the group."

On the basis of above mentioned definitions, it may be concluded that sociometry is a technique to describe social relationships that exists among individuals in a group. The objective of this technique is to establish the pattern of feelings of acceptance and rejection of like and dislike, that is found among the members of a group.

Definition of Terms Used

1. *Popular or star:* He is a person in a group who receives a large number of choices of his fellow members of a group on a sociometric test. He is also referred as star when he gets highest number of choices.
2. *Isolate:* Isolate is the member of the group who receives no choice on a sociometric test i.e., they are not chosen by any of the pupils in the class and they do not have any opportunities for interaction. He is physically a member of the group but psychologically isolated.
3. *Neglectee:* Neglectee is the member of the group who receives usually few positive choices. He is also referred to as a 'fringer' by some investigators.
4. *Rejectee:* Rejectee is the member of the group who receives negative choices. He can only be identified only if the sociometric tool permits negative choice.
5. *Clique:* The term 'Clique' signifies a sub-group within the large group. A sociometric clique is said to be formed when a number of members choose each other on the same sociometric criterion and give few choices to members outside their closcly knit sub-group.
6. *Mutual choices:* It is the selection of two individuals by each other i.e., two members of a group choose to one another.

Sociogram

Findings obtained by means of sociometric technique can be shown graphically in the form is known as a sociogram. A choice may be represented by a single pointed arrow. A mutual choice by an arrow pointing in opposite direction. Rejection may be represented by dotted lines.

Category System

In using a category system the observer classifies or codes the actions of the members of the group into separate categories one of the best known and most widely used category system is that developed by Bales (1950) which he has called Interaction process analysis. Bales set out to develop a standard set of categories for classifying interaction that could be used to study any group. The categories are meant to constitute a mutually exclusive, logically exhaustive system.

Table-13.2

Observation Categories in the Bales Category System

A. *Emotionality Positive Responses*
   1. Shows solidarity, raises others status, gives help reward.
   2. Shows tension release, jokes, laughs, shows satisfaction.
   3. Agree, shows passive acceptance, understands concurs, complies.

B. *Problem-solving Responses : Answers*
   4. Gives suggestion, direction, implying autonomy for others.
   5. Gives opinion, evaluation, analysis, expresses feeling, wish.
   6. Gives orientation, information, respects clarifies, confirms.

C. *Problem-solving Responses Question*
   7. Asks for orientation, information, repetition confirmation.
   8. Asks for opinion, evaluation, analysis, expression of feeling.
   9. Asks for suggestion, direction, and possible ways of action.

D. *Emotionally Negative Responses*
   10. Disagrees, shows passive rejection, formality with holds help.
   11. Shows tension ask for help, withdraws out of field.
   12. Show autogenic, deflates others status, defends or asserts self.

The Bales category system provides a number of scores that describe quantitatively the functioning and structure of groups.

Another kind of category system has been developed by Carter and his associates to study leadership in small laboratory groups.

QUESTIONS

A. Long Answer Type Questions

1. 'Personality is the dynamic organization ....' Discuss.
2. What is personality? Explain its factors that determine it.
3. Heredity and environment both play important role in its development. Discuss.
4. Discuss various methods of assessment of personality.
5. Explain important projective methods/techniques of personality assessment in detail.

B. Short Answer Type Questions

1. Explain rating scale of personality assessment.
2. Discuss objective methods of personality measurement.
3. Discuss MMPI.
4. Heredity is more important than environment in the development of personality comment.
5. Sociometric technique and its importance.

C. **Objective type of Questions**

1. 16 PF Questionnaire was developed by;
   (*a*) Bernreuter (*b*) Allport
   (*c*) Cattell (*d*) Murray
2. Personality has been derived from the word 'Persona, is a word taken from:
   (*a*) French (*b*) Greek
   (*c*) Latin (*d*) Roman.
3. Oedipus complex occurs during the Stage
   (*a*) Oral (*b*) Anal
   (*c*) Latency (*d*) Phallic.
4. MMPI contains items in number of
   (*a*) 100 (*b*) 350
   (*c*) 450 (*d*) 550
5. Birth itself is the first and the greatest universal human frustration. It was stated by:
   (*a*) Freud (*b*) Otto
   (*c*) Adler (*d*) Erikson.
6. Match List I with List II and select correct answer using codes given below the list.

	List I	*List II*
(A)	Self–efficacy	1. Walter Mischel
(B)	Cognitive social learning	2. Freud
(C)	Locus of control	3. Albert Bandura
(D)	Global theory	4. Jullian Rotter

Codes

	A	*B*	*C*	*D*
(*a*)	3	2	1	4
(*b*)	4	3	2	1
(*c*)	1	4	3	2
(*d*)	3	1	4	2

7. The notion of an inferiority complex and compensatory behaviour are associated with:
   (*a*) Adler (*b*) Freud
   (*c*) Horney (*d*) Erikson.
8. According to psycho-analytic theory, the genius is one who

finds outlet of one's unconscious and semi unconscious conflict through the mechanism of:

(a) Projection (b) Redirection
(c) Sublimation (d) Intellectualization.

9. Behavioural micro theory of locus of control was propounded by
(a) Rogers (b) Bandura
(c) Deci (d) Rotter.

10. The work in the field of constitutional psychology is generally credited to:
(a) Sheldon (b) Newman
(c) Hippocrates (d) Kretschmer.

SUGGESTED READINGS

1. Allport, G.W., "Personality: A Psychological Interpretation," New York, Holt Rinhart and Winston, 1937.
2. Vernon, P.E., "Personality Test & Assessment" 1965 Ed. London, Methuen & Co., 1962.
3. Cronbach, Lee J., "Essentials of Psychological Testing," 3rd ed., 1970.
4. Anastasi, A., "Psychological Testing," New York, MacMillan, 1955.
5. Eyesenck, H.J., "Dimensions of Personality," London Kegan Paul, 1947.
6. Kretschmer, E., "Physique and Character," New York, Harcourt Brace, 1925.
7. Lefton, L.A., "Psychology" 3rd edit., Allyan and Bacon Inc., London, 1982.
8. Lindzey, G. and Hall C.S., "Theories of Personality," Wiley Eastern Ltd., 1978, Reprints 1991.
9. Mons, W., "Principles and Practice of Rorschach, Personality Test", London, Faber & Feber 1947.
10. Murray, H.A., "The Thematic Apperception Test," Harvard Uni. Press, Combridge, Mass, 1943.
11. Pareek, Udai Narain, "Development Pattern in Reactions to Frustration, Asia Publications, Bombay, 1964.
12. Thorpe, L.P., Schmuller, A.M., "Personality, and Interdisciplinary Approach." An East-West Students Edition, D.Von Nostrand Company, Inc. New York, 1965.

14

Creativity and its Measurement

No nation can afford to overlook or ignore the significance of creativity in this age of competition. Creative acts not only affect scientific and technological progress but also society in general. It is the responsibility of each nation to identify such talent and encourage and develop creative potential among the students. Now-a-days researchers are eager to study cognitive processes, traits of personality, motivational patterns and background experiences to explain creativity. But to understand creativity, we must look to the social environment too as social factors support creativity. It was Guilford who first focussed on creativity and concluded that creativity is a basic concern in the national interest. Torrance unravel unfailingly the positive domain in educational practice. Modern times, most psychologists and educationists are of the view that all persons have some creative potential, although there may be individual differences in degree.

Creativity is the process of developing original, novel and yet appropriate responses to a problem. An original response is one that is usually not given. A novel response is one that is new or that has not precedence. An original or novel situation should be appropriate, if it is to be termed creative. Teresa Ambile (1996) proposes a three component model of creativity.

1. *Domain-relevant skills:* Include talents and competencies that are valuable for working in the domain. An example would be, one's skills in shaping something while one developed when lived with a family as a child (shaping stone, gold, silver etc.).

2. *Creativity–relevant proceses:* Include work habits and personality traits such as a habit of an individual working 10 hours a day to write and rewrite until he perfected his stories or poems.
3. *Intrinsic task motivation:* This type of creativity is greatly influenced by the social enviroment, by supporting autonomy, stimulating curiosity, encouraging fantasy and providing challenge. Another social factor that influences creativity is whether the field is ready and willing to acknowledge the creative contribution.

The Nature of Creativity

Creativity is considered to be a greatest asset of mankind. It is important to undersand the nature of creativity. It has been explained differently by different philosophers and psychologists.

Philosophically, a creative thinker is one whose thinking leads to a result which conforms to criteria of value in one domain or another. Plato made a distinction between artificial art and true art. Artists deal only with appearances and not reality itself. The true artists bring into birth some new reality. They are creative as they enlarge human consciousness. Some of the Psychologists equated creativity with mental health while some have related it to the personality development. Psycho-analyst like Freud restricted creativity to an interplay of unconscious and conscious mind.

Definitions of Creativity

Murray defined creativity in terms of product. According to him, creativity is the occurrance of something new and valuable. Now he means a certain degree of novelty, originality related to sameness or replication and valuable he means either extrinsically or intrinsically valuable as such to one or more persons or generative of valuable composited in the future.

Guilford (1960) stressed on the divergent production, however he has conceptualized creativity in terms of mental abilities involved in creative pursuits. He defined, "creative thinking is a form of thought that is divergent."

Divergent thinking occurs in response to a problem that as yet not defined, when no set way of solving the problem exists or is available. According to Guilford, the productions of new information from known information, or the generation of logical possibilities, serves as the basis of creativity. The distinctive aspect of creative thinking is divergent thinking which is characterized by flexibility, originality and fluency.

Lefton defined, "Creativity is characteristic of thoughts and of problems solving, generally considered to include originally, novelty and appropriateness."

According to Morris, "Creativity as a process involves three stages:

1. *Hypothesis formation:* People try to formulate a new response to a problem. They have to explore the paths that have not been explored before and to think in new ways.
2. *Hypothesis testing:* The hypothesis is tested using different tools and methods. If the result is novel, original and appropriate, the person can move toward the third stage. i.e.
3. *Communication of results:*

   Rogers defines, "Creativity is the emergence in action of a novel relational product growing out of the uniqueness of the individual." Uniqueness of the person, he means to man's tendency to actualize himself to expose his potentialities.

   According to Stoddard, "The creative act at its highest brings about a notable differences in things, thoughts works of art and social structures."

   Torrance (1962) defined, "Creativity is the process of seeing problems or gaps in information forming ideas or hypotheses testing and modifying these hypothesis and communication of the result."

In view of the above explanations and definitions, some of the Psychologists have expressed creativity in terms of the product, while others in terms of process or a kind of a person. However, it may be stated that there are atleast five components of creativity which have been pointed out as:

1. *The act:* The creative act cannot be described but that is hypothesized as unknowable until it occurs. Rogers (1954) stressed on certain qualities that are associated with creative act. The creative person must undergo certain unique experiences, the first experience of the person is Eureka feeling 'This is so, "I have discovered and this is what I wanted to express. "Wertheimer suggested that creative

thinking involved breaking down and restructuring over knowledge about a phenomenon in order to gain new insights into its nature.

Kelly and Rogers both maintained that we can be creative by gaining an insight into our own understanding of the subject. Actually creativity comes up when we arrange our thoughts in such a way that leads readily to a different understanding of a situation.

2. *The process:* The creative process is the emergence in action of a novel relational product, resulting out of the uniqueness of the person. The creative process generally comes out with product which is novel. Every production is the result of a phased process but regarding to creativity it goes on in the unique manner. Graham Wallas, identified four main stages to describe the creative process.

   (a) *Preparation:* It is the period of accumulating necessary factual knowledge, skills or basic ideas. But there is no guarantee—this stage will lead in generally creative ideas but each creative person has to pass from this stage.
   (b) *Incubation:* This is the stage of relaxation turning attention away from the problem. However, some kind of unconscious/sub-conscious activity is going on although he seeks relaxation from conscious efforts.
   (c) *Illumination :* It is marked with the sudden realization of the meaningful material comes to forefront and includes the Psychological events and accompany the appearance of insight.
   (d) *Verification:* The solution of the problem is tested and refined is known verification. This is the stage where the produced material gets the final form after testing the validity of the concepts.

3. *The object:* The creativity is the object which generally referred to as the product. Here the quality is emphasized which should be originality related to the produced object. This originality is generally associated with four charactertics: (1) Novelty, (2) Unpredictability, (3) Uniqueness, (4) Surprise.
4. *The person:* The person is explained in terms of conditions of self-actualization with reference to the theory of personality of Maslow.

5. *The environment:* Environment is the condition of openness which facilitate the creative persona to move from the actual state of affairs towards the solution of the problem.

Characteristics of Creative Children

Torrance conducted a study to understand the characteristics of creative children. He found the following main characteristics of a creative child:

1. *Courageous in conviction:* He shows strong conviction in his belief and values. He is capable of going beyond socially conformist behaviour.
2. *Curiosity:* Creative child is very curious to know more and more about his environment.
3. *Independent behaviour:* He is able to take independent judgement in crucial matter.
4. *Independent thinking:* Creative child thinks independently to solve various types of problems.
5. *Busy in doing tasks:* He never leaves any task till completes the same. All his energy is concentrated on the tasks in hand.
6. *Intuilion:* He develops intuition in his problem.
7. Unwilling to accept routine solution.
8. High achievement motivation.
9. Willing to take risks.
10. *Visionary:* He has the vision of future problems.

Levels of Creativity

Taylor (1959) suggested for levels of creativity such as:

1. *Expressive creativity:* It involves independent expression having originality in its essence. This is mostly exemplified in the spontaneous drawings of children.
2. *Productive creativity:* This creativity calls for some production and mostly involved in artistic or scientific products.
3. *Inventive creativity:* Ingenuity is displayed with material, methods and techniques. The inventors, explorer and discoverers are the example of using this types of creativity in their production.
4. *Innovative creativity:* This is based upon highly developed abstract conceptualizing skills. Those who make significant modifications in the basic foundations.

5. *Emergent creativity:* This is the highest level of creativity. It is the ability which absorbs commonly provided experiences and produce something unique.

Traits or Characteristics of Creativity

Psychologists have shown that it is the mixture/combination of intellectual factors and personality traits which distinguish the creative person from others. J.P.Guilford made the distinction between two types of thinking abilities one leading to intelligence i.e., convergent thinking and another leads to creativity is called a divergent thinking.

Convergent Thinking

Guilford defines, "Convergent involves thinking towards our right answer. This type of thinking proceeds towards a restricted answer or solution."

Divergent Thinking

Guildford defines, "Divergent thinking, as a kind of mental operation in which we think in different direction. Sometimes seeking variety from known and remembered information. The very unique feature of this kind of thinking is that a variety of responses are produced."

Guilford also mentioned two types of traits:

1. Aptitude Traits

These are primary traits which are related to creativity. These traits have been come out by using factorial analysis.

Sensitivity to Problem

It is an ability that is reflected in a person's detecting something which is missing or lacking in a given situation or needs some modifications.

Fluency

This is quantitative aspect of creativity, coming up with a large quantity of ideas, words and ways of expressing them. There are four factors associated with fluency of thinking such as:

(i) *Word fluency:* It is an ability to express words having a specific letter or combination of words.
(ii) *Associative fluency:* It involves a requirement of meaning for the words given. This ability requires for generating associations or relation, production of analogies or similarities.

(iii) *Expressional fluency:* This is an ability which involves the production of phrases or sentences.

(iv) *Ideational fluency:* This ability involves production of ideas.

Flexibility of Thinking

Flexibility means to think up a variety of ideas and new ways of dealing with situations. It expresses how an individual responds in different ways to a stimulus.

Originality

It is manifested as uncommon with respect to figural, verbal or symbolic transformations. We may say that there are two types of responses, one is obvious and other is remote. Obvious response shows ideational fluency while remote response indicates originality.

Redefinition

It is an ability of rearranging ideas concepts or object or to state the use of parts in new ways. Improvision, reflects this ability of redefinition.

Elaboration

This ability is an expression of detailed steps of production, variety of implications and consequences that can be measured quantitatively.

2. *Non-aptitute Traits*

The traits of motivation and temperament are said to have determining effects upon creative performance. Anne Roe (1946-1953) concluded in her studies that willingness to work hard and to work long hours stood out in common among individuals who showed creativity in arts and science.

Theories of Creative Performance

Different Psychologist and Philosophers tried to answer certain questions related to creativity. The answers constitute various theories of creativity. These are based upon simple assumptions while others have under gone empirical validations. Some important theories on creative performance have been mentioned below:

Divine Inspiration Theory

Some Philosophers have considered creativity as divine inspiration, Plato considers the writer as an agent of some higher power. It is only the higher power which makes him capable of producing anything creative. Most of the creative persons like poets have often experienced that there is some invisible power that makes them to create something new (Houseman, 1933).

Accidental Theory

Much of the creativity is the result of accident or chance. Although this theory fails to provide any scientific bases of explanation however, one thing is sure that no creation is possible unless one is intensely interested and motivated in it. Undoubtedly chance plays important role, but it is only achievement motivation which makes every creation possible.

Besides above, there are some Psychologists who have attempted to explain creative performance in their theories of personality. These are grouped in following categories:

1. *Psycho-Analytic Theory of Personality*

   (a) Sigmund Freud, the father of Psycho–analysis was the first who attempted to analyze the process of creativity. He and his followers lay special stress on his repressed wishes, pregenital and libidinal urges, the sublimation of which largely determines creativity. The creativity owes its origin to conflict within the unconscious mind. According to him, creativity helps a conflict ridden person in releasing his inner conflicts Freudians are also of the view that creativity is a recapitalation of early childhood experiences.

   (b) *Compensatory theory:* Adler is the exponent of this theory. According to him, human beings produce art, science and other aspects of creative performance to compensate for their own inadequacies.

Jung is another very important theoriest whose contribution to creativity is quite substantial. He viewed creativity at two levels:

(i) The psychological mode and
(ii) The visionary mode.

In the *Psychological mode* the content is mainly derived from the domain of human consciousness in relation to family, environment, society and other social institutions, but the release of creativity does not transcend the limits of psychological intelligibility. In the *visionary mode*, the content is derived from the timeless depths which Jung called the collective unconscious.

2. *Humanistic Theory or Motivational Theory*

A group of motivation theorists believe that man's basic motivational tendency is towards self- actualization or self-fulfillment. According to Maslow, creativity is a maximum of self-actualizing which stresses personality and its achievements. Self-actualizing people are highly motivated and unfrightened by the unknown, the mysterious and the puzzling.

For Rogers, motivation is the mainspring of creativity. It is a tendency within a man to actualize himself, to expose/express his potentialities and to activate all the capacities of the organism. According to him, this tendency exists in every individual and awaits only the proper conditions to be exposed. Motivation may be intrinsic or extrinsic, but both are necessary conditions to creativity.

3. *Behaviouristic Theory or Association Theory*

Associationists base their theory of creativity on stimulus response associations. According to them, every creativity results from unusual associations.

Mednick is the exponent of this theory. According to him 'creative' process is the forming of associate elements units into new combinations which either meet specified requirements or are in some way useful. "On the basis of this conceptualization, he developed a test of creativity" – The Remote Association Test.

4. *Cognitive Theory*

Cognitive Psychologists assume that an individual's behaviour is always based on cognition the act of knowing about the situation where the behaviour occurs. Gestalt Psychologists like Wertheimer use the terms productive thinking and problem solving to creativity. According to him, productive thinking involves a process of successive restructuring of a problem.

Guilford also discusses the concept of creativity as a cognitive ability, multivariate in nature. He revealed quite a number of components that constitute creative thinking. His structure of Intellect Model has already been discussed. Guilford analyses the nature of creative thinking ability which he equates with divergent thinkings.

Among the theories discussed in the chapter, the theory/model propounded by Guilford seems to be more rational and widely accepted model as it provides the ground to measure creativity quantitatively with the help of divergent thinking test. Secondly, it considers the motivational factor as an important determinant of creativity. Thirdly, the model assumes that every individual is in possession of creative thinking ability.

Relationship between Creativity and Intelligence

Conceptual Identification

Guilford (1950) conceptualized creativity as divergent thinking process whereas intelligence has been associated with convergent thinking and the difference provides two independent cognitive variables as two independent components (Foster, 1971) between which relationship can be established. Torrance (1963) as well as Getzels and Jackson (1962) believed that the conventional tests of intelligence fail to measure divergent production abilities. The relative difference between intelligence and creativity i.e., between convergent and divergent thinking as conceptualized by Guilford (1950, 1956, 1959) in his S1 Model. It can be best explained in terms of their symbolic presentation. Guilford's concept of structure of intellect stresses on the divergent thinking and transformation rather than the convergent production and evaluation so for as creativity is converned.

Some leading studies that show relationship between Intelligence and Creativity:

1. Getzels and Jackson (1958) found that creativity and intelligence were not synonymous. They compared high school students who were high on creativity tests. (H C upper 20%) put comparatively low on I.Q., with students who were high on I.Q. (H I upper 20%) but not as high on tests of creativity. The researcher found:
   - *(i)* An average difference between the two group of 23 points on I.Q.
   - *(ii)* No significance differences between the two group on standard achievement scores.
   - *(iii)* Teacher's preference for high I.Q. groups.
   - *(iv)* The highly creative group appeared not to value the qualities they recognized as contributing to success as much as the comparison group did.
   - *(v)* The highly creative group showed greater imagination and originality in their writing style and valued human more in themselves than the high I.Q. group did.

2. Wallach and Kogan (1965) criticized the work of Getzels and Jackson (1958) and Torrance (1963). These investigators believe that it is possible to talk about creativity and intelligence only if experimental data show dimension independent of intelligence. However by analyzing their data and Cline Richards and Needham (1963) found that creativity is a unified pervasive, broad *dimension independent of intelligence.* Wallach and Kogan (1956) found very similar inter-correlations within the various creativity measures and between creativity measures and I.Q. scores as given below:

Scores	*Data from Getzels and Jackson*		*Data Cline Richards and Needham*	
	Boy	*Girl*	*Boy*	*Girl*
Intra Creativity	.21	.24	.26	.27
Inter Creativity and I.Q.	.35	.33	.28	.32

Wallach and Kogan conducted experimental study, administered a series of 10 creativity test covering only uniqueness and productivity in the area of fluency. They obtained correlation as below:

Test	*Correlation*
Intra Creativity Test	.40
Intra intelligence Test	.50
Inter creativity – I.Q. Test	.10

Wallach and Kogan analyzed the responses and were able to separate their data into four categories:

1. High Creativity – High I.Q. (HC-H1)
2. High Creativity – Low I.Q. (HC-L1)
3. Low Creativity – High I.Q. (LC-H1)
4. Low Creativity – Low I.Q. (LC-L1)

From this classification, Wallach and Kogan derived the following conclusions:

1. *The girls of HC-H1 group display least doubt and least hesitation about answering:* They have highest attention span, concentration and are interested in academic work. They are high in disruptive attention- seeking behaviour and are

apparently eager to propose novel divergent possibilities in classroom.

2. *The low creativity – High I.Q. (LC-H1)*: Girls have high confidence and assurance. They are sought by others but do not activity seek companionship themselves. They are interested in academic achievement.
3. *Girls with high creativity – Low I.Q. (HC-L1)*: They are cautious and hesitant about expressing themselves in class. They are least confident and assured. They are least able to concentrate and maintain attention.
4. *The low creativity – Low I.Q. (LC-L1)*: Girls show greater confidence and assurance than high creativity – low I.Q. girls. They are more outgoing toward peers than high creativity low I.Q. ones. They seem to compensate for poor academic performance by activities in social sphere.

Measurement of Creativity

The creativity test are usually open ended. The examiners ask how many solutions the subject can see instead of one correct solution.

Types of Creativity Tests:

1. Torrance Test of creative thinking
2. Christensen-Guilford test
3. Mednrick's Remote Association Test.
4. Passi's Battery of creativity test.
5. Baquer Mehanid's test of creativity.

Creativity in the Classroom

Classroom teaching is the most powerful instrument which can help students to develop the creative talent maximum. Teachers are to take that responsibility by shifting from a mere routine type of teaching to creative teaching. Creative teaching is possible when teachers become more creative in helping their learners to be creative. It means teachers should give more attention to creative problem solving skills of the students. The role of the teacher is to stimulate, guide, to provide a conducive environment and the necessary equipments, where students have not to be only passive listeners instead they should be active particulars in teaching-learning process.

Most of the researchers are of the view that creativity should not be left to chance for its development instead it should be fostered through deliberate methods. They should find out methods, approaches and techniques that may be employed to assist students to think creativily. In this regard that teachers must know the factors that inhibit creative thinking in students. Winner (2000) lists four dangers to avoid:

1. Avoid pushing so hard that the child's intrinsic passion to master a field becomes a craving for extrinisic rewards.
2. Avoid pushing so hard that the child later looks back on a missed childhood.
3. Avoid freezing the child into safe, technically perfect way of performing that has led to lavish rewards.
4. Be aware of the psychological wounds that can follow when the child who can perform perfectly becomes the forgotten adult who can do nothing more than continue to perform perfectly without ever creating something new.

Teachers and parents can encourage students with outstanding abilities and creative talents to give back to the society that has provided extra support and resources.

Besides the above dangers teachers should eliminate such obstacles which interferes in developing creativity such as:

1. The pressure to conform, is the main obstacle in eliciting creative responses.
2. Authoritarian attitudes suppress the creative potential.
3. Threats and ridicules injure the feelings of self worth in students and that block in the outlet of their creative potential.
4. External evaluation arouses defensive attitudes among students that inhibit creative responses.
5. Inflexible defense mechanism and compulsive fears from the part of teachers deter the productive thinking among students.
6. Teacher's demand for right answers create an obstacle in creativity.

Creative Teacher

A creative teacher is one who invents such creative techniques which are unforseable and put the students in surprise. Such techniques create interest, sustain the attention and induce to think off in different direction to the students in order to get the large number of solutions to the problem. A creative teacher may apply the following techniques in the classroom to develop creativity amoung students:

1. *Self-initiated learning:* Teachers may provide freedom of thought to elicit creative responses.
2. *Provision of permissive learning environment:* Democratic teaching learning environments facilitates creative learning that also lead to creativity.
3. *Motivation to creative thought process:* The creative teacher motivates students to imagine, to think for various solutions to problems and allow to seek for new associations among existing objects.
4. *Intellectual fluency and flexibility:* The creative teacher stimulates students to store the information and use it in different situations.
5. *Accept and encourage divergent thinking:* Creative teacher lays stress on divergent thinking instead of convergent thinking e.g., during classroom discussion he may ask, can anyone suggest a different way of looking at this question?
6. *Tolerate dissent:* Creative teacher should develop a habit of tolerating dissent expression from the students.
7. Encourage students to trust their own judgement.
8. Emphasis that everyone is capable of creativity in some form.
9. Be a stimulus for creative thinking.
10. *Develop curiosity:* The creative teachers foster curiosity and encourage their students to make the best use of the question. Operational questions always lead to exploration which foster curiosity.
11. Active participation.
12. *To be adventurous:* The creative teacher inculcates the spirit of adventure among his students. He allows them to face uncertainties and ambiguities of life as a challenge which are important traits of personality to be a creative.

Techniques of Development of Creativity

It has been realized that creative thinking abilites can be developed to varying degrees among different individuals through systematically organized programmes in the schools. There are various techniques such as:

1. *Attribute listing:* This technique was developed in 1954 by Robert Platt Crawford. According to him, magic inspiration

is not the only, even major source of creativity, most of the creativity arises from changing the attributes of an object or an activity or from grafting on to the object or an activity of an attribute or attributes of some other object of activity. In 'attribute listing', 'the attempt is made first to list the basic but modifiable attributes or properties or specification of a particular object or activity, after that an attempt is made to search for alternatives to present attribute. This is a kind of search for a better method of solving human problems. This technique is very much applied for improving product design to attract consumers. Crawford laid down the following principle of attribute listing:

1. Creation is largely adaptation and experimentation.
2. Creation is useful modification of an attribute or assimilation of attributes of other objects.
3. Creation is the continuing array of modification suggested by ideas.
4. It is described to search for concrete alternatives during the process of modifying the current attributes of an object.
5. Creativity can be systematized by looking first for closely related substitutes of the current attribute and then progressively going in for more and more far out alternatives.

2. *Morphological analysis:* This is a variant of attribute listing. This technique was developed by Fred Zincky in California in 1957. It provides facilitation of imagination by allowing the individual to focus on one aspect of the object or activity at one time. It combines the modifiable attributes of the major variables of problems into a grid so that all the possible combinations can be considered. In Morphological analysis the basic is to identify the critical modifiable attributes and listing several attributes for each of the attributes enable one to generate a very large number of alternatives of an object or an activity.

The difference between 'attribute listing' and 'Morphological' analysis is that former works best when the object, activity, product is sought to be modified while later can also be applied profitable to modify general objects or activities. Both are not merely techniques, they embody important values and attitude favouring creativity.

3. *Brain storming* : Alex Osborn (1957) developed this method of brain storming which is being widely used and it has now become the tremendous source of generating creative power. It is a technique in which problem is attacked from all possible angles to generate a large number of ideas in order to arrive at the best solution.

   In a brain storming session a group of students sit around a table to brain storm a specific problem. Each participant presents the ideas which come to his mind. No member of the group is allowed to criticize on the idea put forward by another member. The main objective which underline is that offering a person from the usual inhibitions that operate to block his creative process. Encouraging creativity through everyday interaction with students, teachers should use this technique of brain storming. As mentioned earlier, the basic tenet of brain storming is to separate the process of creating ideas from the process of evaluating them because evaluation inhibits creativity. Evaluation, discussion and criticism are postponed until all possible suggestion have been made. In such situation, one idea inspires others; students do not withhold potentially creative solutions out of fear of criticisim. John Bech (1997) give these rules for brain storming:

   1. Defer judgement.
   2. Avoid ownership of ideas.
   3. Feel free to hitchhike on other ideas. This means that one may borrow elements from ideas already on the table, to make slight modifications of ideas already suggested.
   4. Encourage wild ideas.

   This technique is useful and practical. Teachers and students can use it very successfully to find out the best solutions to the problems that are being challenged by the existing system of education.

4. *Inquiry training:* This model was developed by Richard Suchman (1962) to teach students a process of investigating and explaining unusual phenomenon. He identified the components of the inquiry process and built them into the

instrumental model to which he called 'Inquiry Training.' His approach is based on four postulates.

1. *Children are curious by nature:* Any puzzling problem is motivated them to explore the answer of the problem.
2. This process of inquiry can be taught to students as they are increasingly conscious and they can learn scientific procedures directly to solve the problem scientifically.
3. *Team approach:* This approach is more useful than the individual approach to find the solution to a problem.
4. All knowledge is tentative. The students should be make aware of this fact as there is always scope of modification.

5. *Synectics:* The word synectics has been derived from the Greek Word Synecticos which means joining together two different and apparently diverse elements. Gordon (1960) is the originator of this method. It is an operational theory for the conscious use of the preconscious and psychological mechanisms present in man's creative activity. Synectics' is defined as the mental activity in problem solving in order to arrive at solutions of fundamental novelty. Gordon basically put forward three assumption about this creative process viz.

   1. Creative process could be described and it be enhanced by conscious efforts to promote the creative process among students.
   2. Emotional component was more important than the intellectual. Similarly the irrational is more important than the rational.
   3. Emotional and irrational elements must be understood in order to increase the probability of success in a problem solving situation.

Gordon found that there are five interrelated states of mind should be present in an individual to move through the creative process so that he may make a break through to contribute to a final solution. They are:

1. Detachment and Involvement
2. Determinant
3. Speculations
4. Autonomy
5. Hedonic response.

The objective of Synectics training should be provided to teachers in view of the factors mentioned above. The following activities, approaches and techniques should be used to develop creativity among students.

1. *Metaphoric activities:* Metaphors establish a relationship of likeness, the comparison on one object or idea with another object or idea by using one another. It introduces a conceptional distance between the student and the object or subject-matter and allows time to think reflectively. During this activity students innovate and imagine.
2. *Evocative questions:* Teachers may ask such questions which are open ended queries intending to draw all the students of the class into creative process such designed questions may start discussion and arouse interest among students.
3. *Direct analogous questions:* Direct analogous question are a simple comparison of two objects or concepts. Such questions may not be identical in all respects.
4. *Personal analogy:* It involves the students emphatically with the ideas or object to be compared.

QUESTIONS

A. Long Answer Type Questions

1. Explain the concept of creativity. Discuss various factors related to it.
2. Discuss various theories of creativity. Do you agree that every child is creative?
3. Discuss in detail the significance of Creativity in Education.
4. What is creativity? How can it be identified?
5. Discuss in detail the role of the teachers in the development of creativity in children.

B. Short Answer type Questions

1. State the relationship between Creativity and Intelligence.
2. Discuss the role of imagination in creativity.
3. Creativity and creative thinking.
4. Convergent and divergent thinking.
5. Brain storming.
6. Synectics.

C. Objective Questions

1. A technique for problem solving that involves considering all

possible solution with making prior evaluative judgement is know.

(*a*) Mediation (*b*) Hypothesis testing
(*c*) Brain Storming (*d*) Creativity.

2. Creativity is a process involving three stages hypothesis formulation, hypothesis testing and communication of research. It has been defined by:
(*a*) Guilford (*b*) Morris Stein
(*c*) Johnson (*d*) Mackinnon.

3. Thinking occurs in response to a problem that as yet is not defined when no set way of solving the problem exists or is available is called
(*a*) Convergent thinking (*b*) Conceptional thinking
(*c*) Divergent thinking (*d*) Hyphothetical thinking.

4. Consider the statement:
1. Creativity is an expression of the psychologically healthy person.
2. Creative persons are not deliberate non-conformists.
3. Creative person are genuinely independent.
4. Creative persons are more introverted.
(*a*) 1, 2 and 4 are correct (*b*) 2, 3 and 4 are correct
(*c*) All are correct (*d*) 1, 3 and 4 are correct.

5. There is a four stage theory of creative thinking which held that periods of:
1. Incubation 2. Preparation
3. Illumination 4. Verification.
Correct sequence is:
(*a*) 1, 3, 2, 4 (*b*) 1, 2, 3, 4
(*c*) 2, 1, 3, 4 (*d*) 2, 3, 1, 4.

6. Stage of creative thinking was formulated by:
(*a*) Graham Wallas (*b*) Helm Holtz
(*c*) Frank Barron (*d*) Mackinnon.

7. An investigation of (151) fifth grade children was made to establish relationship between intelligence and creativity. It was conducted by:
(*a*) J.P. Guilford (*b*) Wallach and Kogan
(*c*) Barron et al. (*d*) Graham Wallas.

8. Sensitivity to problems, originality and ingenuity are the components of creativity. According to:
(*a*) Wallas (*b*) Johnson
(*c*) Davis (*d*) Barron.

9. Divergent thinking is opposite to:

   1. Autistic thinking 2. Convergent thinking

   (*a*) 1 is true 2 is false (*b*) 2 is true 1 is false

   (*c*) Both are true (*d*) Both are false.

10. Which factors have negative affect on creativity.

    1. Emotional factors 2. Set

    3. Functional fixedness

    (*a*) 1 and 2 are correct (*b*) 2 and 3 are correct

    (*c*) 1 and 3 are correct (*d*) All are correct.

SUGGESTED READING

1. Cattell, R.B. & Butcher, H.J., "Creativity and Personality," Vernon, P.E., Modern Psychological Readings, Penguin, 1970.
2. Getzels, J.W., and P.W. Jackson (1962), "Creativity and Intelligence Exploration with Gifted Students", New York, John Wiley and Sons, Inc.
3. Guilford, J.P. (1959), "Traits of Creativity", In P.E. Vernon (ed.) Creativity Penguin Modern Psychology Readings, England, 1970.
4. Hammer, E.F., "Creativity", New York, Random House, 1961.
5. Johnson, D.M., *Essentials of Psychology,* Mcgraw Hill Book Co., New York 1948.
6. Paramesh, C.R., "Creativity and Personality", Madras, Janta Book House, 1972.
7. Thorndike, R.L., "Measurement of Creativity", New York, Teachers College Record, 1963.
8. Torrance, E.P. (1962), "Guiding Creative Talent" Eaglewood Cliffs, New Jersey, Prentice Hall, Inc.
9. Wallach, M.A. (1971), "The Intelligence–Creativity Distinction", New York, General Learning Press.

15

Achievement and its Measurement

The main focus is given by the educationists and Psychologists is to improve the performance or learning of the students in teaching-learning process. Any educative process is incomplete unless, we have the knowledge of students efficiency or the level of learning the students have reached. The only way to know and understand the product of learning of the children with the help of their achievement or performance in a school subject or as a whole. This assessment is the process of testing or measuring the improvement in learning or mode of change in behaviour of the students at the end of the instruction. It is the responsibility of the teacher to have the knowledge about the achievement or performance of the students i.e. whether he or they acquired the objective of learning in the particular domain of behaviour, as an achievement. The performance is the outcome of the instructions usually with verbal and written performance.

According to Freeman, 'The educational tests seek to measure the products of Training and indirectly to determine the efficiency of the training which the individual has received.

"Cronbach States Achievement testing has been detrimental when it forced schools into training rather than educating pupil."

The child whatever learns in the school is known achiement and to examine his knowledge or efficiency or proficiency in this regard with the help of test is called achievement test. Teacher uses time to time such tests to know the progress of his educans. Now it becomes main objective of the teacher to have knowledge about his students to what extents they have reached to their goals regarding the attaining of their domain of objectives. These tests give emphasis on relative achievement of the students instead of absolute achievement.

A few definitions of achievement test are given below—

Frank, S. Freeman—"A test of educational achievement is one designed to measure knowledge, understanding or skills in a specified subject or a group of subjects."

Lindquist and Mann—"A general achievement test is one' designed to express in terms of a single score a pupil's relative achievement in a given field of achievement."

Bingham defined achievement test, "as measurement of past accomplishment both in and out of school when judged in relation to the lenght and character of the training or experience is called achievement test."

Super "An achievement of proficiency best is used to ascertain what and how much has been learnt or how well a task has been performed."

Ebel—"An achievement test is one designed to measure a student's grasp some knowledge or his proficiency in certain skills."

Characteristics in an achievement test.

1. Achievement tests measure the ability of the students to understand the contents of the curriculum.
2. Achievement tests measure not only the student's grasp of knowledge but also their understanding and application.
3. These tests have level of difficulty as well as power of discriminating.
4. These test have objective questions.
5. These tests are standardized and have their own norms for their interpretation.
6. Tests are reliable and valid.
7. Thest tests have predetermined objectives.
8. Such tests are designed differently for different courses.

Test Construction

Followings are the main step for the test construction

1. Planning
2. Preparation
3. Final Try Out
4. Evaluation

1. Planning

Before doing any action, we must plan to do the work systematically. No work may be considered powerful and effective until we understand the present situations. We should go through the following stages before constructing any achievement test.

1. Reviewing existing tests.
2. Review of related literature.
3. Fixing up the objective in terms of taxonomic categories i.e., cognitive affective, and psycho-motor.
4. Objective to be specified in behavioural terms by using Robert Major or RCEM approach.
5. Content is to be analyzed in sub topic and its elements. Each element is to be related to one behaviour or more than one objectives.
6. Determination of types of items.
7. Types of items and number of items.
8. Time limit
9. Scoring procedure
10. Type of Answer sheet
11. Method of preparing the test.

2. Preparation

Test construction expected to follow the following steps.

1. Table of specification to be prepared to quote the test items.
   (a) Recall type items
   (b) Recognition type items
2. Collection of test items form the various sources.
3. Inclusion of items of different forms.
4. To observe and edit the items by himself as well as with the help of subject expert.
5. To decide scoring procedure.
6. Primary tryout is conducted to check the language difficulty and ambiguity of the items of the test.
7. Individual tryout is to be done. One item should be written on one card. The items should be modified accordingly.

3. Final Tryout

1. After preliminary test is prepared which include more items, than the test.

2. Pre-tryout is done on a large group atleast 100 students representative group.
3. Item analysis is done to obtain difficulty values and discriminating power of the items.
4. Items are selected, rejected and modified on the basis of D.V. or D.P. indices.
5. The desired number of items are prepared for the final draft of the test.

4. Evaluation of the Test

1. Final draft of the test has large number of items (100 items).
2. The final test is administered on 100 students when the test is designed.
3. The reliability and validity of the test are estimated logically and empirically .
4. Norms are to be established.
5. Manual of the test is prepared for the use of the test.

Procedure of Teacher Made Achievement Tests

1. To frame behavioural objectives of the test

The purpose of any instructional process is to develop integrated approach of learning among the students. A teacher must be very clear about his expectation of desired outcomes from his teaching-learning process. He must keep in mind the Blooms taxonomy of behavioural changes which are expected from all three behavioural domain viz cognitive, affective and psycho-motor to achieve from the cognitive domain cognitive.

2. *Cognitive Domain*

The student are taught chemistry.

1. Knowledge

(*a*) The pupil recalls terms concepts and facts etc. related to the subject of chemistry.

(*b*) The pupils recognise terms, facts, concepts, principle used in the subject chemistry.

2. Understanding or Comprehension

1. The pupils illustrate a term, concept principles by examples.
2. The pupils compare and contrast or detect similarities and dissimilarities between closely related concepts.

3. The pupils identify relationship between various facts and concepts.
4. The pupils can translate verbal material into logical written material. They also can translate pictorial material into verbal form.
5. They give explanation of concept and principle acting appropriate examples.

3. Applicaton

1. Students may analyse the situations.
2. They can draw inferences and conclusions from the observed facts.
3. They can give reasons for different concepts.

4. Analysis

1. The pupils can find out the different aspects or parts of a object or material.
2. They can findout the relationship between different parts, points out the parts and able to separate the parts of the object or situation.
3. The students can find out the different parts into components.

5. Synthesis

1. Pupils can give an organised way of solution of the problem.
2. They are capable to develop/create statements.
3. They can propose new plans for experimentation and can rearrange and reconstruct the given material.
4. Pupils can formulate new schemes for categorising, organising and recognising and restructuring of objects, devices and designs.

6. Skills

1. The pupils can express themselves clearly and logically through verbal or in writing.
2. They can develop hand and eye coordination to solve the problem.

Blue Print

Meaning

A blue print is always designed before we construct any test. It is a design oı plan for setting a question paper. It is a kind of a table which shows the number of questions, alongwith the marks pertaining to different sub units of subject are selected. It is a guide for the test construction. It is actually a chart showing list of instructional objectives content areas and types of items of its dimensions. It also depicts the type of questions to be used with reference to each content unit as well as the objective on which, it is based.

A well developed Blueprint has the following characteristics.

1. It has a list of topics in which cognitive domain i.e., knowledge, understand and application of the learners is to be tested.
2. Markwise weightage is given to each topic is view of importance.
3. Marks are allotted to each domain of instructional objectives.
4. Classification of questions into various categories viz—objective type, short answer type and long answer type.
5. Proportion of easy, average and difficult question.

Preparations of the Blueprint

The construction of a good test has to follow a definite design or plan. The steps in designing a test via a blueprint followed in the following pattern.

1. Allocation of Marks to Various Level

Objectives	*% marks*
Knowledge	40
Understanding	36
Application	24

2. Allocation of Marks of Various Questions

Types of questions	*% of marks*
Very Short Answer (V.S.A.)	32
Short Answer (S.A.)	48
Long Answer (L.A.)	20

3. Allocation of Marks to Various Units

Units	*% of marks*
Water	32
Air	26
Elements, compounds and mixtures	22
States of matter	20

Blue Print

Domain / Unit	Knowledge V.S.A.	Knowledge S.A.	Knowledge L.A.	Understanding V.S.A.	Understanding S.A.	Understanding L.A.	Application V.S.A.	Application S.A.	Application L.A.	Total V.S.A.	Total S.A.	Total L.A.	Grand Total
Water	4 (1)	1 (3)	X	1 (1)	1 (3)	X	X	X	1 (5)	5	6	5	16
AIR	1 (1)	1 (3)	X	1 (1)	1 (3)	X	X	X	1 (5)	2	6	5	13
Elements Compounds and Mixture	2 (1)	1 (3)	X	2 (1)	1 (3)	X	1 (1)	X	X	5	6	X	11
State of Matter	1 (1)	1 (3)	X	2 (1)	1 (3)	X	1 (1)	X	X	4	6	X	10
Total Marks	8	12	X	6	12	X	2	X	10	16	24	10	50
Percentage of Total	16%	24%	X	12%	24%	X	4%	X	20%	32%	48%	20%	100%
	40%			36%			24%						

Construction of a Question Paper

The construction of a question is done on the basis of the blueprint as explained earlier. This process involves the following steps.

Designing of the Question Paper

The test is to be designed in accordance with the purpose of the teaching, learning achievement. This may include.

1. Identification of aims and objectives.
2. Weightage is to be given to each objective.
3. Proportionate weightage to each unit, and sub-unit is to be given.
4. Decision is to be taken to the weightage for different type of questions or items.
5. Time allocation in view of the length of the questions.
6. Blueprinting of the achievement test A blueprint is to be prepared on the basis of the design of the test.

Framing of the Items

Blueprint guides the framing of questions. It the technical competency of teacher to frame questions of the required involves variety as indicated in the blueprint. Each question should be framed to examine a particular objective using the relevant content of the unit.

Assembling of the Items

The items framed should be grouped together according to the form used. Objective type questions are to be played at one and short type at another and essay or long type quesions separately

(*a*) content wise
(*b*) difficulty wise
(*c*) objective wise.

Preparing of Instructions

Preparing instructions being as a part of the test are meant directly the examinees to attempt the questions in a particular manner besides indicating some restrictions.

Marking Scheme

A marking scheme is the scheme to assess the answers script of the learner, It states the following—

(*i*) Correct answer and value point for each question.
(*ii*) Marks to be assigned for each correctly written answer.

Merits

(i) It increases the objectivity.

(ii) It provides uniformity in assessing the answer of the question.

ACHIEVEMENT TEST
Subject–Chemistry
Class–VII

M.M. : 50 **Time. 90 min**

NOTE:

(i) All questions are compulsory.

(ii) Each part of question 1 to 3 carries 3 marks.

(iii) Question 4 to 11 are short answer type carrying 3 marks each.

(iv) Question 12 and 13 are long answer type, carrying 5 marks each.

Q1. Give one word answer of each of the followings?

(a) Which gas is necessary to form proteins in plants?

(b) Which state of matter has a definite volume but no definite shape?

(c) Which will evaporate faster water at 10°C or water at 20°C.?

(d) Does water expand or contract when it changes to ice?

(e) Is sea water, a compound or a mixture?

(f) Why carbon-dioxide is used in fire extinguisher and not the oxygen?

Q2. Fill in the blanks.

(a) Baking powder when heated gives out__________gas.

(b) Water does not change the colour of the litmus paper because it is__________.

(c) The process by which water can be broken into its constituent elements is called__________.

(d) The smallest particle of a compound is__________.

(e) The inter molecular distance between the particles__________when the liquid was solidifies due to low temperature.

Q3. State the following statements as True or False.

(a) The boiling point of water can be used as a test for the purity of water. ☐

(b) Solubility of most solids in water increase with temperature. ☐

(c) Most plants directly take nitrogen from the air. ☐

(d) The gas used to release energy from food inside air body is carbon-dioxide. ☐

(e) Water and sugar are mixed together and heated to give a solution which is a compound of sugar and water. ☐

Q4. Why do climbers to high mountains carry cylinder with them?

Q5. A dirty cloth when washed under a hand pump water does not form lather with the soap.

Q6. Mention three ways in which air gets polluted.

Q7. Is hard water safe for drinking? State its two disadvantages.

Q8. A perfume sprayed at one corner of the room, can be smelt at the other corner. Explain why?

Q9. Why naphthalene balls kept open for some time start reducing without changing into liquid? Explain the process.

Q10. Why is nitrogen essential for plants as well as animals? Can it be used directly by the living organisms from air?

Q11. Water is a compound and hydrogen is an element. State two diferences on this basis, between water and hydrogen.

Q12. How is it possible for the fish and other acquatic animals to survive even when the temp. goes below 0° C and the water freezes? Support your answer with the help of a diagram.

Q13. What is desalination? Explain the procedure by which it is done to get pure water.

Marking scheme for Achievement test

Question No.	*Correct Answer of the question*	*Marks Allotted*	*Total mark of the quest.*
1	2	3	4
1.	(a) nitrogen (b)	1	6
	(b) liquid	1	
	(c) Water at 20°C	1	
	(d) Expands	1	
	(e) Mixture	1	
	(f) It is notes supporter of comubustion	1	
2.	(a) Carbon dioxide	1	5
	(b) Neutral	1	
	(c) Eectrolysis	1	
	(d) Atom	1	
	(e) decreases	1	
3.	(a) True	1	5
	(b) True	1	
	(c) False	1	

Q.	Part	Answer	Marks	Total
	(d)	False	1	
	(e)	False	1	
4.	(a)	Amount of air is less on high attitudes	1	3
	(b)	Amount of oxygen is also less	1	
	(c)	It also causes breathing problems so they carry cylinder	1	
5.	(a)	Hand pump water is hard water	1	3
	(b)	It does not form lather with the soap	1	
	(c)	As it contains calcium and magnesium salts in it	1	
6.	(a)	By carbon dioxide from various sources	1	
	(b)	By sulphuric-di-oxide from industrial wate	1	3
	(c)	By nitrogen-di-oxide and lead from the automobiles and industries	1	
7.	(a)	Yes, It is safe for drinkng purpose	1	
	(b)	Disadvantages at reduced clearing efficiency of soap	1	3
	(c)	When used in geysers or boiling industry causes deposition on the miner wall	1	
8.	(a)	The particles of perfume difuse into the air	1	
	(b)	And the sprayed perfume on diffision through the air reaches the corner of the room.	2	3
9.	(a)	*(i)* It is the process of changing of solid decrease into gas without being changed into liquid.	1 2	3
		(ii) They subline		

10. *(i)* Nitrogen is essential for protein synthesis in plants and animals. Plants form nitrates from it which goes in the body of animals to form proteins which are necessary for growth and development of the body. 2

(ii) It can not be used directly by the organism 1

11.

	Water		Hydrogen	Marks
(a)	Can be broken into its constituents elements	(i)	Can not be broken into more sample constituents	1½
				3
(b)	Does not show the property of its constituents	(ii)	shows the property of its constituents	1½

12.	(a)	Since the ice is lighter than water so its floats upon the bottom			1
	(b)	and saves inner layer from freezing so the aquatic animals survive	1		
	(c)	The density of frozen ice at 0°C is less than the water	1	5	
	(d)	Correct diagram with variation of density with temperature	2		
Q13.	(a)	The process of removal of salt from sea water is desalination	1		
	(b)	This can be done by the method distillation	1		
	(c)	Explanation of proper correct procedure with	1	5	
	(d)	Correct apparatus to be mentioned	2		
		Total		**50**	

Uses of Achievement test

Tests of educational achievements have widely been used in educational institutions at all stages. They are used in elementary and secondary schools to evaluate teachers effectiveness of different teaching methods. They serve and are helpful in maintaining standards in pupils performance and progress for a general evaluations of all part of a school system. Achievement tests are generally used in the field of education industry, civil services and also for guidance and counselling and for clinical purpose. The achievement tests are used to fulfill the following purpose.

1. *Assignment of grades*: More often such tests are used to assign grades in on the basis of achievement in tests.
2. *Promotional to next class*: In education institutions, the students are promoted to higher class on the basis of achievement test scores. In some services, promotion for next higher post is done in the basis of test score in achievement tests.
3. *Classification of Individuals:* Achievement tests are often used to classify students into special course on curriala within the school or college.
4. *Counselling and Remedial Teaching*: Achievement tests are very useful to the school psychologists and chinical psychologists to understand the school problems, difficulties of a particular child and his behaviour if he is deviant too. These tests are

used to indicate the school performance, progress and effectiveness of teaching learning process.

The diagnostic and achievement tests are designed primarily to help in counselling the remedial teaching of students who show difficulty in mastering certain school subject or topics. Achievement tests some times also indicate the causes of students training or poor conduct in the class and school.

5. *Vocational guidances*: Achievement tests in combination with course grades are useful in helping the students to choose future programmes of school work or vocational training.
6. *Helpful in Effective School Administration:* Achievement tests help the administrators to judge the extent to which the objectives of the school are being achieved to find out strengths and weaknesses of the curriculum and arranging special school programmes. It also helps in decisions concerning admission grouping and promotion of the students.
7. *Helpful in Curriculum Development*: Curriculum development is an significant aspect of the teaching-learning process. Evaluation of achievement data enable the curriculum development, to determine the effectiveness of new procedures to identify areas where revision of the curriculum is essential. Evaluation of the same helps to determine the degree to what extent an existing curriculum is effective. The evaluation data in this regard are helpful in constructing the new and revised curriculum.

Difference between standardized and Teacher made Achievement Test.

Standardized Tests	*Teacher made Tests*
1. Standardized tests meant their application of comparing with the students of the same grade for which they were standardized	1. Such test are consctructed by the school teacher to judge the effectiveness of his teaching-learning process.
2. Standard of the grade as whole is the main consideration	2. Teacher's job is to construct such test to understand the achievement in subject concerned.
3. Standardized test's construction requires vast knowledge, experience and expertise.	3. It is easy to construct

(Contd.)

Standardized Tests	Teacher made Tests
4. These test are reliable, valid.	4. These test are not reliable and valid to that extent of standard tests.
5. Such test have their own norms.	5. Norms are established by the teacher to classify students in different category.
6. These tests serve the purpose of prognostic teaching-learning process.	6. These tests are constructed from the diagnostic point of view.
7. These tests are useful for all.	7. These tests are used only in the school for which they are constructed.
8. Standardized tests are only one type.	8. Such tests are of three types: *(i)* essay type *(ii)* objective and diagnostic.

Essay Type Tests

The essay type tests are not reliable and valid as compared to objective type tests even though it is not possible to eliminate them from the field of educational measurement and evaluation. These type of tests are widely used to measure the higher learning objectives.

Characteristics of Essay Type Tests

1. An essay type test questions require the students to plan his own answer and to express it in their own words.
2. An essay test consists of relatively a few, more general questions which require extended answers.
3. Examinees are supposed to spend their time in thinking and writing the answer of the essay type questions.
4. The quality of an essay type test is determined and depend largely upon the skill of the teacher who examines the answer of the students.
5. Evaluation of the answer of the essay type question require subject expert.
6. An essay type test is relatively very easy to prepare and at the same time it is tedious and difficult to score accurately.
7. A essay type tests provide opportunity to express student's his own view point in the answer as to give more freedom to the scorer to be guided by his individual performances in scoring the answer.
8. Essay type test permits opportunity and encouraged bluffing.

9. Essay type tests are less reliable and less content coverage.
10. There is no scope of guessing the answer which would be cent per cent correct as it is seen in the objective type of tests.

Diagnostic Test

An achievement test is one kind of educational test which have two purposes prognostic and diagnostic purpose.

The prognostic means to measure and evaluate the extent and level of learning outcomes or attainments of the students in a specific subjects which has been taught to them. Diagnostic means to identify the causes of their weaknesses of their poor performance of the students.

Meaning of Diagnostic Test

Diagnostic test is also a kind of achievement test which measures of acquired learning experiences and weaknesses. In the try to measures find out the difficulties faced the content of the subject. Teacher tries to understand the causes of their difficulty so that he may problems and difficultives.

Defìnitons

A diagnostic test is one designed to reveal a person's strength and weakness in one or more areas of the field being tested.

Ross, Prevention is the highests level of diagnosis and its value depends more upon the teacher who uses than upon the test used.

Diagnostic Process

1. Selection of students who need diagnosis.
   (i) Students who have poor achievement score in the subject.
   (ii) Teacher may also select students whom he considered poor in intelligence and adjustment.
   (iii) Selection of those students who have high I.Q. but poor performance in a particular subject or subjects as a whole.
2. Identification of student's difficulty points of each student. It will help one to identify students difficulty correctly. Such informal and observations charts usually indicate the correct level on which to start remedial instruction (Durrell).
3. *Analysis of difficult point:* A teacher should analyse the difficult point of the student by asking from him the proofing questions, interview and should seek the help of his friends too.

4. *Remedial process:* Teacher shared follow the effective method of teaching by providing him remedial instructions. Only teacher knows the drawbacks and weaknesses of his students.
5. *Preventive measure*: "Prevention is better than cure. Teacher must know the difficult points of his topics which should be made clear by following the objectvies of cognitive Hemain.

Educational Age

The educational age index (E.A.) indicates a student's average level of performance or achievement in a group of school subjects measured by means of standardized tests and in terms of the average, for various chronological ages in school. Suppose a pupils achievement on the tests is at the 10-year level, his E.A. = 10. Educational ages obtained are not comparable even if the performance in the same school subject is measured, but with different tests, the EAs might still not be comparable because of differences in the standardization process.

Index used with Educational Achievements Tests

Educational Age and Achievement Age—The Educational age (E.A.) designates a pupil's average standing in the several subjects in which he has been tested. Suppose a student has been given a test of battery on which his scores were as follows:

Reading rate and comprehension	8 year level
Arithmetic fundamentals	9 year level
Spelling	9 year level
Language	8 year level
His E.A. would be average	34 ÷ 4 = 8.5 Years

i.e.,

Each of the separate ages represents the measured average level of educational achievement of pupils of that age.

Achievement age (AA) designates a pupils level of performance in a single school subject.

Educational Quotient (E.Q.)

The educational quotient indicates, whether a pupil's knowledge of a group of school subjects is commensurate with his C.A.

(Chronological Age) or whether it is above or below the level to be expected of him for his age. The formula is

$$E.Q. = \frac{E.A.}{C.A.} \times 100$$

Achievement Quotient (A.Q.)

It is found by dividing educational age by mental age. The formula becomes A.Q.

$$= \frac{E.A.}{M.A.} \times 100$$

indicates whether or not the student is working up to his mental capacity as found by intelligence test.

AQ is more valuable index than the EQ in judging whether or not a pupil's school achievement is commensurate with the quantity and quality of learning that might by expected of him.

Types of Items

Test items may be classified into one or another of the following types—1. Recall Type, 2. Recognition Type.

(i) *Recall type:* Student's power of memory is judged with the help of simple recall type questions. These are two types.

(a) *Simple recall*—Students are asked questions whose answer are supposed to be written on place in a single word. Such as—

(i) How many square root of 25 --------
(ii) What is the formula of area of circle.
(iii) Who was first Prime Minister of India.

(b) *Completion Type recall*—In such type of tests a place is left blank to write with a answer to complete the same

(i) $a^2 - b^2 = (a - b)(\quad)$
(ii) Mode = 3 Median ---------
(iii) 12, 24, 36, ---------

(ii) *Recognition Type Questions*—In such type of questions, examinees are supposed to recognise the answer among written answer of the questions.

(a) **Alternate Response Type**

There are certain statements which may correct or incorrect.

Examinees are to recognize the true or false, right or wrong answer of the statement such as:

(*i*) Circumference of a circle = r^2 True/False
(*ii*) $4A^2 - (\ ) B^2 = (2A-3B)(2A+3B)$ True False

(b) Multiple Choise Test Items

In such type of list, there are 4 or more than four possible answers of the question, testee is to recognize correct answer of the question.

(*i*) Square root of 625 is 15, 25, 35, 45
(*ii*) Value of $(A^2)^3$ is A^5, A^6, A^8, A^{23}
(*iii*) Which of the following methods can provide cause and effect conclusions
(*a*) Case study (*b*) Experimental
(*c*) Observational (*d*) Correlational

(c) Matching type questions—

After each name write the number of topic which intimately associate with that psychologist

1.	Conditioned reflex	Titchener ....
2.	Psycho-analysis	Hall ....
3.	Psychology of adolescence	Pavlov
4.	Existential Psychology	Cattell J.M.
5.	Reaction time experiment	Freud

(*d*) **Classification Type Questions.** In this type of question, some words or group of objects are put up before the examinees, who are to select that word which is not related at all with other words such as:

(*i*) 2, 5, 8, M, 13, 17, 21
(*ii*) Interest, Straight line, Rate, Compound interest, Time

(*e*) **Analogy type Questions**—

(*i*) Sky : Blue :: Grass :
(*ii*) 1 : 2 :: 50 :
(*iii*) Ocean : Pearl :: Sky :

(*f*) Check Lists: Place a check mark in front of each of the following items which is a part of an automobile.

Throttle

gear shift

periscope

generator

distributor

stabilizer

aileron

QUESTIONS

A. Long Answer Type Questions?

1. Describe the functions of Achievement tests. Distinguish between teacher made and standardized test.
2. Explain the steps of test construction of an achievement test.
3. What is achievement test? Describe its utility in the evaluation of the students.
4. What do you understand by diagnostic tests. Describe its utility for a class room teacher.
5. Explain with suitable examples the different type of objective questions.

B. Short Answer Type Questions?

1. Explain the importance of achievement test.
2. Differentiate between standardized and Teacher made tests.
3. Diagnostic tests are significant for a teacher. Why?
4. Explain the different type of objective questions.
5. Objects of objective questions.

C. Objective Questions

1. Importance is given to the wrong answers in diagnostic test. True/False
2. Importance is given to the right answers in achievement test. True/False
3. Essay type and objective type of tests are complementing to each other. True/False
4. Achievement and diagnostic test are complementary to each other. True/False
5. In diagnostic test-importance is given:
   (*a*) right answers (*b*) wrong answer
   (*c*) both above (*d*) none of these.
6. A standardized test has its.............

Bibliography

Anastasi, A. (1958) *"Psychological Feasting"*, New York, The Mcmillan Corr.pany.

Cronbach, L.J. (1970) *"Essentials of Psychological Testing"*, New York; Hasper and Rao, Publishers.

Ebel, R.L. (1970) *"Measuring Educational Achievement"*, Englewood Cleffs, N.J. Pventice–Hall Inc.

Garrett, H.E. (1967) *"Statistics in Pychology and Education"*, Bombay; Vakils Feffer and Simons Pvt. Ltd.

Gronlund, N.E. (1976) *"Measurement and Evaluation in Teaching"*, New York, Mcmillan Company.

Hoyt, C (1941) "Test Reliability Estimated by Analysis of Vananice, Psychometrica, 6, pp. 153-160.

Lindqust, E.F. (ed.) (1951) "Educational Measurement Washingtion, D.C. American Council on Education.

Thorndike, E.L. and E.P. Hagen. (1969) Measurement and Evaluation in Psychology and Education, New York: John Wiley and Sons. Inc.

Metha, P.H. (1966) "First Measurement; Handbook for India" New Delhi, NCERT.

Nunnally, J.C. (1967) "Psycho-metric" Theory New York McGraw Hill Book Company.

Table—A

Fractional Parts of the Total Area (Taken as 10,000) Under the Normal Probability Curve, Corresponding to Distances on the Base-Line Between the Mean and Successive Points Laid off from the Mean in Units of Standard Deviation

Example: Between the mean and a point 1.38 σ ($x/\sigma = 1.38$) are found 41.62 per cent of the Entire ear under the cure.

x/σ	*.00*	*.01*	*.02*	*.03*	*.04*	*.05*	*.06*	*.07*	*.08*	*.09*
0.0	0000	0040	0080	0120	0160	0199	0239	0279	0319	0359
0.1	0398	0438	0478	0517	0557	0596	0636	0675	0714	0753
0.2	0793	0832	0871	0910	0948	0987	1026	1064	1103	1141
0.3	1179	1217	1255	1293	1331	1368	1406	1443	1480	1517
0.4	1554	1591	1628	1664	1700	1736	1772	1808	1844	1879
0.5	1915	1950	1985	2019	2054	2088	2123	2157	2190	2224
0.6	2257	2291	2324	2357	2389	2422	2454	2486	2517	2549
0.7	2580	2611	2642	2673	2704	2734	2764	2794	2794	2823
0.8	2881	2910	2939	2967	2995	3023	3051	3078	3106	3133
0.9	3159	3186	3212	3238	3264	3290	3315	3340	3365	3389
1.0	3413	3438	3461	3485	3508	3531	3554	3577	3599	3621
1.1	3634	3665	3686	3708	3729	3749	3770	3890	3810	3830
1.2	3849	3869	3888	3907	3925	3944	3962	3980	3997	4015
1.3	4032	4049	4066	4082	4099	4155	4131	4147	4162	4177
1.4	4192	4207	4222	4236	4251	4265	4279	4292	4306	4319
1.5	4332	4345	4357	4370	4383	4394	4406	4418	4429	4441
1.6	4452	4463	4474	4484	4495	4505	4515	4525	4535	4545
1.7	4554	4564	4573	4582	4591	4599	4608	4616	4625	4633
1.8	4641	4649	4656	4664	4671	4678	4686	4693	4699	4706
1.9	4713	4719	4726	4732	4738	4744	4750	4756	4761	4767
2.0	4772	4778	4783	4788	4793	4798	4803	4808	4812	4817
2.1	4821	4826	4830	4834	4838	4842	4846	4850	4854	4857
2.2	4861	4864	4868	4871	4875	4878	4881	4884	4887	4890
2.3	4893	4896	4898	4901	4904	4906	4909	4911	4913	4916
2.4	4918	4920	4922	4925	4927	4929	4931	4932	4934	4936
2.5	4938	4940	4941	4943	4945	4946	4948	4949	4951	4952
2.6	4953	4955	4956	4957	4959	4960	4961	4962	4963	4964
2.7	4965	4966	4967	4968	4969	4970	4971	4972	4973	4974
2.8	4974	4975	4976	4977	4977	4978	4979	4979	4980	4981
2.9	4981	4982	4982	4983	4984	4984	4985	4985	4986	4986
3.0	4986.5	4986.9	4987.4	4987.8	4988.2	4988.6	4988.9	4989.3	4989.7	4990.0
3.1	4990.3	4990.6	4991.0	4991.3	4991.6	4991.8	4992.1	4992.4	4992.4	4992.9
3.2	4993.129									
3.3	4995.166									
3.4	4996.631									
3.5	4997.674									
3.6	4998.409									
3.7	4998.922									
3.8	4999.277									
3.9	4999.519									
4.0	4999.683									
4.5	4999.966									
5.0	49999.997133									

Table—B
Normalized Biserial Coefficients of Correlation as Determined from Proportions of Correct Responses in Upper and Lower 27 Per cent of the Group

PROPORTION OF CORRECT RESPONSES IN THE LOWER 27 PER CENT	PROPORTION OF CORRECT RESPONSES IN THE UPPER 27 PER CENT																									
	02	06	10	14	18	22	26	30	34	38	42	46	50	54	58	62	66	70	74	78	82	86	90	94	98	
02	00	19	30	37	43	48	51	55	58	61	63	66	68	70	72	73	75	77	79	80	82	84	86	88	91	02
06		00	11	19	26	31	36	40	44	47	50	53	56	59	61	64	66	68	71	73	76	78	81	84	88	06
10			00	08	15	21	26	30	34	38	41	45	48	51	54	57	60	63	65	68	71	74	77	81	86	10
14				00	07	12	18	22	27	31	34	38	42	45	48	51	54	57	60	63	67	70	74	78	84	14
18					00	06	11	16	20	25	28	32	36	39	43	47	49	53	56	60	63	67	71	76	82	18
22						00	06	10	15	19	23	27	31	34	38	42	45	49	52	56	60	63	68	73	80	22
26							00	05	09	14	18	22	26	30	33	37	41	44	48	52	56	60	65	71	79	26
30								00	04	09	13	17	21	25	29	33	37	40	44	49	53	57	63	68	77	30
34									00	04	09	13	17	21	25	29	33	37	41	45	49	54	60	66	75	34
38										00	04	08	13	16	20	25	29	33	37	42	47	51	57	64	73	38
42											00	04	08	12	16	20	25	29	33	38	43	48	54	61	72	42
46												00	04	08	12	16	21	25	30	34	39	45	51	59	70	46
50													00	04	08	13	17	21	26	31	36	42	48	56	68	50
54														00	04	08	13	17	22	27	32	38	45	53	66	54
58															00	04	09	13	18	23	28	34	41	50	63	58
62																00	04	09	14	19	25	31	38	47	61	62
66																	00	04	09	15	20	27	34	44	58	66
70																		00	05	10	16	22	30	40	55	70
74																			00	06	11	18	26	36	51	74
78																				00	06	12	21	31	48	78
82																					00	07	15	26	43	82
86																						00	08	19	37	86
90																							00	11	30	90
94																								00	19	94
98																									00	98
	02	06	10	14	18	22	26	30	34	38	42	46	50	54	58	62	66	70	74	78	82	86	90	94	98	

This table is abridged from J.C. Flanagan's table of normalized biserial coefficients originally prepared for the Cooperative Test Service. It is included here with the generous permission of Dr. Flannagan and the Educational Testing Service of Princeton, New Jersey. This version is taken from Merle W. Tate, *Statistics in Education* (New York: The Macmillan Co., 1955), p. 364. Reproduced by permission.

Decimal points are omitted.

If the proportion of correct responses in the lower 27 per cent exceeds that in the upper, enter the table with the lower 27 per cent proportion at the top and attach a negative sign to the coefficient.

Index